OFFICIAL FOOTBALL RECORDS 2012

First published by Carlton Books Limited 2011
Copyright © 2011 Carlton Books Limited

Carlton Books Limited
20 Mortimer Street
London W1T 3JW

A CIP catalogue record for this book is available from the British Library.
10 9 8 7 6 5 4 3 2 1

ISBN: 978-1-84732-870-0

Editors: Martin Corteel, Conor Kilgallon
Editorial Assistant: David Ballheimer
Designers: Darren Jordan, Stefan Morris, Sally Bond
Picture Research: Paul Langan
Production: Rachel Burgess

Written by: Press Association Sport

PRESS
ASSOCIATION
Sport

Manufactured under licence by Carlton Books Limited

Printed in Dubai

*Players, from left to right: Ian Harte, Reading; Jack Wilshere, Arsenal;
Anthony Pilkington, Huddersfield Town; Mark Wright, Shrewsbury Town*

OFFICIAL FOOTBALL RECORDS 2012

CARLTON
BOOKS

CONTENTS

Overleaf: Everton's Louis Saha (right) has a shot blocked by Chelsea's Ramires during a match at Goodison Park in January 2011.

INTRODUCTION

Welcome to the second edition of the *Barclays Premier League and npower Football League Official Football Records* – a book crammed full of stats and facts covering every aspect of our beautiful game.

English football has witnessed many memorable moments, matches, players and personalities since the first Football League season way back in 1888 – and all of those are covered here. From the amazing 32-game winning record that helped one side to the fourth-tier title back in 1976 to the Premier League game that broke new ground when it finished 7–4, no detail has been spared. In fact, each division and every one of the 92 clubs that make up the npower Football League and the Barclays Premier League have their own dedicated entries, containing every record and piece of trivia you could wish to know.

The top flight is covered in the most detail, with reviews of the 2010/11 campaign in all four divisions and domestic cup competitions followed by a comprehensive look at the all-time stats that have lit up the Premier League since its formation in 1992. Look out for interesting sections on things such as top goalscorers, leading appearance makers, transfers and attendances.

As well as all-time records for every division, each Premier League and Football League club's history has been explored in detail – from Arsenal to Yeovil – with some fascinating stats and key moments picked out.

You will also discover interesting and quirky facts about England's major cup competitions including the oldest association football competition in the world, the FA Cup, as well as the Carling Cup and the Football League Trophy, currently called the Johnstone's Paint Trophy, which has been running since 1983.

Obviously, writing a book of this nature presents plenty of challenges. To avoid confusion, anything concerning the top division before the Premier League came into being will be referred to as the top flight, while the Championship, as it is now commonly known, will be covered largely as the second tier and League 1 and 2 will be encompassed in the third and fourth-tier sections.

A book like this has to have a cut-off point. Football is never standing still, and such is the fast-paced nature of the modern game that when the season is in progress, records can be set or broken every week. That is why all the stats and information used here are correct up to and including the end of the 2010/11 campaign.

Every effort has been made to ensure that all appearance data and goalscoring records are 100 per cent accurate, although anomalies in the records pre-dating the modern era, particularly involving players from the late 1800s and early 1900s, are unavoidable and have to be taken into account.

Hopefully you will have great fun reading this book.

Action from the Barclays Premier League clash between Newcastle and Blackpool at St James' Park. The visitors won 2–0 with goals from Charlie Adam and DJ Campbell.

REVIEW OF THE SEASON 2010/11

The 2010/11 campaign witnessed a number of significant achievements for clubs throughout English football's top four divisions. Manchester United won a record 19th top-flight title, npower Championship runners-up Norwich made it back-to-back promotions, while Stevenage managed the same feat to land a place in the third tier for the first time in their history.

In what was another campaign of thrills and spills, Manchester City won the FA Cup and also claimed a much-coveted UEFA Champions League spot, while Swansea became the first-ever Welsh club to make it into the Premier League following a stunning play-off success.

A whole host of other teams enjoyed a season to remember, but Sir Alex Ferguson stole the headlines in the Barclays Premier League, cementing his place as the ultimate manager with yet another title victory. It was the Scot's 12th during his time at Old Trafford and made Manchester United the most successful club in the domestic game, overtaking Liverpool.

Chelsea, who parted company with coach Carlo Ancelotti at the end of the campaign, finished nine points off the pace in second, while Manchester City managed the same total to secure their highest-ever Premier League placing of third.

Arsenal took the final UEFA Champions League spot by finishing fourth, leaving fifth-place Tottenham with a UEFA Europa League place.

It could not have been closer at the bottom, with five teams in contention to be relegated on the final day. In the end, Blackpool – who won many admirers for their attacking style of play – and Birmingham joined West Ham in dropping into the npower Championship.

Replacing them were champions QPR, Norwich and Swansea. The Hoops, under the management of Neil Warnock, made it back to the top flight for the first time in 15 years, while Paul Lambert led the Canaries to a second successive promotion. Swansea finished third and went up via the play-offs, with Scott Sinclair scoring a hat-trick as they beat Reading 4–2 at Wembley to make history for Wales.

Phil Brown could not keep Preston in the npower Championship, and they were joined by Sheffield United and Scunthorpe in suffering relegation to npower League 1. Three northern teams were replaced by three from the south, as Brighton, Southampton and Peterborough came up.

Gus Poyet's Seagulls eased to the title, while Saints held off a stern challenge from Huddersfield to snatch the second automatic spot. The Terriers were 27 games unbeaten when they took on Peterborough in the Play-Off Final at Old Trafford, but three second-half goals cruelly ended their impressive run.

In npower League 2, champions Chesterfield finished five points ahead of Bury, while Wycombe also went up in third. Stevenage, who had ended the campaign in sixth, achieved their second straight promotion by beating Torquay 1–0 in the Play-Off Final, while The Football League bid a fond farewell to Lincoln and Stockport – who tasted relegation for the second successive season.

Yaya Toure scored the only goal of the FA Cup final as Manchester City beat Stoke 1–0, Birmingham stunned Arsenal in the Carling Cup and Carlisle lifted the Johnstone's Paint Trophy.

↓ Birmingham striker Obafemi Martins celebrates in spectacular style with a trademark back-flip after scoring the winning goal in the 2011 Carling Cup final against Arsenal at Wembley.

↑ Manchester United became the most successful club in English top-flight history in 2010/11 after winning a record 19th league championship by nine points from Chelsea.

↓ Yaya Toure only arrived at Manchester City in July 2010, but 10 months later he scored the winner as they secured a first major trophy since 1976.

↑ QPR earned the right to play in the top flight for the first time in 15 years with their npower Championship title success.

BARCLAYS PREMIER LEAGUE REVIEW

The 2010/11 Barclays Premier League campaign will forever be remembered for Manchester United's record-breaking 19th title win, which meant they surpassed Liverpool as England's most successful domestic side.

The triumph helped Sir Alex Ferguson – who has overseen 12 of those title successes – realise his ultimate dream at Old Trafford, although the Scotsman still shows no sign of calling time on his distinguished career. Indeed, there are still two more UEFA Champions League crowns to be won in order for United to equal the Reds' achievements in Europe – something that the veteran boss is acutely aware of.

When Ferguson looks back upon his lofty achievements, he may count the 2010/11 season's success as the jewel in his crown.

Chelsea were flying high after making an excellent start, opening up a five-point lead at the summit by the end of October. But when the Blues unravelled around the hectic Christmas period, United showed the kind of ruthlessness seen so often during Ferguson's reign to capitalise.

With United moving top, Chelsea responded by splashing out £75million in January, smashing the British transfer record for a buying club to snatch Liverpool's Fernando Torres for £50million while also swooping for Benfica's David Luiz. However, the Blues' efforts proved in vain as Torres could not halt their slide – scoring just once in 14 appearances – with the Red Devils proving increasingly rampant.

Such was the quality of their late charge, Arsenal – who for much of the year were United's biggest threat – saw their challenge pale into insignificance, and they eventually had to settle for a fourth-place finish. That paved the way for FA Cup winners Manchester City to claim third and an automatic place in the UEFA Champions League.

With United wrapping up the title with a game to spare, all eyes moved to the bottom of the table as one of the most dramatic climaxes to a season unfolded.

Five teams – Blackpool, Birmingham, Blackburn, Wolves and Wigan – were fearing the drop heading into the final round of fixtures. Only Rovers managed to avoid being in the bottom three at some stage during 'Survival Sunday', and in the end it was Ian Holloway's Blackpool and Birmingham who joined bottom club West Ham in dropping out of the top flight.

The biggest shock of the campaign came at Anfield, where a club legend made a dramatic return to management. When Roy Hodgson's stay on Merseyside ended after just six months, Kenny Dalglish made a sensational return to the hotseat.

The Scotsman brought new optimism to the red half of the city, earning himself the role permanently after a strong second half to the season. Hodgson, meanwhile, took the reins at relegation-threatened West Brom, turning their fortunes around to ensure a hugely-impressive 11th-place finish.

TOP SCORERS

Dimitar Berbatov	Manchester United	20
Carlos Tevez	Manchester City	20
Robin van Persie	Arsenal	18
Darren Bent	Aston Villa	17
Peter Odemwingie	West Brom	15

⤍ A high-five from Dimitar Berbatov salutes the striker's record five-goal haul against Blackburn in November 2010, a game Manchester United won 7–1.

WINNERS AND LOSERS

Champions	Manchester United
Runners-up	Chelsea
UEFA Champions League qualifiers	Manchester United, Chelsea, Manchester City, Arsenal
UEFA Europa League qualifiers	Tottenham, Birmingham, Stoke, Fulham
Relegated	West Ham, Blackpool, Birmingham

⇡ West Ham's Jack Collison has that sinking feeling after seeing his side relegated from the Barclays Premier League.

⇠ Blackpool's Charlie Adam was one of several Barclays Premier League rookies to impress in 2010/11.

⇠ Club legend Kenny Dalglish returned to the Liverpool dugout after a 20-year absence during the 2010/11 campaign.

BARCLAYS PREMIER LEAGUE TABLE & AWARDS

Team	P	Home					Away						GD	Pts
		W	D	L	F	A	W	D	L	F	A		
Man Utd	38	18	1	0	49	12	5	10	4	29	25	+41	80
Chelsea	38	14	3	2	39	13	7	5	7	30	20	+36	71
Man City	38	13	4	2	34	12	8	4	7	26	21	+27	71
Arsenal	38	11	4	4	33	15	8	7	4	39	28	+29	68
Tottenham	38	9	9	1	30	19	7	5	7	25	27	+9	62
Liverpool	38	12	4	3	37	14	5	3	11	22	30	+15	58
Everton	38	9	7	3	31	23	4	8	7	20	22	+6	54
Fulham	38	8	7	4	30	23	3	9	7	19	20	+6	49
Aston Villa	38	8	7	4	26	19	4	5	10	22	40	-11	48
Sunderland	38	7	5	7	25	27	5	6	8	20	29	-11	47
West Brom	38	8	6	5	30	30	4	5	10	26	41	-15	47
Newcastle	38	6	8	5	41	27	5	5	9	15	30	-1	46
Stoke	38	10	4	5	31	18	3	3	13	15	30	-2	46
Bolton	38	10	5	4	34	24	2	5	12	18	32	-4	46
Blackburn	38	7	7	5	22	16	4	3	12	24	43	-13	43
Wigan	38	5	8	6	22	34	4	7	8	18	27	-21	42
Wolves	38	8	4	7	30	30	3	3	13	16	36	-20	40
Birmingham	38	6	8	5	19	22	2	7	10	18	36	-21	39
Blackpool	38	5	5	9	30	37	5	4	10	25	41	-23	39
West Ham	38	5	5	9	24	31	2	7	10	19	39	-27	33

HART-WARMING SEASON FOR JOE

Goalkeeper Joe Hart capped a superb season by claiming the Barclays Golden Glove prize. He kept 18 clean sheets for Manchester City as they secured a UEFA Champions League berth as well as lifting the FA Cup. Hart managed three more clean sheets than his nearest rival, Petr Cech, while Manchester United's Edwin van der Sar and Liverpool's Pepe Reina both managed 14. Hart's impressive performances also made him an England regular.

⇢ The 2010/11 campaign marked the emergence of Joe Hart as Manchester City and England's undoubted number one. The young shot-stopper appeared in every league game.

SCOTT HAS GOT THE LOT

Scooping the Football Writers' Player of the Year gong was one bright spot for Scott Parker in a season that saw his West Ham side suffer relegation. It underlined the quality of Parker's performances that, while playing in a side that finished bottom of the table, he impressed the top UK newspaper journalists enough to claim one of the highest individual honours in English football.

‣ Scott Parker's dynamic midfield displays were not enough to save West Ham from relegation.

⇐ Recognition from his peers completed a remarkable turnaround for Gareth Bale, who was only on the fringes of the Spurs team at the start of 2010.

DUO HAVE GOLDEN BOOTS

The 2010/11 Barclays Golden Boot was shared after a late charge from Carlos Tevez saw him finish level with Manchester United striker Dimitar Berbatov on 20 goals. Berbatov looked on course to win the accolade for much of the season, despite struggling for a starting place in the latter part of the campaign. But Tevez had other ideas and, after overcoming an injury, he scored twice against Stoke in Manchester City's penultimate game of the season to ensure the prize was shared.

‣ Carlos Tevez reached the 20-goal mark for the second straight season to share the Barclays Golden Boot award, having netted 23 in 2009/10.

BALE'S HAPPY TALE

Gareth Bale scooped the PFA Player of the Year award following an impressive season with Tottenham. The former Southampton winger lit up Spurs' first UEFA Champions League campaign while also playing a key role as Harry Redknapp's side finished fifth in the Barclays Premier League. Bale became the fourth Welshman to win the gong, following in the illustrious footsteps of Ian Rush, Mark Hughes and Ryan Giggs. Jack Wilshere scooped the Young Player of the Year prize after an excellent breakthrough campaign at Arsenal.

FERGIE IS TOP BOSS

Sir Alex Ferguson led Manchester United to their 19th top-flight title and won himself the Barclays Manager of the Year prize in the process. It was perhaps the most important championship of the Scottish tactician's reign, as it meant that United overtook Liverpool's haul of 18 league championships.

‣ Alex Ferguson was named the Premier League's top boss for the 10th time after masterminding another title success with Manchester United in May 2011.

NPOWER CHAMPIONSHIP REVIEW

QPR secured a return to the top flight after a 15-year absence as Neil Warnock led the west Londoners to the npower Championship title. The Hoops asserted their authority over the league from start to finish, sealing promotion to the Barclays Premier League with a 2–0 victory at Watford in the penultimate game of the season.

Ironically, it was the Hornets who had ended Rangers' astonishing 19-game unbeaten run with a 3–1 win at Loftus Road in December. Warnock's side only lost once more at home all season, with Leeds securing a 2–1 victory on the final day.

Summer signing Adel Taarabt scored 19 goals and made 16 assists on his way to winning The Football League's Player of the Year award for the npower Championship.

Norwich completed back-to-back promotions to guarantee top-flight football at Carrow Road for the first time since 2005. Simeon Jackson scored six goals – including a dramatic winner deep into injury time against Derby on April 25 – as a six-game unbeaten end to the campaign secured Paul Lambert's side the runners-up spot.

Swansea became the first-ever Welsh club to reach the Premier League after they claimed a 4–2 victory over Reading in the Play-Off Final. The Swans survived a nervy semi-final first leg against Nottingham Forest to stun the Reds 3–1 in the second tie, with Darren Pratley scoring from inside his own half.

The Royals had been the surprise package in the second half of the season, with a run of eight consecutive wins earning a fifth-place finish. Despite an impressive 3–0 aggregate success over Cardiff in the semi-finals, Brian McDermott's men fell short at Wembley.

Brendan Rodgers' Swans stormed into a three-goal lead before half-time thanks to Scott Sinclair's brace and a powerful strike from Stephen Dobbie. Reading rallied to close the gap to a single goal after the break, with Joe Allen putting through his own net and Matt Mills heading home, but Sinclair scored from the penalty spot 10 minutes from time to complete a hat-trick and send Swansea into the promised land.

Leeds were expected to challenge for promotion following their return to the second tier from npower League 1, but boss Simon Grayson was ultimately unable to snatch a play-off place. The Whites generated the biggest crowd of the 2010/11 season as 33,622 fans turned out at Elland Road to watch a 1–0 victory over Sheffield United on September 25.

The Blades will play in the third tier of English football for the first time in 23 years after four different managers were unable to prevent a slide into npower League 1. The South Yorkshire club parted company with Kevin Blackwell after two games, with his replacement Gary Speed then leaving to take over as Wales manager in December.

Caretaker boss John Carver made way for boyhood Blades fan Micky Adams, who oversaw a 14-game winless run before relegation was finally confirmed following a 2–2 draw with local rivals Barnsley on April 30.

Preston and Scunthorpe accompanied the Blades through the exit door.

WINNERS AND LOSERS

Champions	Queens Park Rangers
Runners-up	Norwich
Play-off winners	Swansea
Play-off runners-up	Reading
Relegated	Scunthorpe, Sheffield United, Preston

← QPR and Norwich go head to head in their npower Championship clash in October 2010. The game ended 0–0, but both sides were ultimately promoted.

↑ A return of 24 goals in the npower Championship ensured that Danny Graham completed his best scoring season as a professional. He has now scored 86 times in total during his career.

↑ There was plenty to celebrate for experienced boss Neil Warnock in 2010/11, as he led his QPR team back into the top flight.

← Brendan Rodgers emerged as one of the best young managers in the game after leading Swansea into the Barclays Premier League via the npower Championship Play-Off Final.

TOP SCORERS

Danny Graham	Watford	24
Grant Holt	Norwich	21
Shane Long	Reading	21
Luciano Becchio	Leeds	19
Scott Sinclair	Swansea	19
Adel Taarabt	QPR	19
Jay Bothroyd	Cardiff	18
Max Gradel	Leeds	18

NPOWER LEAGUE 1 REVIEW

Brighton surpassed the wildest expectations of their fans and even manager Gus Poyet in his first full season in charge, winning promotion at a canter with five games to spare and the npower League 1 title in their next match.

The Seagulls went top of the table in late September following a 2–1 home win over Oldham and stayed there. By the time that promotion to the npower Championship had been secured, they held a 16-point advantage over closest rivals Southampton.

There had been little to suggest that the Seagulls would be so dominant in their final season at the Withdean – they moved into their new 22,500-seater Falmer Stadium in time for the 2011/12 campaign – but it is evident that Poyet brought the best out of his squad of players.

Defenders Inigo Calderon and Gordon Greer and winger Elliott Bennett were standout performers throughout the campaign, while Ashley Barnes and leading scorer Glenn Murray fired 40 goals between them.

And yet, despite Brighton's dominance, Southampton fans will feel that their side could have caught them had the season lasted a few games longer. Nigel Adkins took over from Alan Pardew as manager at St Mary's with the season already seven games old, and after a faltering start, one of the leading promotion favourites began to gather momentum.

Saints lost four of their first half-dozen league games, but only six more defeats followed and a remarkable nine wins from their last 10 matches saw them overhaul Huddersfield to clinch the second automatic promotion slot.

Huddersfield's season drew to a cruel conclusion as they went on to lose to Peterborough in the Play-Off Final at Old Trafford. Had Southampton not finished like a steam train, Lee Clark's Terriers would have comfortably claimed automatic promotion. Having led the chase of Brighton all season, Huddersfield did little wrong in the run-in, setting a new club record of 27 league games unbeaten, but their first defeat in 28 against Peterborough proved costly.

Posh fans will argue that their Play-Off Final win was merited after they finished the season as the division's top scorers with 106 goals – 27 of them from League 1 Player of the Year Craig Mackail-Smith. It was a triumphant return to London Road for manager Darren Ferguson, who steered his side back to the second tier at the first attempt.

At the other end of the table, Walsall manager Dean Smith, who replaced Chris Hutchings in January, pulled off a great escape with two wins and as many crucial draws in their last six matches to condemn Dagenham & Redbridge to an immediate return to npower League 2 on the final day.

Bristol Rovers, Plymouth – who failed to shoulder the burden of a 10-point deduction after going into administration in February – and Swindon endured difficult seasons on their way to relegation.

TOP SCORERS

Craig Mackail-Smith	Peterborough	27
Glenn Murray	Brighton	22
Rickie Lambert	Southampton	21
Bradley Wright-Phillips	Charlton	21
Ashley Barnes	Brighton	18
Jamie Cureton	Exeter	17
Gary Jones	Rochdale	17
Will Hoskins	Bristol Rovers	17

⤑ Bradley Wright-Phillips enjoyed a season to remember for Charlton with 21 league goals, but that was still not enough to dislodge npower League 1's top scorer, Craig Mackail-Smith.

↑ Dejected Plymouth players troop off the pitch following another defeat in 2010/11. The Pilgrims went on to suffer relegation to npower League 2.

WINNERS AND LOSERS

Champions	Brighton
Runners-up	Southampton
Play-off winners	Peterborough
Play-off runners-up	Huddersfield
Relegated	Swindon, Plymouth, Bristol Rovers, Dagenham & Redbridge

⤑ Gus Poyet won the FA Cup and the UEFA Cup Winners' Cup as a player, but guiding Brighton to the npower League 1 title marked his breakthrough as a manager.

↑ Brighton do battle with Dagenham & Redbridge in their April 2011 clash at the Withdean Stadium. Ashley Barnes scored late on to win it 4–3 and secure the Seagulls' promotion.

NPOWER LEAGUE 2 REVIEW

Chesterfield had a season to remember as they celebrated their move into a new home by romping to the npower League 2 title. The Spireites, who ended a 139-year stay at Saltergate by moving to the brand new b2net Stadium, finished five points clear at the summit, and their dominance was shown by the fact that they occupied top spot from early December onwards.

John Sheridan's side played an attacking brand of football and had no problem settling in to their new surroundings. They plundered 59 goals in front of their own fans – easily the best record in the division.

A late-season surge from Bury saw them push Chesterfield close for the title, with victory over the Spireites on the penultimate weekend sealing a promotion spot. Inspired by the goals of Ryan Lowe, who scored 27 and was named npower League 2 Player of the Year at The Football League Awards, the Shakers' achievement was all the more impressive considering they lost manager Alan Knill to Scunthorpe in March.

Wycombe grabbed the final automatic promotion spot, ensuring just a one-year stay in the bottom tier, as their consistency throughout the second half of the campaign saw them drop out of the top three just once from February.

Stevenage perhaps provided the real story of the season, though, as they secured back-to-back promotions with a Play-Off Final victory over Torquay. After finishing as runaway winners of the Conference in 2009/10, Boro produced a strong finish to the campaign, losing just twice in their final 15 games.

Despite the final defeat for Torquay, it was still a successful season for the Gulls, as they shook off their pre-season tag as one of the relegation favourites to stay in the upper echelons of the division for much of the campaign.

There were also mixed emotions for the two other sides to miss out in the play-offs. Having failed to secure automatic promotion by a point after being one of the favourites to go up, Shrewsbury ended up disappointed. Accrington, meanwhile, took pride from their efforts after losing just one of their final 19 games in the regular season to make the end-of-season shake-up.

It was a campaign of two halves for Rotherham, Port Vale and Gillingham. The Millers and Vale were both in the top three at the start of 2011 but endured poor runs to slip out of promotion contention. The Gills looked to be in relegation danger at one point before Christmas, but a fine second half of the season put them in the top seven, before a late dip in form cost them.

At the other end of the table, Stockport suffered a second successive relegation to lose their Football League status after 106 years. It was a difficult term for the Hatters, who won only nine games all season and were joined in the Conference by Lincoln.

The Imps were 15th in mid-March and looking safe, but a run of nine defeats from their final 10 games saw them slip into the bottom two on the final day, while Barnet produced a miraculous recovery to retain their League status, climbing out of the relegation zone for the first time in 12 games on the last weekend.

WINNERS AND LOSERS

Champions	Chesterfield
Runners-up	Bury
Promoted	Wycombe
Play-off winners	Stevenage
Play-off runners-up	Torquay
Relegated	Stockport, Lincoln

↑ It all proved too much to bear for the dejected Stockport County players as the club dropped out of The Football League after 106 years.

⋯› The 2010/11 campaign marked a high point for Ryan Lowe and his Bury team-mates, with the club returning to third tier for the first time since 2002.

TOP SCORERS

Clayton Donaldson	Crewe	28
Ryan Lowe	Bury	27
Cody McDonald	Gillingham	25
Adam Le Fondre	Rotherham	23
Craig Davies	Chesterfield	23

↓ Crewe striker Clayton Donaldson was virtually unstoppable last season, finishing top of the scoring charts with 28 goals. That was the best return of anyone across all four divisions.

↑ Chesterfield's players, led by Mark Allott (front), celebrate their npower League 2 title success with the championship trophy. The Spireites won the league by five points from Bury.

NPOWER FOOTBALL LEAGUE TABLES & AWARDS

Championship table

Team	P	Home					Away					GD	Pts
		W	D	L	F	A	W	D	L	F	A		
QPR	46	14	7	2	43	15	10	9	4	28	17	+39	88
Norwich	46	13	6	4	47	30	10	9	4	36	28	+25	84
Swansea	46	15	5	3	41	11	9	3	11	28	31	+27	80
Cardiff	46	12	7	4	41	25	11	4	8	35	29	+22	80
Reading	46	12	7	4	43	25	8	10	5	34	26	+26	77
Nottm Forest	46	13	8	2	43	22	7	7	9	26	28	+19	75
Leeds	46	11	8	4	47	34	8	7	8	34	36	+11	72
Burnley	46	12	6	5	40	30	6	8	9	25	31	+4	68
Millwall	46	12	6	5	39	22	6	7	10	23	26	+14	67
Leicester	46	13	6	4	48	27	6	4	13	28	44	+5	67
Hull	46	7	8	8	21	19	9	9	5	31	32	+1	65
Middlesbro	46	10	7	6	37	32	7	4	12	31	36	0	62
Ipswich	46	10	3	10	33	37	8	5	10	29	31	-6	62
Watford	46	9	7	7	39	32	7	6	10	38	39	+6	61
Bristol City	46	10	4	9	30	29	7	5	11	32	36	-3	60
Portsmouth	46	8	9	6	31	26	7	4	12	22	34	-7	58
Barnsley	46	11	6	6	32	23	3	8	12	23	43	-11	56
Coventry	46	9	5	9	27	26	5	8	10	27	32	-4	55
Derby	46	8	4	11	35	32	5	6	12	23	39	-13	49
C Palace	46	11	6	6	28	24	1	6	16	16	45	-25	48
Doncaster	46	7	9	7	26	31	4	6	13	29	50	-26	48
Preston	46	7	4	12	27	36	3	8	12	27	43	-25	42
Sheff Utd	46	7	5	11	27	36	4	4	15	17	43	-35	42
Scunthorpe	46	5	5	13	21	40	7	1	15	22	47	-44	42

League 1 table

Team	P	Home					Away					GD	Pts
		W	D	L	F	A	W	D	L	F	A		
Brighton	46	17	4	2	54	22	11	7	5	31	18	+45	95
Southampton	46	16	4	3	44	13	12	4	7	42	25	+48	92
Huddersfield	46	12	8	3	38	21	13	4	6	39	27	+29	87
Peterboro	46	15	5	3	69	40	8	5	10	37	35	+31	79
MK Dons	46	14	5	4	35	23	9	3	11	32	37	+7	77
Bournemouth	46	13	5	5	47	24	6	9	8	28	30	+21	71
L Orient	46	12	6	5	37	25	7	7	9	34	37	+9	70
Exeter	46	12	5	6	40	31	8	5	10	26	42	-7	70
Rochdale	46	9	8	6	36	30	9	6	8	27	25	+8	68
Colchester	46	12	7	4	38	30	4	7	12	19	33	-6	62
Brentford	46	9	5	9	24	28	8	5	10	31	34	-7	61
Carlisle	46	9	7	7	34	26	7	4	12	26	36	-2	59
Charlton	46	10	6	7	29	29	5	8	10	33	37	-4	59
Yeovil	46	8	6	9	27	30	8	5	10	29	36	-10	59
Sheff Wed	46	10	5	8	38	29	6	5	12	29	38	0	58
Hartlepool	46	9	6	8	32	32	6	6	11	15	33	-18	57
Oldham	46	7	9	7	29	31	6	8	9	24	29	-7	56
Tranmere	46	9	4	10	28	27	6	7	10	25	33	-7	56
Notts Co	46	9	3	11	24	25	5	5	13	22	35	-14	50
Walsall	46	9	3	11	33	36	3	9	11	23	39	-19	48
Dag & Red	46	8	6	9	28	27	4	5	14	24	43	-18	47
Bristol R	46	6	7	10	24	35	5	5	13	24	47	-34	45
Plymouth	46	9	4	10	27	33	6	3	14	24	41	-23	42
Swindon	46	5	9	9	20	27	4	5	14	30	45	-22	41

*Plymouth deducted 10 points for going into administration

League 2 table

Team	P	Home					Away					GD	Pts
		W	D	L	F	A	W	D	L	F	A		
Chesterfield	46	16	3	4	59	31	8	11	4	26	20	+34	86
Bury	46	11	6	6	35	23	12	6	5	47	27	+32	81
Wycombe	46	12	6	5	38	25	10	8	5	31	25	+19	80
Shrewsbury	46	11	9	3	36	18	11	4	8	36	31	+23	79
Accrington	46	15	5	3	53	24	3	14	6	20	31	+18	73
Stevenage	46	9	11	3	37	24	9	4	10	25	21	+17	69
Torquay	46	10	8	5	36	22	7	10	6	38	31	+21	68
Gillingham	46	10	7	6	29	24	7	10	6	38	33	+10	68
Rotherham	46	10	8	5	41	26	7	7	9	34	34	+15	66
Crewe	46	13	6	4	49	18	5	5	13	38	47	+22	65
Port Vale	46	11	7	5	32	22	6	7	10	22	27	+5	65
Oxford Utd	46	11	4	8	32	25	6	8	9	26	35	-2	63
Southend	46	10	7	6	37	28	6	6	11	25	28	+6	61
Aldershot	46	8	8	7	26	26	6	11	6	28	28	0	61
Macclesfield	46	6	7	10	25	36	8	6	9	34	37	-14	55
Northampton	46	8	9	6	40	33	3	10	10	23	38	-8	52
Cheltenham	46	6	6	11	24	32	7	7	9	32	45	-21	52
Bradford	46	10	3	10	27	30	5	4	14	16	38	-25	52
Burton	46	9	8	6	36	31	3	7	13	20	39	-14	51
Morecambe	46	6	8	9	26	31	7	4	12	28	42	-19	51
Hereford	46	4	11	8	23	30	8	6	9	27	36	-16	50
Barnet	46	8	5	10	30	35	4	7	12	28	42	-19	48
Lincoln City	46	7	4	12	18	41	6	4	13	27	40	-36	47
Stockport	46	4	12	7	31	51	5	2	16	17	45	-48	41

*Torquay deducted 1 point for fielding an ineligible player
**Hereford deducted 3 points for fielding an ineligible player

PLAYER OF THE YEAR

Championship	Adel Taarabt (QPR)
League 1	Craig Mackail-Smith (Peterborough)
League 2	Ryan Lowe (Bury)

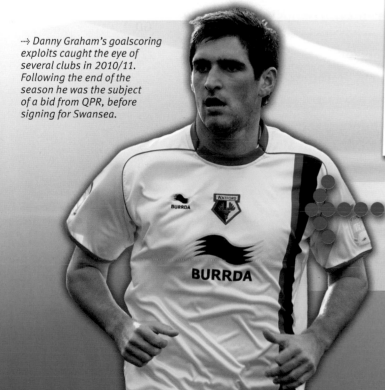

--→ Danny Graham's goalscoring exploits caught the eye of several clubs in 2010/11. Following the end of the season he was the subject of a bid from QPR, before signing for Swansea.

←--- Adel Taraabt was the standout player in the npower Championship as QPR romped to the title. The tricky forward made a total of 44 appearances, scoring 19 times.

YOUNG PLAYER OF THE YEAR

Connor Wickham (Ipswich)

GOLDEN BOOT

Championship	Danny Graham (Watford)	24 goals
League 1	Craig Mackail-Smith (Peterborough)	27 goals
League 2	Clayton Donaldson (Crewe)	28 goals

GOLDEN GLOVE

Championship	Paddy Kenny (QPR)	24 clean sheets
League 1	Casper Ankergren (Brighton),	
	Kelvin Davis (Southampton)	20 clean sheets
League 2	Nikki Bull (Wycombe)	17 clean sheets

CUP COMPETITIONS REVIEW

Manchester City and Birmingham ended lengthy waits for silverware in 2010/11, while Carlisle returned to Wembley to claim the Johnstone's Paint Trophy a year after suffering final heartbreak.

In the FA Cup, Yaya Toure etched his name into Manchester City folklore with the decisive goal in a 1–0 Wembley victory. A single flourish of the Ivory Coast midfielder's left boot was enough to banish 35 trophyless years against Stoke – who had impressively demolished Bolton 5–0 to reach the final.

City knocked out Manchester United in the last four, with the Red Devils having earlier been pushed to the limit in their 1–0 win over non-League Crawley in the fifth round. Steve Evans' side finished the season as Conference champions, and the cup scalps of Swindon, Derby and Torquay made their dream day out at Old Trafford possible.

Fans were treated to their share of giantkillings elsewhere, with Evo-Stik Premier League outfit FC United of Manchester overcoming Rochdale 3–2 at Spotland in front of a fervent travelling support in the first round, while Football League new-boys Stevenage served up a 3–1 third-round humbling for Newcastle, whose fierce rivals Sunderland fell to Notts County at the same stage.

Leyton Orient were eventually undone by Arsenal in the fourth round, but not before Jonathan Tehoue's 89th-minute equaliser at Brisbane Road earned them a lucrative replay against the Gunners and a luxury trip to Las Vegas at the personal expense of charismatic chairman Barry Hearn.

Arsene Wenger's side also struggled to shake off lower-league opposition en route to the Carling Cup final. Tamas Priskin gave Ipswich a 1–0 advantage going into the second leg of the npower Championship side's semi-final with the Gunners, and the return game remained goalless for an hour before Nicklas Bendtner, Cesc Fabregas and Laurent Koscielny broke the Tractor Boys' hearts.

Koscielny could not look back on the final with such fondness, though, as a mix-up between him and goalkeeper Wojciech Szczesny allowed Obafemi Martins to steal a last-gasp 2–1 victory and Birmingham's first major prize since 1963.

Arsenal's Robin van Persie levelled Nicola Zigic's opener, but the deserved nature of Blues' triumph made their subsequent relegation from the Barclays Premier League all the more surprising.

In the Johnstone's Paint Trophy, holders Southampton were still reeling from the sacking of manager Alan Pardew when they lost 3–0 at home to Swindon in the first round but their 2010 opponents, Carlisle, managed to hold off Huddersfield's second-leg comeback to make the final again – this time claiming the trophy against Brentford thanks to Peter Murphy's goal.

FA CUP

Winners Manchester City
Runners-up Stoke
Top scorers Scott McGleish (Leyton Orient),
Mathieu Manset (Hereford/Reading) 6

↑ Stoke City's Jermaine Pennant (left) and Manchester City's Adam Johnson challenge for the ball during the 2011 FA Cup final at Wembley.

CARLING CUP

Winners Birmingham
Runners-up Arsenal
Top scorers Carlton Cole (West Ham),
Scott Sinclair (Swansea) 4

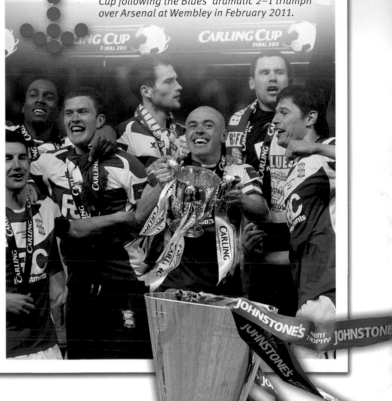

↓ Birmingham's Stephen Carr (centre) is flanked by his team-mates as he holds aloft the Carling Cup following the Blues' dramatic 2–1 triumph over Arsenal at Wembley in February 2011.

←⋯ Stoke's players got pats on the back all around following their stunning performance to see off Bolton 5–0 in the FA Cup semi-final, but they couldn't repeat the feat in the showpiece.

JOHNSTONE'S PAINT TROPHY

Winners Carlisle
Runners-up Brentford
Top scorer Peter Murphy (Carlisle),
Neil Mellor (Sheffield Wednesday),
Jordan Rhodes (Huddersfield) 4

⋯→ Carlisle captain Paul Thirlwell gets to grips with one of the largest cups in English football as he lifts the Johnstone's Paint Trophy. The Cumbrians beat Brentford 1–0 in the final.

ENGLISH LEAGUE RECORDS

The Football League has changed dramatically since the first ball was kicked back in 1888.

In that inaugural season, the competition was made up of just one division consisting of 12 teams. Now, almost 125 years on, there are four divisions, with 92 clubs competing in total.

The top flight is the pinnacle of the English game. It is revered and respected right around the world and attracts some of the best players on the planet. It has always been held up as a shining example of how football should be organised, and over the years it has gone from strength to strength.

The arrival of the Premier League in particular has helped to take the game to new heights. The competition was formed in May 1992 as part of a restructuring designed to help football in England grow and flourish. Initially, the league was composed of 22 teams, but it was always the intention to reduce that number to 20 to promote development and excellence at club and international level, and this was achieved in 1995.

Throughout its history, the top flight has been the setting for some amazing matches and feats of individual and collective brilliance – from the first title winners, Preston North End, and their top scorer, John Goodall, right through to the 2010/11 Barclays Premier League champions, Manchester United, whose team is packed with world-class stars.

Further down the pyramid, the action is just as enthralling. The second tier – which came into being in 1892 – was rebranded as the Championship in 2004 with the third tier, formed in 1920, and the fourth tier – a relatively new addition, having first been introduced in 1958 – becoming known as League 1 and League 2 at the same time. Throughout all the divisions, fans have got used to seeing edge-of-the-seat drama and superb individual skill week in, week out.

The expanded number of teams and structure of the competition is just one of many changes to have affected The Football League down the years. In 1981, for example, following a proposal by television pundit and former Coventry chairman Jimmy Hill, the decision was made to award three points for a win, rather than two as had previously been the case. The idea was that this would encourage greater attacking play, with more at stake for clubs involved in promotion and relegation battles.

The play-offs were another exciting introduction in 1986, offering teams who finished in the top six or seven places in their respective divisions the chance to compete in an end-of-season shootout for promotion. The play-offs now mean that even long after the titles have been handed out, supporters are guaranteed a nail-biting climax to the campaign.

It all adds up to a fast-paced, modern and exciting game that makes English football the envy of the world.

It's all too much to bear for Liverpool players and fans alike as another chance goes begging during the Reds' 3–2 home defeat to arch-rivals Manchester United on September 11 1999.

BARCLAYS PREMIER LEAGUE ALL-TIME RECORDS

The Premier League was formed in 1992 and originally consisted of 22 teams, although that was cut to 20 for the start of the 1995/96 season. The competition is now the most watched, and the most lucrative, league in world football. Swansea are the 45th different team to compete in the division, but only four have won the title, with Manchester United leading the way as the most successful club.

Wayne Rooney chose the perfect game to score arguably his best goal yet in February 2011 as his stunning overhead kick helped Manchester United beat arch-rivals City, and set the Red Devils on the way to the Barclays Premier League title.

CHAMPIONS & RUNNERS-UP

DEVILISHLY GOOD

Manchester United became the most successful club side in English league football by claiming their 19th top-flight title in 2010/11. Liverpool have 18 championships to their name but have now been overtaken by their north-west rivals, who had only won seven titles before the Premier League began in 1992. The Red Devils were crowned champions at Ewood Park following a 1–1 draw with Blackburn on May 14. Chelsea had closed the gap at the top to three points when the two sides met at Old Trafford at the start of the final month, but a 2–1 win for United in that game pretty much sealed the trophy.

←··· Manchester United captain Nemanja Vidic holds the Barclays Premier League trophy aloft. No one has been able to come close to matching the Red Devils in the Premier League era.

UNITED UP AND RUNNING

Manchester United were the first winners of the Premier League in 1992/93. Sir Alex Ferguson's men claimed the title in style, finishing 10 points ahead of Aston Villa. The season started badly for the Red Devils, who took just one point from their opening three games. However, they improved dramatically to win 24 games and lose just six times over the course of the campaign. Eric Cantona and Mark Hughes were joint top scorers for the Red Devils that season with 15 goals each.

PREMIER LEAGUE TITLE WINNERS

1992/93	Manchester United
1993/94	Manchester United
1994/95	Blackburn
1995/96	Manchester United
1996/97	Manchester United
1997/98	Arsenal
1998/99	Manchester United
1999/00	Manchester United
2000/01	Manchester United
2001/02	Arsenal
2002/03	Manchester United
2003/04	Arsenal
2004/05	Chelsea
2005/06	Chelsea
2006/07	Manchester United
2007/08	Manchester United
2008/09	Manchester United
2009/10	Chelsea
2010/11	Manchester United

TITLE DECIDER

The Premier League era has witnessed many memorable title races, but arguably the most exciting and dramatic decider of recent times actually came three years before the league was formed. Arsenal were vying for the championship with Liverpool in 1989, and amazingly the two sides found themselves playing each other in the last game of the season to decide who won the trophy. The Gunners needed a 2–0 win but were only leading through an Alan Smith header going into the last minute. Michael Thomas, who later went on to play for Liverpool, then scored a crucial second right at the end of the game to snatch the trophy for the Londoners.

RUNNER-UP GUNNERS

Arsenal have been runners-up in the Premier League on five occasions. They finished second four times between 1999 and 2003, with Manchester United beating them to the title on each occasion. United have themselves been runners-up four times, as have Chelsea. Newcastle have finished second twice and Aston Villa, Blackburn and Liverpool once since the league began.

ROVERS MISS OUT

Blackburn claimed the title in 1994/95 but finished seventh the following season. That is the lowest finish by the defending champions in the competition's history. Kenny Dalglish, who had been in charge for the title-winning campaign, took up a director of football role at Ewood Park at the end of that season and his assistant, Ray Harford, was named as the club's manager.

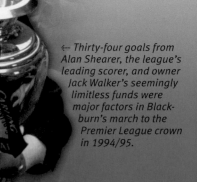

←··· Thirty-four goals from Alan Shearer, the league's leading scorer, and owner Jack Walker's seemingly limitless funds were major factors in Blackburn's march to the Premier League crown in 1994/95.

← Newcastle manager Kevin Keegan holds his head in his hands as his team draw 1–1 against Nottingham Forest on May 2 1996 to lose further ground to Manchester United in the title race.

↓ It's celebration time for Chelsea after Didier Drogba (left) scores the only goal of the game in the 2010 FA Cup final against Portsmouth. Victory for the Londoners saw them win the double for the first time in the club's history.

BLUES DOUBLE UP

Chelsea became the third team in Premier League history to win the double in 2009/10. In English football this means winning the Barclays Premier League title and the FA Cup. The Blues finished one point ahead of Manchester United to win the league and then claimed a 1–0 victory in the FA Cup final against Portsmouth, with Didier Drogba scoring the only goal of the game. Manchester United and Arsenal have both done the double twice since the competition was formed – while United also achieved the treble, including the Champions League, in 1999. Going further back, Preston, Aston Villa, Tottenham and Liverpool have also achieved the feat.

MAGPIES' WINGS CLIPPED

Newcastle threw away a 12-point lead at the top of the table to finish second to Manchester United in 1995/96. The Magpies won many admirers that term for their attacking brand of football, but they struggled to keep it tight at the back and were eventually overtaken by United, who finished four points ahead. Kevin Keegan's side were runners-up to the Red Devils again the following season.

DOUBLE AND TREBLE WINNERS

Treble

Manchester United	1998/99

Double

Preston	1888/89
Aston Villa	1896/97
Tottenham	1960/61
Arsenal	1970/71, 1997/98, 2001/02
Liverpool	1985/86
Manchester United	1993/94, 1995/96
Chelsea	2009/10

UNITED'S TREBLE TRIUMPH

Manchester United claimed an amazing treble in 1999, winning the league title, the FA Cup and the UEFA Champions League in the same season. They came out on top in one of the closest title races in the competition's history, with both Arsenal and Chelsea pushing them all the way. United then beat Newcastle 2–0 in the FA Cup final, with Teddy Sheringham and Paul Scholes on target, but they saved the best for last when they scored two goals in injury time to snatch a dramatic 2–1 win against Bayern Munich in the Champions League final in Barcelona.

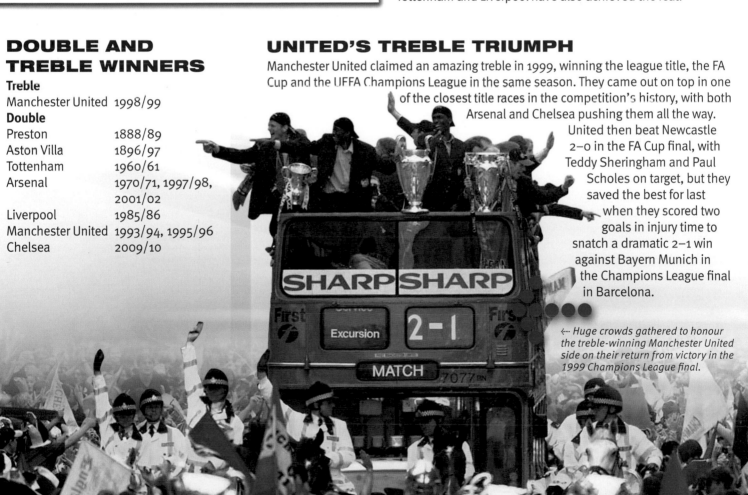

← Huge crowds gathered to honour the treble-winning Manchester United side on their return from victory in the 1999 Champions League final.

PARTICIPATION, UPS & DOWNS, WINS, DEFEATS & DRAWS

IMPRESSIVE DEBUTS

Newcastle and Nottingham Forest share the record for the highest Premier League finish by a newly-promoted team. The Magpies claimed the second-tier title in style in 1993/94, with Andrew Cole scoring 12 goals in 11 games and fellow forward David Kelly netting 24. They then took that momentum into the following campaign, finishing third in the top flight. Forest matched that feat in 1994/95, despite having finished as runners-up to Crystal Palace in the second tier. Stan Collymore and Bryan Roy fired the Reds to a UEFA Cup spot.

← Bryan Roy (left) with 13 goals and Stan Collymore with 22 combined with deadly effect in 1994/95 to take newly-promoted Nottingham Forest to an unlikely third place.

PREMIER LEAGUE EVER-PRESENTS

Arsenal
Aston Villa
Chelsea
Everton
Liverpool
Manchester United
Tottenham

THE GREAT ESCAPE

West Brom are the only team in Premier League history to have avoided relegation having been bottom of the table at Christmas. They pulled off 'The Great Escape' in 2004/05 with a last-day win at home to Portsmouth. Geoff Horsfield and Kieran Richardson, who had impressed on loan from Manchester United, scored the goals in a decisive 2–0 victory. The Baggies finished that season a point ahead of both Crystal Palace and Norwich and two in front of bottom club Southampton, who all failed to win their last match.

SURVIVAL SUNDAY

The last day of the 2010/11 Barclays Premier League season was gripping – and nerve-shredding for supporters of the five clubs who were in danger of being relegated at the start of play! Positions in the drop zone changed an amazing 14 times during the 90 minutes before Blackpool and Birmingham were confirmed as the two teams joining West Ham in slipping into the second tier. Wolves survived by just a single point, despite suffering a 3–2 defeat at home to Blackburn. Hugo Rodallega's second-half header earned Wigan a 1–0 win at Stoke which also ensured their survival.

BIG FOUR

Arsenal, Chelsea, Liverpool and Manchester United have traditionally been known as the 'Big Four'. This stems from the fact that since season 2003/04, these sides have dominated the division, finishing in the first four places, albeit in a different order, in all but three seasons. Everton snatched fourth spot in 2004/05, Tottenham managed the feat in 2009/10 and Manchester City finished third in 2010/11, with Liverpool the side to miss out each time. Manchester United are the only club never to have finished outside of the top four.

↑ It was agony for Barry Ferguson and his Birmingham City team-mates on the final day of the 2010/11 campaign, as they suffered relegation from the Barclays Premier League.

↓ Manchester United and Chelsea players make their way onto the pitch for their Barclays Premier League match in May 2011. Manchester City and Tottenham are trying to break the Big Four's monopoly for good.

RED DEVILS PLAY IT STRAIGHT

Manchester United went on a run of nine straight victories without conceding a goal between Boxing Day 2008 and February 2009. The sequence started with a 1–0 win at Stoke, with Carlos Tevez scoring the only goal, while Paul Scholes, Dimitar Berbatov and Wayne Rooney were on target in a 3–0 victory against Fulham on February 18 – the last game of the streak.

RAMS RECORD

Derby hold the record for being relegated from the division with the least amount of points. The Rams endured a difficult campaign in 2007/08, taking just 11 points from 38 matches. They managed just one win – a 1–0 success against Newcastle in September – and suffered 29 defeats. Nottingham Forest went down with the highest points total in the first Premier League season. They took 40 points, although they did play 42 games.

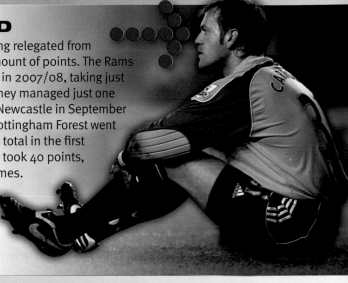

⋯⋯→ *Derby keeper Roy Carroll looks dejected after Arsenal striker Emmanuel Adebayor completes his hat-trick during the Gunners' 6–2 victory at Pride Park in April 2008.*

✝ *Thierry Henry slots home his second goal, and Arsenal's third, during the Gunners' 4–3 win over Everton at Highbury in May 2002.*

GUNNERS ON A ROLL

Arsenal set the record for the most consecutive Premier League wins in 2002. The Gunners managed 14 over two seasons, with the impressive run starting with a 1–0 victory at Everton in February and continuing until the end of the 2001/02 campaign when Thierry Henry bagged a brace to help beat the Toffees 4–3 at Highbury. Arsene Wenger's side won the opening game of the 2002/03 season at home to Birmingham, but the sequence was ended on August 24 with a 2–2 draw at West Ham.

UNLUCKY RUN FOR BLACK CATS

Sunderland endured 15 straight defeats on their way to suffering relegation in 2002/03. That record number of consecutive losses started with a 2–1 reverse at Everton on January 18 2003, despite the Black Cats having taken the lead through Kevin Kilbane. The miserable sequence continued until the end of the season – they were thumped 4–0 at home by a Freddie Ljungberg-inspired Arsenal on the last day. The Wearsiders went down with 19 points that term.

⋯⋯→ *Sunderland's Gavin McCann experiences that sinking feeling after 15 straight defeats in the 2002/03 season condemned the Black Cats to relegation.*

THE CHEIK OF IT

Cheik Tiote completed one of the most dramatic comebacks in Premier League history as Newcastle took a point against Arsenal having been 4–0 down at half-time in February 2011. Wing wizard Theo Walcott had fired the Gunners ahead after just 44 seconds. They were three up inside the first 10 minutes and then four ahead at the break. A red card for Abou Diaby changed the game, with Joey Barton scoring two penalties and Leon Best making it 4–3 before Tiote's stunning 25-yard strike. It was the 12th game in Premier League history to finish 4–4.

←⋯⋯ *Cheik Tiote roars with delight after hauling Newcastle level with Arsenal – one of the most amazing games ever in the Premier League.*

SCORELINES & POINTS RECORDS

SEVEN-UP POMPEY

Portsmouth and Reading were involved in the highest-scoring match in Premier League history on September 29 2007. There were 11 goals scored as the game finished 7–4 to the home side. Pompey were leading 2–1 at the break, with Benjani Mwaruwari scoring both of their goals. Dave Kitson levelled for the Royals, who then found themselves 5–2 behind – Benjani completing his hat-trick. There were two goals in injury time, with Sulley Muntari scoring a penalty and Sol Campbell putting through his own net.

⤎ Sean Davis celebrates after scoring the sixth of Portsmouth's goals in their 7–4 victory over Reading in September 2007.

TOWN TUMBLE

Ipswich endured an afternoon to forget in March 1995 when they were beaten 9–0 by Manchester United at Old Trafford. Roy Keane opened the scoring for the home side before Andrew Cole took over. Cole, who had only joined the club from Newcastle two months earlier, helped himself to a hat-trick before Mark Hughes got in on the act, adding a brace to make it 6–0. Cole netted another two goals, with a Paul Ince strike sandwiched in between.

⤏ Andrew Cole became the first player in Premier League history to score five goals in a match during Manchester United's 9–0 demolition of Ipswich in March 1995.

BIGGEST PREMIER LEAGUE WINS

Manchester United	9–0	Ipswich	(04/03/1995)
Tottenham	9–1	Wigan	(22/11/2009)
Newcastle	8–0	Sheff Wed	(19/09/1999)
Chelsea	8–0	Wigan	(09/05/2010)
Nottingham Forest	1–8	Manchester United	(06/02/1999)
Middlesbrough	8–1	Manchester City	(11/05/2008)

COLLYMORE CLOSING IN

Liverpool's 4–3 win over Newcastle on April 3 1996 is regarded by many as the greatest Premier League game of all time. The Magpies' title challenge had faltered going into the match, and the night started badly when Robbie Fowler scored after two minutes. They hit back to lead 2–1 through Les Ferdinand and David Ginola, only for Fowler to level. Faustino Asprilla restored Newcastle's lead but Stan Collymore broke their hearts, equalising in the 68th minute before netting a dramatic injury-time winner.

⤏ Stan Collymore nets the winner in Liverpool's dramatic 4–3 victory over Newcastle in April 1996. Many consider this to be the greatest Premier League match ever played.

SIX POINTERS

The term 'six-pointer' is often heard when the football season enters its final few weeks. Teams obviously still only get three points for a win, but if they are struggling at the bottom of the table or battling it out for promotion at the top and come up against one of their rivals, getting those points can significantly boost a team's hopes of beating the drop or going up.

BAGGIES BEAT THE DROP

West Brom took just 34 points during the 2004/05 season but managed to avoid relegation. That was the lowest points total to beat the drop in Premier League history. The battle for survival went to the last day of the season, with Crystal Palace and Norwich relegated with 33 points and Southampton finishing bottom with 32. Hull stayed up with 35 points in 2008/09.

RED DEVILS MAKE THEIR POINT

Perhaps unsurprisingly, Manchester United have gathered the most points in Premier League history. The Red Devils have only finished outside of the top two in three seasons since the competition began – in 2001/02, 2003/04 and 2004/05 – and that is reflected in their total of 1,574 points. Arsenal are second in the list 195 points behind, while Chelsea are third with a total of 1,338.

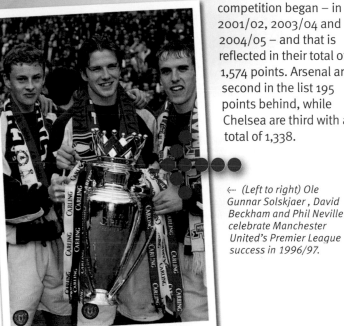

← (Left to right) Ole Gunnar Solskjaer , David Beckham and Phil Neville celebrate Manchester United's Premier League success in 1996/97.

BLUES ON A HIGH

Chelsea recorded the highest points total in Premier League history when they won the title in 2004/05. The Blues finished the campaign with 95 points, 12 more than second-place Arsenal and three more than Manchester United had managed in 1993/94. They won 29 of their 38 games, drew eight and lost just once that year. Their sole defeat came at Manchester City in October.

↓ (Left to right) Chelsea's Robert Huth, Tiago, Mateja Kezman, Jiri Jarosik, Arjen Robben, Didier Drogba and Ricardo Carvalho celebrate with the Barclays Premier League Trophy in 2004/05.

↓ United goalkeeper Peter Schmeichel looks downcast after Alan Shearer scores Newcastle's fourth during the Magpies' 5–0 win at St James' Park in October 1996.

UNITED KEEP IT TIGHT

Manchester United set a new record when they went 14 consecutive games without conceding a goal during the 2008/09 season. The run started on November 15 2008 with a 5–0 win against Stoke, with Cristiano Ronaldo opening the scoring early and sealing the rout late on. United were also 5–0 winners at West Brom at the end of January, with the Portuguese winger again bagging a brace. Roque Santa Cruz ended the sequence when he scored for Blackburn after 32 minutes of a 2–1 United win at Old Trafford on February 21.

COMPETITION LOW

Manchester United claimed the 1996/97 title with a competition-low total of 75 points. Sir Alex Ferguson's side recorded 21 victories – the least amount of wins of any Premier League champions – drew 12 games and lost five, including a 5–0 thumping at Newcastle and 3–2 defeat at home to Derby. They still scooped the trophy by seven points from Newcastle, Arsenal and Liverpool, who all finished that season with 68 points.

TOP SCORERS

THE BOOT FITS

Thierry Henry has won the Premier League Golden Boot a record four times. Arsenal legend Henry first scooped the award in season 2001/02 when he netted 24 goals, edging out Jimmy Floyd Hasselbaink, Alan Shearer and Ruud van Nistelrooy, who all scored 23 times. The Frenchman finished second to Van Nistelrooy the following season but claimed the accolade for the next three terms. Henry hit 30 goals in 2003/04 – eight more than his nearest rival. He bagged 25 in 2004/05 and 27 the season after that.

BERBATOV BAGS FIVE

Dimitar Berbatov became the fourth player in the league's history and the second Manchester United striker to score five goals in one game in November 2010. The Bulgarian equalled the record during a stunning 7–1 win against Blackburn. Former Old Trafford hero Andrew Cole, Alan Shearer, who was playing for Newcastle, and more recently Jermain Defoe are also in the unique club. Berbatov also scored hat-tricks against Liverpool and Birmingham during an impressive 2010/11 season.

↑ Bulgarian hot-shot Dimitar Berbatov joined an exclusive club of players when he fired home five goals against Blackburn Rovers.

←... Thierry Henry was a goalscoring king for the Gunners, netting 174 goals in 254 Premier League appearances for Arsenal between 1999 and 2007.

PREMIER LEAGUE GOALSCORERS

Alan Shearer	260
Andrew Cole	187
Thierry Henry	174
Robbie Fowler	163
Les Ferdinand	149
Michael Owen	149
Teddy Sheringham	147
Frank Lampard	139
Jimmy Floyd Hasselbaink	127
Robbie Keane	123

SUB OF THE DAY

Ole Gunnar Solskjaer holds the record for scoring the most goals in a single Premier League game after coming on as a substitute. The Norwegian striker came off the bench for Manchester United at Nottingham Forest on February 6 1999 to score four goals in the last 10 minutes as the Red Devils won 8–1 at the City Ground.

DUO SHARE LANDMARK

Andrew Cole and Alan Shearer share the landmark for the most goals scored in a Premier League season. Cole was first to set the record when he netted 34 in 42 games for Newcastle in 1993/94. Shearer equalled that haul the following season to help fire Blackburn to the title.

RAMPANT ROONEY

Wayne Rooney is the only Englishman to have scored more than 25 goals in a Premier League season since 1999/00. Kevin Phillips had been the last player to achieve the feat, scoring 30 for Sunderland at the turn of the millennium, before Rooney hit 26 in 2009/10 as Manchester United finished runners-up in the title race.

RED-HOT BLUES

Chelsea scored 68 times at Stamford Bridge during their title-winning season of 2009/10 – a record for the most home goals in a single Premier League campaign. The Blues went goal crazy, enjoying big wins against Blackburn (5–0), Wolves (4–0), Sunderland (7–2), Aston Villa (7–1), Stoke (7–0) and Wigan (8–0). Manchester United netted a record 47 goals away from home in 2001/02 but had to settle for third place.

SHEAR CLASS

Alan Shearer is the Premier League's leading all-time goalscorer, having netted 260 times in 441 appearances from the league's first season in 1992/93 until the end of the 2005/06 campaign. The former Blackburn and Newcastle striker tops the chart by 73 goals from Andrew Cole, who scored 187 overall. Shearer bagged his first Premier League goals for Rovers in a 3–3 draw at Crystal Palace on August 15 1992, while his last came for the Magpies – a penalty in a 4–1 win against fierce rivals Sunderland at the Stadium of Light on April 17 2006.

IMPRESSIVE GIG FOR RYAN

Ryan Giggs has scored in all 19 Premier League seasons since the competition began in 1992. The winger has spent his entire career at Manchester United and netted his first goal in the Premier League in September 1992 to put his side ahead in a 1–1 draw at Tottenham. Welshman Giggs scored two top-flight goals in 2010/11, bagging in United's first game against Newcastle and the 5–0 demolition of Birmingham in January.

⤶ A model of consistency, Giggs has scored in every Premier League season. He has netted 105 times in the league for the Red Devils.

TEVEZ AT THE TOP

Carlos Tevez topped the Barclays Premier League goalscoring charts in 2010/11, despite having bagged three goals less than the previous season. The Manchester City striker netted 20 times to share the Golden Boot with Manchester United's Dimitar Berbatov. Both players had one goal taken away from them by the Dubious Goals Committee. Argentinian Tevez managed 23 goals in 2009/10, but the goalscoring exploits of Chelsea's Didier Drogba (29), Wayne Rooney of Manchester United (26) and Darren Bent (24) – then of Sunderland – meant he was only fourth in the list that year.

⤴ A legend at both Blackburn and Newcastle, Alan Shearer scored an all-time Premier League record 260 goals in only 441 appearances – at a rate of a goal every 1.7 matches.

⤳ Carlos Tevez could have won the Golden Boot outright in 2010/11 had it not been for his strike against Newcastle later being ruled as an own goal.

GOALS

PANTS RECORD FOR JOHN

Fulham defender John Pantsil scored three goals during the 2010/11 season – unfortunately all of them were at the wrong end of the pitch! The unlucky Ghana international became only the second player in Premier League history to score three own goals in a single season, matching the unwanted record set by Andreas Jakobsson while playing for Southampton in 2004/05. Pantsil's first blunder gifted Blackpool an equaliser at Bloomfield Road in August, his second handed Liverpool a 1–0 win at Anfield in January and he made it a hat-trick at Aston Villa in a 2–2 draw a month later.

THROW-IN WOE

Aston Villa goalkeeper Peter Enckelman saw a throw-in roll under his foot and into the back of the net during a derby clash with Birmingham at St Andrew's in 2002. Villa defender Olof Mellberg threw the ball back to the shot-stopper, who missed it completely. A goal was given, although rules actually state that if the ball is not touched by another player from a throw-in before going into the net then a corner kick should be awarded.

⤙ Aston Villa goalkeeper Peter Enckelman had a night to forget on September 16 2002, conceding a bizarre own goal as Birmingham ran out 3–0 winners in the first Birmingham derby for 16 years.

DIRK'S LATE SHOW

A football match is only meant to last for 90 minutes, but incredibly Dirk Kuyt's equaliser for Liverpool at Arsenal in April 2011 was scored after 102 minutes! The Dutchman's penalty goes down as the latest goal ever scored in the Premier League. Bizarrely, Robin van Persie's strike for the Gunners – also a spot-kick – had come in the 98th minute. A clash of heads between Reds defenders Jamie Carragher and John Flanagan had brought about the long spell of injury time.

⤓ No one has ever scored later than Liverpool's Dirk Kuyt in a Premier League game.

TAKING IT TO THE MAXI

Maxi Rodriguez scored two hat-tricks in three games during the last few weeks of the 2010/11 Barclays Premier League season. The Liverpool winger had only netted three times before Birmingham visited Anfield in April but a treble against Blues signalled the start of a crazy run for the Argentinian. He scored again in a 3–0 win against Newcastle before grabbing another three-goal haul at Fulham in his next match to finish with 10 for the campaign. A record-breaking 17 hat-tricks were scored in total in the Barclays Premier League last season.

KING OF THE GOALSCORERS

Ledley King scored after just 10.2 seconds of a Premier League game at Bradford in December 2000. King tried his luck with a shot from outside the area that deflected off a defender and found the bottom corner. It was the England centre-back's first goal for Tottenham. The game ended 3–3.

SUPER SATURDAY

The Barclays Premier League went goal crazy on February 5 2011, with the net bulging 41 times in eight matches – a record for a 38-game season. Five games saw four or more goals scored, with Newcastle and Arsenal sharing eight in a remarkable draw. Everton beat Blackpool 5–3 – Toffees striker Louis Saha scoring four – while Wigan claimed a 4–3 win against Blackburn. A new record was also set for the most penalties scored in one matchday. Seven were converted, while Spurs' Rafael van der Vaart also missed a re-taken spot-kick.

FOWLER ON FIRE

Robbie Fowler scored the fastest hat-trick in Premier League history in August 1994. Fowler, playing for Liverpool in a home clash against Arsenal, bagged a treble in just four minutes and 33 seconds. The ball fell kindly in the box for his opener, with the prolific forward adding a second with a neat finish into the bottom corner. Fowler practically walked in his third following a fortunate rebound. Liverpool won the game 3–0.

✝ Goals in the 26th, 29th and 31st minutes for Liverpool against Arsenal on August 28 1994 secured Robbie Fowler a place in the record books. It remains the fastest hat-trick in Premier League history.

LONG-RANGERS

Goalkeeper Paul Robinson scored a free-kick from almost 90 yards for Tottenham against Watford in March 2007. The former England shot-stopper launched his kick upfield, with the bounce deceiving his opposite number, Ben Foster, before the ball flew over his head and into the net. Earlier that same season, Matthew Taylor had scored a long-range volley from more than 40 yards for Portsmouth against Everton and Xabi Alonso had netted from 65 yards in Liverpool's 2–0 win at home to Newcastle.

⋯➤ Ben Foster (left) and Paul Robinson swap stories at the end of a game in which the latter had fortuitously beaten the former with a 90-yard free-kick.

FIVE STAR

Five players have scored in the Premier League for six different clubs. Nick Barmby, Craig Bellamy, Marcus Bent, Andrew Cole and Les Ferdinand have all managed the feat. Bellamy, who last played in the top flight with Manchester City, has also scored Premier League goals for Liverpool, Newcastle, West Ham, Coventry and Blackburn. He netted his first Premier League goal for Coventry in a 2–1 win at Southampton in August 2000.

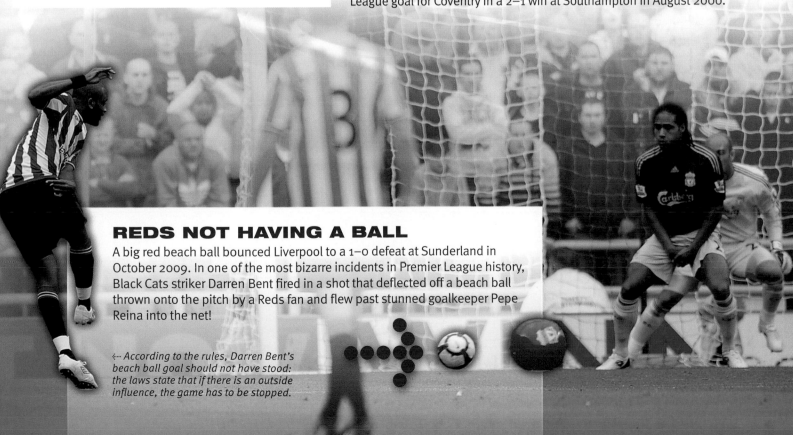

REDS NOT HAVING A BALL

A big red beach ball bounced Liverpool to a 1–0 defeat at Sunderland in October 2009. In one of the most bizarre incidents in Premier League history, Black Cats striker Darren Bent fired in a shot that deflected off a beach ball thrown onto the pitch by a Reds fan and flew past stunned goalkeeper Pepe Reina into the net!

⟵⋯ According to the rules, Darren Bent's beach ball goal should not have stood: the laws state that if there is an outside influence, the game has to be stopped.

GOALKEEPERS

FRIEDEL'S A FIXTURE

Veteran goalkeeper Brad Friedel holds the record for the most consecutive Premier League appearances. At the end of season 2010/11, the American shot-stopper had featured in 266 unbroken top-flight games. He set the record on November 30 2008 when he played for the 167th time against Fulham and made his 250th straight appearance on January 16 2011. Friedel thought his run had been ended when was sent off at Liverpool in a 5–0 defeat in March 2009, but the red card was overturned, allowing him to play in Villa's next game.

Brad Friedel has been a permanent feature in the Barclays Premier League since August 2004, making an all-time record 226 consecutive appearances.

SPOT OF BOTHER

Craig Gordon and Shay Given share the record for having the most penalties scored past them in a single Premier League season. Sunderland goalkeeper Gordon was beaten eight times during the 2007/08 campaign, including two in one game against Wigan. Given matched that feat in 2008/09, with Xabi Alonso on target from the spot in a 5–1 win for Liverpool. Dean Kiely had seven penalties put past him while playing for Charlton in 2002/03 and was sent off conceding one against Fulham on the last day.

Wigan's Denny Landzaat successfully slots a penalty past Sunderland's Craig Gordon. The Scotland keeper conceded a record eight penalties during the course of the 2007/08 season.

GOLDEN GLOVE WINNERS

2004/05	Petr Cech	(Chelsea)
2005/06	Pepe Reina	(Liverpool)
2006/07	Pepe Reina	(Liverpool)
2007/08	Pepe Reina	(Liverpool)
2008/09	Edwin van der Sar	(Manchester United)
2009/10	Petr Cech	(Chelsea)
2010/11	Joe Hart	(Manchester City)

BLUNDERFUL GOALS

Goalkeeping blunders are pretty common in football, and the Premier League has seen its fair share over the years. The normally unflappable Edwin van der Sar was guilty of one last season when he gifted West Brom a point at Old Trafford by spilling the ball at the feet of Somen Tchoyi, who tapped home. Tim Flowers was deceived by a divot on the pitch as a Stan Collymore strike looped over him and into the net in February 1996. And Shay Given was left red-faced by Dion Dublin in November 1997 when he failed to realise that the striker was behind him and put the ball down, allowing Dublin to nip in and score.

SCHMEICHEL LANDS AWARD

Peter Schmeichel was awarded the Premier League's Save of the Decade award in April 2003. The Danish shot-stopper, who was also named in the Team of the Decade, landed the prize for a stunning reflex stop to keep out a John Barnes header in a game against Newcastle in December 1997. Schmeichel is also one of only three goalkeepers to have scored in the Premier League. He pulled a goal back for Aston Villa in a 3–2 defeat at Everton in October 2001.

RISKY BUSINESS

Petr Cech wears a protective headguard in goal following an incident during a match with Reading in October 2006 that saw him fracture his skull. He came off worst as he challenged for the ball with Stephen Hunt. The midfielder's knee hit the goalkeeper's head. Cech was immediately taken to hospital, where he underwent surgery. Thankfully, he was able to make a comeback against Liverpool in January 2007.

←··· Petr Cech's collision with Stephen Hunt during Chelsea's match against Reading on October 14 2006 left the Czech keeper with serious head injuries.

SAVES OF THE SEASON

Birmingham's Ben Foster made more saves than any other top-flight goalkeeper in 2010/11. Foster's total of 245 stops was 19 more than Robert Green, who was part of a West Ham side that, like Blues, suffered relegation at the end of the season. Title-winner Edwin van der Sar made 117 saves.

METHOD IN THE MADNESS?

Most goalkeepers claim to have a technique for trying to save penalties. Former Arsenal stopper David Seaman famously claimed to have a system, although he refused to reveal what it was! David James, who played in the top flight for a string of clubs, said: 'Sometimes it's just instinctive. There have been a couple times when I have known which way the ball was going as soon as the guy put it on the spot. Then the only thing you have to do is stand up long enough to save it.'

⟶ Flamboyant, erratic and brilliant in equal measure, 1998 World Cup winner Fabien Barthez never quite managed to establish himself as Peter Schmeichel's long-term successor at Manchester United.

BURRIDGE IS GOLDEN OLDIE

Goalkeeper John Burridge is the oldest player to have featured in the Premier League. Burridge was at Manchester City when he claimed the record, coming on to replace the injured Tony Coton at half-time against Newcastle in April 1995 aged 43 years, four months and 26 days. He kept a clean sheet as the game ended goalless. Keepers hold the top six positions in the oldest player chart, with Alec Chamberlain, Steve Ogrizovic, Neville Southall, Kevin Poole and Jens Lehmann – following his return to Arsenal in 2010/11 – making up the list.

↑ Golden oldie John Burridge made the last of his appearances in English football's top flight in April 1995, 26 years after he made his debut as a professional footballer, with Workington.

ECCENTRIC KEEPERS

Goalkeepers are often seen as eccentric characters, and the Premier League has witnessed some of the most colourful. Fabien Barthez, formerly of Manchester United, was known to attempt step-overs or dribble past opposing strikers. And Liverpool's Bruce Grobbelaar was once involved in a disagreement with his own team-mate, Steve McManaman, in a clash against Everton in 1993/94.

APPEARANCES

PREMIER LEAGUE APPEARANCES

Ryan Giggs	573
David James	572
Gary Speed	535
Sol Campbell	503
Frank Lampard	491
Emile Heskey	488
Paul Scholes	465
Jamie Carragher	463
Phil Neville	460
Alan Shearer	441

2010/11 EVER-PRESENTS

Brad Friedel	(Aston Villa)
Petr Cech	(Chelsea)
Leighton Baines	(Everton)
Tim Howard	(Everton)
Jose Reina	(Liverpool)
Martin Skrtel	(Liverpool)
Joe Hart	(Manchester City)

ALI'S ONE GAME

Ali Dia is one of the Premier League's most memorable figures, despite making just one appearance in the competition back in 1996. The story goes that Dia's agent phoned Southampton's manager at the time, Graeme Souness, and convinced him that he was speaking to legendary striker George Weah. He claimed Dia was his cousin, who had played for Paris St Germain in France and was a regular for his country. Souness subsequently signed Dia on a one-month contract to give him a chance to show his skills, and the forward was thrown into action after 32 minutes of a home game against Leeds. He lasted less than an hour before being hauled off, and he was released soon afterwards!

↑ Ryan Giggs has more medals, and more appearances, than any other player in the history of the Premier League.

RYAN SNATCHES RECORD

Ryan Giggs moved above David James as the Premier League's record appearance holder at the end of the 2010/11 season – but only just! The veteran winger featured in his 573rd game for Manchester United in the 1–1 draw at Blackburn which clinched his side a 19th top-flight title. That meant he overtook goalkeeper James, playing for Bristol City in the npower Championship, by just one game going into the 2011/12 campaign. Giggs is the most successful player in Premier League history and was named PFA Player of the Year in 2009 at the age of 36.

⋯→ Marcus Bent has appeared for more Premier League clubs than any other player – a remarkable seven since he first appeared for Crystal Palace in the 1997/98 season.

BENT MAKES HIS MARC

Much-travelled striker Marcus Bent has turned out in the Premier League for seven different clubs. Since making his bow for Crystal Palace in January 1998, Bent has also played for Blackburn, Ipswich, Leicester, Everton, Charlton and Wigan. He enjoyed his best top-flight goalscoring seasons in 2001/02 and 2003/04, netting nine times for Ipswich and then Leicester.

VAN THE MAN FOR GUNNERS

Arsenal hot-shot Robin van Persie scored in a record-breaking nine consecutive away games between New Year's Day and the last game of the 2010/11 season. The Dutch striker netted 18 goals in total during that spell – a feat only previously matched by Thierry Henry and Cristiano Ronaldo. Van Persie started the run with the opening goal in a 3–0 win at Birmingham. He scored twice in games against West Ham and Newcastle and his stunning run continued until the last day, when he helped the Gunners to a point with a 2–2 draw at Fulham.

---> *Robin Van Persie scored more goals than any other player in the second half of the 2010/11 Barclays Premier League season, but it was not enough to lead Arsenal to silverware.*

LONG SEASON FOR DUO

Merseyside rivals Leighton Baines and Martin Skrtel were the only outfield players to play every single minute of the 2010/11 Barclays Premier League season. Left-back Baines scored five goals and provided 11 assists for his Everton team-mates during another impressive campaign for the England international. Slovakia centre-half Skrtel managed two goals, both of which came in 2–1 defeats – at Tottenham and West Brom – but he was a rock in the heart of Liverpool's defence. Five goalkeepers also featured in all 38 games from start to finish, including the Toffees' Tim Howard and Reds shot-stopper Jose Reina.

RANGER HAS BENCH ROLE

Nile Ranger was the most used substitute in the Barclays Premier League in 2010/11. Newcastle manager Alan Pardew brought the young striker off the bench 23 times in all, but he failed to score a goal in the top flight. Ranger was handed his full Premier League debut in the 1–0 defeat at Aston Villa in April 2011 following an injury to Shola Ameobi. It was his only start of the campaign.

<--- *Consistency was the watch-word on Merseyside last season, but Leighton Baines came off best when he and fellow ever-present Martin Skrtel played each other in October, as Everton beat Liverpool 2–0.*

↓ *Few players go from the Premier League to League 2 and back again, but that is exactly what Sol Campbell did to keep up his record of appearing in consecutive top-flight seasons.*

OLE, OLE, OLE!

Ole Gunnar Solskjaer scored a record 17 Premier League goals as a substitute during his 11-year spell at Manchester United. The Norwegian striker famously netted four times after coming off the bench in a game against Nottingham Forest in 1999, while he also made an impact as a sub in the UEFA Champions League, snatching a late winner in the final against Bayern Munich that same year.

PAIR REACH 19 NOT OUT

Ryan Giggs and Sol Campbell are the only players to have featured in all 19 Premier League seasons. Giggs' first appearance in the competition came in Manchester United's 3–0 defeat at home to Everton in August 1992, where he played 81 minutes before being substituted for Dion Dublin. Campbell looked set to lose his proud record in 2009/10 when he left Portsmouth and joined fourth-tier Notts County. However, he re-joined former club Arsenal later that season and then moved to Newcastle for the 2010/11 campaign.

PLAYERS

HAIR-RAISING STORIES

Everton ace Marouane Fellaini is undoubtedly one of the most recognisable players in the Barclays Premier League due to his stand-out hairstyle. Toffees' assistant manager Steve Round once even claimed that the midfielder's afro was contributing to the Belgian picking up more bookings. 'He's put it down to inexperience, but we've also put it down to the fact that he's quite recognisable,' Round said. Other bizarre hairstyles to crop up in the top flight over the years have included Djibril Cisse's variety of patterned cuts and Javier Margas, who dyed his hair claret and blue – the same colour as his West Ham shirt.

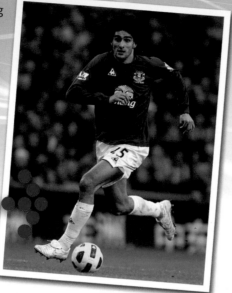

⸺⸽ Marouane Fellaini joined Everton for £12million (rising to £15million) from Standard Liege in September 2008 and has achieved cult status with the Goodison Park faithful.

↑ Gary Neville (Manchester United, right) and younger brother Phil (Everton) lead out their teams prior to the north-west rivals' top-flight clash at Old Trafford on January 31 2009.

MIDDLE MEN

Some interesting middle names have cropped up during the Premier League years, such as Peter Boleslaw Schmeichel and Emile William Ivanhoe Heskey. Last season's squad lists threw up plenty more, with Newcastle striker Peter Rosenkrands Lovenkrands joining Everton duo Phil Nikodem Jagielka and John Gijsbert Alan Heitinga and Mario Barwuah Balotelli of Manchester City in adding to the records of those with unusual names. England trio Wayne Mark Rooney, Rio Gavin Ferdinand and John George Terry have slightly less exotic middle names!

⸺⸽ At 27 letters it's unlikely that many Newcastle fans will be getting Peter Lovenkrands' full name on the back of their shirts.

SIBLING RIVALRY

No fewer than five sets of brothers played in the top flight at the same time back in 2009/10. Gary and Phil Neville are arguably the most famous siblings to have graced the Premier League, with Phil leaving Manchester United – and his sibling – for Everton in 2005. Twin brothers Rafael and Fabio Da Silva are following in the Nevilles' footsteps at Old Trafford, while Manchester United team-mate Rio Ferdinand has a brother, Anton, who plays for Sunderland. Michael and Andy Dawson turned out for Tottenham and Hull respectively, while Gary and Steven Caldwell were brought together in the top flight with Burnley and Wigan in 2010.

FOREIGN DIGNITARIES

During the most recent season, players from 65 different countries (including the four home nations) featured in Barclays Premier League matches. There have been many foreigners who have graced the top flight and at the end of the 2001/02 season, to help mark the 10th anniversary of the Premier League, a vote was taken to decide the best overseas players. A star-studded list included Arsenal's French duo Thierry Henry and Patrick Vieira, Danish goalkeeping legend Peter Schmeichel and his former Manchester United team-mate, French hero Eric Cantona.

JOBS FOR THE BOYS

Football is, or can be, a relatively short-lived career, meaning that some players need to find alternative employment after hanging up their boots. Former Sweden international Tomas Brolin played for Leeds and Crystal Palace in the Premier League and starred at World Cup USA 1994, but after retiring from football aged 32, he reportedly started selling nozzles for vacuum cleaners! Other unusual career choices include that of ex-Nottingham Forest midfielder Neil Webb, who became a postman, and Wimbledon legend Vinnie Jones, who has featured in a number of Hollywood movies.

MOST REPRESENTED NATIONALITIES 2010/11 (number of players from each country)

England	233
France	34
Ireland	24
Scotland	19
Spain	17
Wales	14
Brazil	12
Netherlands	12
United States	12
Argentina	9
Belgium	9
Ivory Coast	9
Northern Ireland	9
Senegal	8
Nigeria	7
Portugal	7
Australia	6
Denmark	6
Ghana	6
Serbia	6

A TOAST TO SHERI

Former England striker Teddy Sheringham holds the record as the oldest player, other than goalkeepers, to have featured in the Premier League. Sheringham was 40 years and 272 days old when he made his last top-flight appearance – a 1–0 defeat for West Ham against Manchester City at Upton Park on December 30 2006.

LAND OF THE GIANTS

Nikola Zigic jointly holds the record as the tallest player to have played in the competition. The giant Serbian striker, who signed for Birmingham from Spanish side Valencia for £6million in May 2010, is 202 centimetres tall. That's the same height as Stefan Maierhofer, who played a handful of games for Wolves during the 2009/10 campaign. Zigic scored five Barclays Premier League goals last season and also opened the scoring for Blues in the Carling Cup final.

Nikola Zigic is 202 centimetres tall, but keeping Birmingham in the Barclays Premier League was too tall an order for him in 2010/11.

The oldest outfield player ever to appear in the Premier League, Teddy Sheringham made his final top-flight appearance 18 years after he had made his first.

WELCOME MATT

Matthew Briggs became the youngest player to appear in the Premier League when he came off the bench for Fulham in their clash with Middlesbrough in May 2007. Briggs was 16 years and 65 days old when he came on for Moritz Volz in the 77th minute of a 3–1 defeat at the Riverside Stadium. That was Briggs' only top-flight appearance until last season, when he started three games.

ALL THE SMALL THINGS

They say that great things come in small packages, but pint-sized players have traditionally struggled to make an impact in the Premier League. Since the competition began in 1992, six players have measured up at 163 centimetres. Left-back Alan Wright was the most prominent of those – he made 260 appearances for Aston Villa in an eight-year spell between 1995 and 2003. The remaining five players – Danny Wallace, Paul Brayson, Andres D'Alessandro, Andrew Ducros and Clint Marcelle – only made 43 appearances between them. Tottenham winger Aaron Lennon was the smallest player playing in the Barclays Premier League in 2010/11, measuring up at 165cm, with Manchester City's Shaun Wright-Phillips one centimetre taller.

STADIUMS & ATTENDANCES

THEATRE OF DREAMS

Manchester United's Old Trafford home is the largest stadium in the Barclays Premier League. The 'Theatre of Dreams', as it is commonly known, has a capacity of 75,797, which is over 15,000 more than Arsenal's Emirates Stadium can hold. The capacity had been just over 76,000 until the seating was reorganised in 2009. Wembley, which plays host to all the major domestic cup finals and also the England national team, has a capacity of 90,000. Both stadiums have been given a five-star rating by UEFA.

MAINE VENUE

The record attendance for any top-flight game came at Maine Road – Manchester City's old stadium – on January 17 1948. City's derby rivals, Manchester United, took on Arsenal, with Old Trafford being rebuilt after sustaining damage during the Second World War. Reported figures range from 81,962 to 83,260, and although the total number of spectators cannot be confirmed, the 1–1 draw has gone down in history as having the highest attendance of any Football League match.

RECORD LOW FOR DONS

Wimbledon attracted the lowest attendance in Premier League history, with only 3,039 spectators turning up for a game against Everton in January 1993. The record-low crowd witnessed a 3–1 win for the visitors, with Tony Cottee scoring twice and Ian Snodin adding a third before the Dons pulled a goal back through John Fashanu. Wimbledon were sharing Selhurst Park with Crystal Palace at the time.

⌄ Empty terraces for Wimbledon's home match against Everton in the 1992/93 season – it was the lowest attendance in Premier League history.

⤑ A revamped Old Trafford was fully opened for the first time on March 31 2007, when a crowd of 76,098 saw Manchester United beat Blackburn 4–1.

DRAWING A CROWD

Manchester United set a Premier League attendance record when 76,098 spectators watched them ease to a 4–1 win against Blackburn at Old Trafford on March 31 2007. There were just 214 empty seats as second-half goals from Paul Scholes, Michael Carrick, Park Ji-Sung and Ole Gunnar Solskjaer earned United victory. Matt Derbyshire had fired Rovers ahead in the 29th minute. There has since been a reduction in capacity at the stadium.

TOP HOME ATTENDANCES 2010/11

Manchester United (v Bolton)	75,486
Arsenal (v Chelsea)	60,112
Newcastle (v Sunderland)	51,988
Sunderland (v Newcastle)	47,864
Manchester City (v Arsenal)	47,393

STANLEY PARK DIVIDE

The stadiums of Merseyside rivals Liverpool and Everton are only separated by Stanley Park. Anfield, the home of the Reds, and Everton's Goodison Park are the closest two grounds in the top flight, although Nottingham Forest and Notts County's stadiums are actually the closest in English football.

↓ *Separated by Stanley Park, Merseyside's two great football arenas, Goodison Park (left) and Anfield (right), are only 0.586 miles (0.944km) apart.*

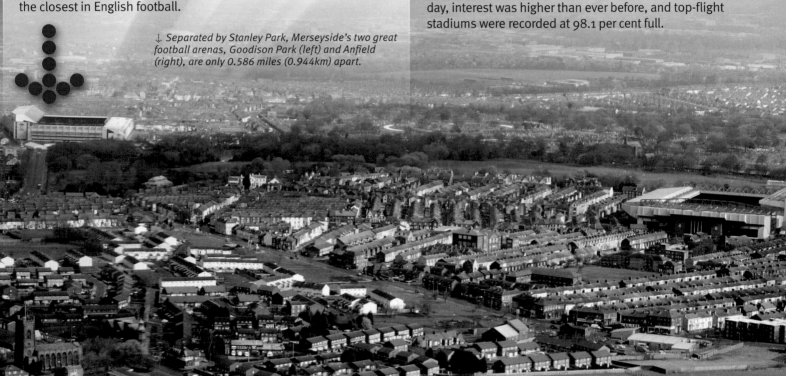

FULL HOUSE FOR FINAL DAY

Eight Barclays Premier League matches sold out on the last day of the 2010/11 season. Overall matchday attendances maintained the high levels of recent years, with grounds 92.2 per cent full throughout the course of the campaign. With five clubs battling to beat the drop on the final day, interest was higher than ever before, and top-flight stadiums were recorded at 98.1 per cent full.

AVERAGE ATTENDANCES 2010/11

Manchester United	75,109
Arsenal	60,025
Newcastle	47,718
Man City	45,778
Liverpool	42,775
Chelsea	41,435
Sunderland	40,011
Aston Villa	37,220
Everton	36,039
Tottenham	35,689
West Ham	29,198
Wolverhampton	27,696
Stoke	26,858
Birmingham	25,462
Fulham	25,043
Blackburn	25,000
West Brom	24,683
Bolton	22,870
Wigan	16,812
Blackpool	15,780

RISE AND SHINE

The earliest kick-off ever in the competition's history was on October 2 2005 when a clash between Manchester City and Everton started at 11.15am. The game had been moved from its original Saturday afternoon slot due to the Toffees' UEFA Cup commitments. Two fixtures had already been scheduled for the Sunday, so the game started early. A crowd of 42,681 were in attendance – one fan turning up in pyjamas as a joke – as a stunning 25-yard strike from Danny Mills and an injury-time goal from Darius Vassell secured City a 2–0 win.

NEW HOME FOR GUNNERS

Arsenal's Emirates Stadium is the newest stadium in the Barclays Premier League, having been officially opened in July 2006. It is the third biggest stadium in London after Wembley and Twickenham – the home of England's rugby union team. The ground was initially known as Ashburton Grove until a multi-million pound sponsorship deal was struck. It has a capacity of 60,361 spectators, although the highest attendance currently stands at 60,161. That was for a 2–2 draw against Manchester United in November 2007.

↓ *Arsenal's Emirates Stadium is one of the first sights that visiting fans from the north of the country see of London as they make their way into the capital on the train.*

MANAGERS

MANAGER OF THE YEAR SINCE 2002

2001/02	Arsene Wenger	(Arsenal)
2002/03	Sir Alex Ferguson	(Manchester United)
2003/04	Arsene Wenger	(Arsenal)
2004/05	Jose Mourinho	(Chelsea)
2005/06	Jose Mourinho	(Chelsea)
2006/07	Sir Alex Ferguson	(Manchester United)
2007/08	Sir Alex Ferguson	(Manchester United)
2008/09	Sir Alex Ferguson	(Manchester United)
2009/10	Harry Redknapp	(Tottenham)
2010/11	Sir Alex Ferguson	(Manchester United)

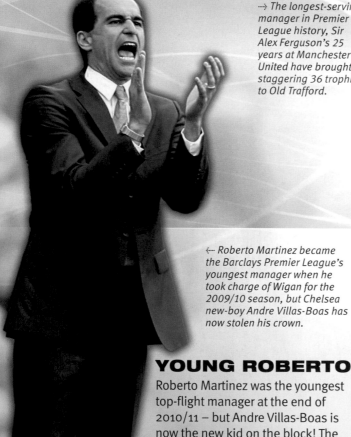

---> The longest-serving manager in Premier League history, Sir Alex Ferguson's 25 years at Manchester United have brought a staggering 36 trophies to Old Trafford.

<--- Roberto Martinez became the Barclays Premier League's youngest manager when he took charge of Wigan for the 2009/10 season, but Chelsea new-boy Andre Villas-Boas has now stolen his crown.

YOUNG ROBERTO

Roberto Martinez was the youngest top-flight manager at the end of 2010/11 – but Andre Villas-Boas is now the new kid on the block! The Chelsea coach was only 33 when he replaced Carlo Ancelotti at Stamford Bridge. Spaniard Martinez is 38 – 169 days younger than Brendan Rodgers of Swansea. At the start of 2011/12, there were five managers in their 60s. Sir Alex Ferguson is the oldest top-flight boss at 69, while Tottenham boss Harry Redknapp is five years younger.

FERGIE IS PART OF THE FURNITURE

Sir Alex Ferguson is currently the longest-serving manager, as well as the most successful, in English football. He was appointed boss of Manchester United in November 1986, meaning that the season just gone was the Scot's 25th in the Old Trafford dugout. Arsene Wenger has just completed his 15th campaign at Arsenal, putting him second in the list, with Everton's David Moyes fourth overall throughout the divisions after spending the last 10 terms at Goodison Park. Moyes took charge of his 350th game in May 2011 – a 1–0 defeat at West Brom.

THE NAME GAME

Jose Mourinho was dubbed 'The Special One' by the media on his arrival at Chelsea in June 2004, but he is not the only boss to have been given a nickname by fans and the press. Another former Chelsea coach, Claudio Ranieri, earned the tag of 'The Tinkerman' for his constant experimentation with the Blues' line-up, while new West Ham boss Sam Allardyce is affectionately known as 'Big Sam', Alex McLeish is 'Big Eck' and Sir Alex Ferguson is 'Fergie'.

MULTI-NATIONAL MANAGERS

Managers from seven different countries were in charge of Barclays Premier League teams at the end of the 2010/11 campaign. Of the 20 top-flight clubs, England had six bosses, Scotland had five and Italy, France, Wales and the Republic of Ireland each had two. Bolton chief Owen Coyle was born in Paisley, Scotland, and Wolves boss Mick McCarthy hails from Barnsley, but both represented Ireland during their playing careers. Spaniard Roberto Martinez completes the multi-national line-up, although Israeli Avram Grant was also in charge of West Ham until the penultimate game of the season.

SHORT AND NOT SO SWEET

Roy Hodgson was sacked after just 20 games in charge of Liverpool last season, but that was by no means the shortest Premier League managerial reign. Les Reed was manager of Charlton for just six weeks in late 2006. Reed had been Iain Dowie's assistant at The Valley but was promoted on November 14 when Dowie left the club. He managed just one victory and saw his side knocked out of the League Cup by fourth-tier outfit Wycombe before leaving his post on Christmas Eve. Sammy Lee spent 11 games in charge of Bolton between April and October 2007, while Colin Todd lasted 17 matches as boss of Derby in 2001/02.

↓ Kevin Keegan watches on as Newcastle's faint Premier League title hopes fade following their 1–1 draw against Nottingham Forest on May 2 1996.

KEEGAN LOSES HIS COOL

Top-flight bosses are always good for a memorable soundbite, but perhaps the most famous is Kevin Keegan's emotional outburst following Newcastle's 1–0 win at Leeds in April 1996. The Magpies had seen a significant lead at the top of the Premier League overturned by Manchester United, meaning that the title race was really hotting up. Keegan, hitting back at a comment made by United boss Sir Alex Ferguson, ended his televised rant with the now immortal line: 'I would love it if we beat them, love it!'

BROWN'S DRESSING DOWN

A manager's half-time team-talk can play a big part in how a side performs in the second half of a game. Normally, it's held in the dressing room, but on Boxing Day 2008, Hull boss Phil Brown took the unusual step of telling his players his thoughts on the pitch in front of the club's travelling fans. The Tigers were 4–0 down at the time against Manchester City, but they improved after the break to go down 5–1.

⋯⋯▸ Already 4–0 down in the match against Manchester City in December 2008, Phil Brown reads the half-time riot act to his Hull players.

PORTERFIELD WINS SACK RACE

Ian Porterfield was the first managerial casualty of the Premier League era. He left his job at Chelsea in February 1993 and was replaced on a temporary basis by David Webb. However, chairman Ken Bates opted to bring in Glenn Hoddle for the start of the 1993/94 campaign. Three more managers left their jobs at the end of that inaugural season, with Steve Coppell resigning at Crystal Palace, Brian Clough retiring at Nottingham Forest and Doug Livermore being replaced by Ossie Ardiles at Tottenham.

⋯⋯▸ On February 15 1993, Ian Porterfield paid the price for Chelsea's dramatic slump in form by becoming the first managerial casualty of the Premier League era.

MOYES MAKES HIS MARK

David Moyes became an instant hit with Everton fans when he labelled the Toffees 'The People's Club' on his arrival in March 2002. Glasgow-born Moyes said: 'I am from a city that is not unlike Liverpool. I am joining the people's football club. The majority of people you meet on the street are Everton fans.' That statement went down well with the blue half of Merseyside, although not so much with Liverpool fans!

TRANSFERS

COLE IS OUT OF TOON

Andrew Cole broke the British transfer record in January 1995 when he swapped Newcastle for Manchester United. It was the first record-breaking move since the introduction of the Premier League. Cole had scored 34 top-flight goals for the Magpies in season 1993/94 and added nine more in 18 games in 1994/95 before making the move to Old Trafford. The Red Devils paid £6.25million cash for Cole and also sent Keith Gillespie in the opposite direction.

SHEAR MAGIC FOR MAGPIES

Newcastle broke the world transfer record to land Alan Shearer from Blackburn in July 1996. The Magpies paid Rovers £15million to sign the prolific England striker, who had finished the 1995/96 campaign with 31 league goals. Shearer netted 25 times in the Premier League in his first season with his boyhood club to top the goalscoring charts for the third consecutive term. He also scooped the PFA Player of the Year award for the second time.

← A crowd of 15,000 diehard fans braved the rain to salute Alan Shearer's world-record transfer to Newcastle in 1996.

↑ Fernando Torres' move from Liverpool to Chelsea was part of a spending spree on January transfer deadline day in 2011.

DEADLINE-DAY MADNESS

Transfer deadline day always creates a buzz, with clubs attempting to push through deals at the last minute. However, the events of January 31 2011 were even more crazy than normal. Chelsea, who had seen their title bid falter, agreed an amazing move for Liverpool hot-shot Fernando Torres. The Reds, who were only willing to sell if they had a replacement, splashed out on two big names – Newcastle's Andy Carroll and Luis Suarez of Ajax. Manchester United have left it late to complete moves for both Wayne Rooney and Dimitar Berbatov in recent years.

GROVES STARTS A TREND

Big-money transfers may be commonplace in English football nowadays, but Willie Groves was actually the first player to be transferred for over £100. The Scottish forward moved from Celtic to West Brom in 1890, but it was his switch from the Baggies to rivals Aston Villa three years later that set the record. Groves went on to help the Villans to the First Division title in 1894.

BRITISH TRANSFER RECORDS SINCE 1995*

Player	Transfer	Fee	Date
Andrew Cole	(Newcastle to Manchester United)	£6.25million	Jan 1995
Dennis Bergkamp	(Inter Milan to Arsenal)	£7.5million	June 1995
Stan Collymore	(Nottingham Forest to Liverpool)	£8.5million	June 1995
Alan Shearer	(Blackburn to Newcastle)	£15million	July 1996
Nicolas Anelka	(Arsenal to Real Madrid)	£22.5million	Aug 1999
Juan Sebastian Veron	(Lazio to Manchester United)	£28.1million	July 2001
Rio Ferdinand	(Leeds to Manchester United)	£29.1million	July 2002
Andriy Shevchenko	(AC Milan to Chelsea)	£30.8million	July 2002
Robinho	(Real Madrid to Manchester City)	£32.5million	Sept 2008
Cristiano Ronaldo	(Manchester United to Real Madrid)	£80million	June 2009

* Reported fees

RECORD-BREAKING RONALDO

Cristiano Ronaldo holds the world transfer record following his incredible £80million move from Manchester United to Real Madrid in June 2009. The Portugal winger enjoyed a stunning season at Old Trafford in 2007/08, scoring 42 goals in all competitions – 31 of those in the league – but United rejected Madrid's advances that summer. However, Ronaldo expressed his desire to leave the club after another impressive campaign in 2008/09 – he scored 18 top-flight goals and 25 in total – and the record-breaking deal was sealed that summer.

It took a world-record transfer fee of £80million for Real Madrid to prise Cristiano Ronaldo away from Old Trafford.

FIRMANI'S ITALIAN JOB

The cosmopolitan nature of the English game frequently sees players come and go from overseas, but Eddie Firmani was the first player to move abroad from a British club. He set a British transfer record when he left Charlton for Italian side Sampdoria in July 1955.

SWITCHING SIDES

Transfers between derby rivals have caused a few stirs over the years. Sol Campbell's move from Tottenham to Arsenal in July 2001 didn't go down well with the White Hart Lane faithful, while Ashley Cole was given a tough time by Gunners fans following his switch to Chelsea in August 2006. Nick Barmby moved from Everton to Liverpool in a £6million deal in July 2000 – the highest fee the Reds have ever paid to their Merseyside rivals.

Eric Cantona's arrival galvanised Manchester United, who won the Premier League title in four of the Frenchman's five seasons at the club.

Injury plagued Paul Gascoigne's spell at Lazio – the England star made just 47 appearances in three seasons at the club before joining Rangers in July 1995.

BARGAIN BUYS

Everybody loves a bargain, and that's what Manchester United got when they signed Eric Cantona from Leeds for £1.2million in November 1992. The Frenchman had helped the Yorkshire club to the First Division title before leaving for Old Trafford. Cantona went on to become a United legend, scoring 64 Premier League goals. Fellow Frenchman Christophe Dugarry also proved to be a steal for Birmingham in 2003 when he scored five goals in as many games during a loan spell from Bordeaux to help the club avoid relegation.

GAZZA GOES TO LAZIO

Paul Gascoigne was one of the last big-money movers before the start of the Premier League. He left Tottenham to join Italian club Lazio in a reported £5.5million deal in 1992. Gascoigne, whose first goal for the club was an 89th-minute equaliser in the Rome derby against Roma, struggled with injuries and was sold to Glasgow Rangers in July 1995.

OWNERS & CHAIRMEN

CITY SLICKERS

Manchester City are regarded as having one of the most expensive teams in the Barclays Premier League. The club is owned by Sheikh Mansour bin Zayed Al Nahyan, a member of the Abu Dhabi royal family. In Sheikh Mansour's first summer, City announced their bold intentions in the transfer market by buying six players, including striker Carlos Tevez. And before the first transfer window closed in August 2010, David Silva, Yaya Toure, Mario Balotelli, Jerome Boateng, Aleksander Kolarov and James Milner had arrived. Wolfsburg striker Edin Dzeko in January 2011.

↑ Manchester City's transfer market policy paid off in 2010/11 as boss Roberto Mancini led his team of stars to qualification for the UEFA Champions League.

SMITH COOKS UP A HALF-TIME TREAT

Celebrity chef Delia Smith memorably made an impassioned plea for support from Norwich fans on the Carrow Road pitch at half-time of a game against Manchester City in February 2005. The Canaries were leading 2–0 when Smith, the club's joint majority shareholder, grabbed a microphone and came onto the field. After praising the Norwich fans as the best in the division, she then urged them to be more vocal in the second half, asking: 'Where are you? Let's be having you!' City went on to lose the game 3–2.

↓ A former season-ticket holder at Norwich, Delia Smith (along with husband Michael Wynn-Jones) became the club's joint majority shareholder in 1996.

↑ It's little wonder QPR supremo Lakshmi Mittal is all smiles given the staggering amount of cash he has to spend!

JUMPING THROUGH HOOPS

Barclays Premier League new-boys QPR have the financial backing to compete with the big-boys. Lakshmi Mittal and his family, who own a 20 per cent stake in the London club, are billionaires, while F1 supremo Bernie Ecclestone, who has a 15 per cent stake in the Hoops, is also a billionaire. Both men featured in the top 10 of the Barclays Premier League Rich List for 2010/11.

YOU'RE FIRED!

Lord Alan Sugar, star of the television show *The Apprentice*, was chairman of Tottenham between 1991 and 2001. Spurs won just one trophy during his reign – the League Cup in 1999 – but he did break the club's transfer record to bring Les Ferdinand to White Hart Lane in 1997. Lord Sugar sacked several bosses during his time in charge – presumably giving him an early chance to perfect his now famous 'You're fired' catchphrase!

⇠ Lord Alan Sugar's 10-year reign as Tottenham chairman saw seven different managers at the White Hart Lane club.

THE AMERICAN DREAM

There has been an influx of American businessmen into the Barclays Premier League over the last few years. Three of the perceived 'Big Four' – Manchester United, Arsenal and Liverpool – have either an American owner or a large shareholder from the USA. The Glazer family own United, Fenway Sports Group run Liverpool and Stan Kroenke now holds just over 66% of the Gunners' shares. Missouri-born Ellis Short is the majority shareholder at Sunderland, while Randy Lerner – who also owns the Cleveland Browns American football team – has been in charge at Aston Villa since 2006.

A VOTE OF CONFIDENCE

It's nice to have the support of the powers-that-be, but getting a vote of confidence from your chairman is not always a sign that things are going well as a manager. That normally happens if a team is under pressure due to poor results or performances. Blackburn owner Anuradha Desai went public to give her backing to Steve Kean in March 2011 following a fifth loss in six games. Gianfranco Zola, meanwhile, was also given a vote of confidence by joint West Ham owner David Sullivan in 2009/10, only to be sacked that summer.

A FAN WITH A PLAN

Steve Gibson helped his boyhood club to reach new heights in the Premier League. The Middlesbrough chairman took over the Teessiders in 1994 having become a director at just 26. He raised the club's profile by building a brand new all-seater stadium and bringing in big-name players such as Juninho and Fabrizio Ravanelli, and he guided them to a seventh-place finish in the top flight in 2004/05.

⇠ A self-made millionaire and a lifelong Boro fan, Steve Gibson is one of the most respected chairmen in English football.

DIRECTORS IN THE PICTURE

The role of director of football may be a common one on the continent but it is relatively new to the English game. Those in the job are normally seen as a go-between from the manager to the club's board and the owner, and they rarely get involved in the coaching of players. Avram Grant held the position at both Chelsea and Portsmouth and went on to take over as manager on both occasions. Liverpool brought in Damien Comolli to help Roy Hodgson with the recruitment of players in November 2010 and he now works alongside Kenny Dalglish.

ROMAN'S EMPIRE

Roman Abramovich took English football to a new level when he bought Chelsea in July 2003. That summer, the Russian billionaire immediately brought in world-class players such as Claude Makelele and Arjen Robben. In May 2006, he smashed the British transfer record to sign Andriy Shevchenko. Since Abramovich took over, Chelsea have won the Barclays Premier League title three times, the FA Cup three times, the Carling Cup twice and have been beaten finalists in the UEFA Champions League.

⇡ Russian billionaire Roman Abramovich has invested heavily in Chelsea since buying the west London club in July 2003.

SUPPORTERS

↑ *Everton fan Sylvester Stallone acknowledges the Goodison Park fans before the Toffees' match against Reading in January 2007.*

SONGS OF PRAISE

Supporters can be cruel at times. Managers struggling for a win to save their jobs are often on the receiving end of 'You're getting sacked in the morning' chants from opposition fans. Some of the Premier League's top stars have also been immortalised in song by supporters down the years. 'Ooh-Ahh, Cantona' could regularly be heard ringing around Old Trafford when 'King Eric' turned out for Manchester United, while Ryan Giggs can also boast his own chant. To the tune of Joy Division's Love Will Tear Us Apart, the Stretford End sing: 'Giggs... Giggs will tear you apart, again.'

↓ *Manchester United's fans pack out the famous Stretford End of Old Trafford as the teams are led out for the Manchester derby.*

PREMIER LEAGUE A-LISTERS

Some of Hollywood's biggest stars support Barclays Premier League clubs. Tom Hanks is an Aston Villa fan, Samuel L. Jackson fell in love with Liverpool while shooting a film there, and Sylvester Stallone – star of Rocky and Rambo – watched Everton draw 1–1 with Reading in January 2007. Brad Pitt is said to be a Manchester United fan, while pop star Justin Timberlake was once photographed at Old Trafford. Funnyman Will Ferrell wore a Chelsea shirt when he watched the Blues beat Inter Milan in a pre-season friendly in America.

ON THE BOX

More football fans tuned in to watch Barclays Premier League action than ever before during the most recent campaign. The BBC's Match of the Day programme peaked at 5.4million viewers in February, while Tottenham's home clash with Manchester United posted Sky's biggest figures for a live game at 3.23million. United's trip to Wolves on February 5 2011 attracted 806,000 ESPN subscribers. They were the best figures since the detailed data was first recorded in 2004/05.

BLUE-NOSE CARRAGHER

Jamie Carragher may turn out for Liverpool every week, but he was an Everton fan growing up. He revealed: 'Everton controlled my life and dominated my thoughts 24/7. I went to the away games, followed them across Europe and in the mid-80s went to Wembley so often it began to feel like Alton Towers!' The Reds defender is not the only player to reveal his boyhood idols. Robbie Keane grew up as a Liverpool supporter, Manchester City's Adam Johnson is a Sunderland fan and Joleon Lescott, who used to play for Wolves, apparently has a soft spot for Aston Villa!

THE LOUDEST PREMIER LEAGUE FANS

Liverpool	97 decibels
Manchester United	94 decibels
Aston Villa	89 decibels
Everton	86 decibels
Blackpool	85 decibels
Stoke	83 decibels
Newcastle	82 decibels
West Ham	81 decibels
Chelsea	80 decibels
Sunderland	80 decibels

↑ The noise generated at Anfield when Liverpool supporters are in full voice is equivalent to a Boeing 737 coming in to land.

ASIA AND BEYOND

The Barclays Premier League is the most popular and most watched league in the world, and it has a particularly strong following in Asia. The Barclays Premier League Asia Trophy was introduced in 2003 as a way of giving fans across the continent the chance to catch a glimpse of their heroes in action. It has taken place in a different country once every two years since, with Chelsea, Bolton, Portsmouth and Tottenham all having won the event. The tournament returned to Hong Kong in 2011, with Aston Villa, Blackburn and Chelsea taking part.

REDS MAKE A RACKET

Liverpool fans are officially the loudest in the Barclays Premier League. The Reds reached an average of 97 decibels when crowd noise was measured up and down the country during the 2010/11 season. A decibel meter was set up inside every top-flight ground on three separate occasions, with an average taken to give a table of the loudest supporters. Manchester United fans were second in the table, reaching 94 decibels.

DO THE POZNAN

Manchester City took more than Europa League points off Polish side Lech Poznan in October 2010. The Lech Poznan fans turned out to have an unusual way of celebrating goals, turning away from the pitch, waving their scarves above their heads and bouncing up and down. City fans decided to take the dance as their own, chanting 'Let's all do the Poznan' as they got stadiums rocking up and down the country. Fans from other clubs, including West Ham, have since joined in the craze.

↓ Tottenham's Wilson Palacios (left) and Hull's Geovanni (right) battle for the ball during the two sides' Barclays Asia Trophy clash in Beijing in July 2009.

⇢ Manchester City fans show how the dance is done after their team score the only goal of the game against Stoke City in the 2011 FA Cup final at Wembley.

THE SOCIAL NETWORK

Social networking sites such as Twitter have brought players and fans closer together. Big names such as Rio Ferdinand, Jack Wilshere and Cesc Fabregas regularly 'tweet', sometimes offering supporters the chance to win money-can't-buy prizes, while occasionally replying to questions from fans. Players also use these sites to update fans and media on their lives.

BRAGGING RIGHTS

Derby games are always exciting and some of biggest take place in the Barclays Premier League. Last season there were 94 matches which could be classed as derbies but in 2011/12 that figure dropped to 74, given the teams in the division. The Manchester derbies, Merseyside derby and a host of London clashes are just some that earn fans of the winning team bragging rights on a Monday morning.

DISCIPLINARY & REFEREE RECORDS

CAMEO APPEARANCES

Three players have been sent off in the Premier League era without even touching a ball! Swedish defender Andreas Johansson's first act after coming on for Wigan on the last day of the 2005/06 season was to bring down Freddie Ljungberg in the penalty area. His second was to walk off the pitch after being shown a red card! Keith Gillespie was playing for Sheffield United when he was dismissed for elbowing Reading's Stephen Hunt in January 2007, just a few seconds after entering the action. And Dave Kitson lasted less than a minute of Reading's clash with Manchester United in August of that same year before he was sent off for a late challenge on Patrice Evra.

⋯⋯▸ Reading's Dave Kitson sees red less than a minute after coming on as a substitute during the Royals' 0–0 draw against Manchester United in August 2007.

↑ Dermot Gallagher was on the Premier League's referee roster for 15 years before his retirement in 2007.

GALLAGHER IS A HIT

Dermot Gallagher spent a record 15 years refereeing in the Premier League between 1992 and 2007. Gallagher's first game in the competition was a 2–0 win for Coventry at Tottenham on August 19 1992, while his final fixture was a 2–2 draw between Liverpool and Charlton at Anfield on May 13 2007. He didn't dish out a single yellow or red card during that match. Graham Poll officiated in the Premier League for 14 years, while Mike Riley managed 13.

REDS HAVE BEST RECORD

Liverpool have the best disciplinary record of the seven clubs who have been involved in the Premier League since the start. At the end of the most recent campaign, the Reds had totalled 879 bookings and 41 red cards from 734 matches. Manchester United have had 48 players sent off since 1992 and have recorded 65 more yellow cards than the Merseysiders.

RESPECT CAMPAIGN

The Football Association launched the Respect campaign in the summer of 2008 aimed at improving the behaviour of players and coaches towards referees and officials. Guidelines were set out that now mean only the team captain is allowed to approach the referee, while all players are asked to adhere to a basic code of conduct governing their behaviour on the pitch.

OLDEST AND YOUNGEST

Peter Walton is the Barclay's Premier League's oldest referee, while Michael Oliver is the youngest. Walton, who turned 52 in October 2011, took charge of his first game in the competition in 2003 – a 4–3 win for Wolves against Leicester. Oliver became the youngest person ever to officiate in the Premier League when he took charge of Birmingham's 2–1 win at home to Blackburn in August 2010. He was 25 years and 182 days old, beating Stuart Attwell's record.

NOTE OF CAUTION

Newcastle midfielder Cheik Tiote was shown the yellow card 14 times during the 2010/11 season, equalling the record for the most bookings received in a single Premier League campaign. Mark Hughes was playing for Southampton and Olivier Dacourt turned out for Everton when they reached that number during the 1998/99 campaign. Robbie Savage equalled that total in 2001/02 while at Leicester, and Paul Ince repeated the feat in season 2003/04 when he was bossing the Wolves midfield.

⤓ It's yet another yellow card for Everton's Olivier Dacourt, this time against Leeds on September 12 1998.

DUNNE AND DUSTED

Richard Dunne joined Duncan Ferguson and Patrick Vieira on eight top-flight red cards when he was sent off in Manchester City's 1–0 win against Wigan in January 2009. The Republic of Ireland international was dismissed shortly after Pablo Zabaleta had put City ahead. That was Dunne's second league dismissal of the 2008/09 season, and he was sent off for a third time in the UEFA Cup clash against Hamburg the following April.

⇢ Manchester City defender Richard Dunne has his head in his hands after being shown a red card in the final moments of his side's 2–1 defeat to Tottenham in November 2008.

BLUES TOP FAIR PLAY TABLE

Chelsea topped the Fair Play table in 2010/11. The table is decided via a points system, with various aspects of a club's performance being assessed after every game. The amount of bookings and red cards, as well as positive play and respect towards referees, are taken into consideration. The top three national associations in UEFA's Fair Play League are given an extra Europa League place, with Fulham taking the additional spot this year. Chelsea, Tottenham and Manchester United had already qualified for Europe via the Barclays Premier League, so the Cottagers were the ones who benefited.

FAIR PLAY TABLE 2010/11

Chelsea	1297
Tottenham	1288
Manchester United	1271
Fulham	1264
Blackpool	1263
West Ham	1259
West Brom	1253
Arsenal	1251
Liverpool	1244
Manchester City	1243

⇢ A record 94 yellow cards and five red cards make Lee Bowyer, now with Birmingham, perhaps the most combative player in Premier League history.

BOWYER IS BOOKED UP

Lee Bowyer is the most booked player in Premier League history. Bowyer, who is known for his tough-tackling approach, was shown a yellow card on seven occasions while playing for Birmingham in 2010/11 to take his overall total to 101 cautions. That figure is four more than Bolton striker Kevin Davies, whose 10 bookings last season moved him up to second on the all-time list.

ATKINSON SEES RED

Martin Atkinson dished out 10 red cards in the Barclays Premier League in 2010/11 – the most by any top-flight referee. He sent off two players in a single game on two occasions. The first was on the first weekend of the season when Liverpool drew 1–1 with Arsenal, with Joe Cole and Laurent Koscielny both dismissed. Atkinson then sent off Antolin Alcaraz and Hugo Rodallega as Wigan lost 2–0 and ended the game with nine men at Manchester United in November.

CHAMPIONSHIP ALL-TIME RECORDS

The second tier was first introduced in 1892, starting out with 12 clubs. That number has doubled under the current format, with the npower Championship – as it is now known – continuing to go from strength to strength. Over the years, big guns such as Manchester United and Liverpool have competed in the division, alongside smaller teams like Darwen and Loughborough – both of whom left their mark, albeit for the wrong reasons!

Queens Park Rangers' captain Adel Taarabt lifts the npower Championship trophy in 2011. Until 1992 this trophy, known as The Lady, was actually awarded to the champions of England's top tier but since the advent of the Premier League the trophy has gone to the champions of the second tier.

CHAMPIONS, PARTICIPATION, UPS & DOWNS

LOUGHBOROUGH LAND RECORD

Loughborough managed just one victory during the 1899/00 season – a second-tier record. The Leicestershire club were elected to The Football League for the start of the 1895/96 campaign but lasted just five seasons before dropping out. Loughborough's sole win that term came with a 2–1 victory at home to Burton United. They finished rock bottom with eight points and having scored just 18 times – also a Football League landmark for the fewest goals scored in a season.

BLACK CATS POUNCE

Sunderland romped to the league title in 1998/99, finishing a massive 18 points ahead of runners-up Bradford. Peter Reid was in charge as the Black Cats lost just three games – against Barnsley, Tranmere and Watford – to end the campaign with a then-record 105 points. Reading broke that when they went a point better in 2005/06.

⬇ Peter Reid won The Football League championship as a player at Everton in the top flight in 1985, and then was boss of Sunderland when they finished top of the second tier 14 years later.

SMALL HEATH STAY PUT

Small Heath, or Birmingham as they are now known, finished top of the very first second-tier table in 1892/93 – but they missed out on promotion. Before automatic promotion was introduced, the bottom three teams in the top flight took on the top three from the second tier each season to determine who went up. Small Heath played Division One's bottom club, Newton Heath (now Manchester United), and were beaten 5–2 in a replay after the initial clash had finished 1–1. Bizarrely, both the runners-up, Sheffield United, and Darwen, who finished third, did win promotion.

DONNY DOWN AND OUT

The 1904/05 season ended in disappointment for Doncaster, with their eight-point total equalling Loughborough's record for the lowest ever. However, Rovers managed treble the amount of wins, beating Barnsley, Leicester and Glossop and drawing with Blackpool and Port Vale in a league that also included Manchester United and Liverpool. Cambridge hold the record for the lowest total since three points for a win was introduced, taking just 24 in 1983/84.

SECOND NOT THE BEST

Norwich finished second to Queens Park Rangers with a healthy 84 points in 2010/11, but that is not the highest total for a runner-up in the division. In the 2002/03 campaign, a Leicester side managed by Micky Adams finished six points behind champions Portsmouth to gain automatic promotion with an impressive 92-point haul.

⬆ Norwich celebrate their return to the Barclays Premier League for the 2011/12 season by finishing second in the npower Championship.

LOSING LIONS

Millwall lost a record 12 games during the 1987/88 season but still managed to win the league. Runners-up Aston Villa, Middlesbrough, who finished third, Bradford in fourth and even fifth-place Blackburn all lost fewer matches than the Lions. However, John Docherty's side won 25 games – three more than their closest rivals – to win the title by four points and earn a place in the top flight for the first time in the club's history.

↓ Under manager John Docherty, Millwall took the policy of win some, lose some to new levels in 1987/88. They lost more games than four other rivals, but still won the second-tier title.

SEVEN UP FOR WARNOCK

Neil Warnock secured a record-equalling seventh promotion when he led QPR to the npower Championship title in 2010/11. Warnock's first achievement in management was to guide Scarborough into the Football League in 1987, while his most impressive feat was back-to-back promotions with Notts County, which resulted in them reaching the top flight in 1991. He also tasted success with Huddersfield, Plymouth and Sheffield United. Dave Bassett and Graham Taylor had been the only bosses to spearhead seven promotion-winning campaigns before Warnock.

⇢ Guiding QPR to the npower Championship title was one of a line of achievements for Neil Warnock, who has won promotion a record number of times.

SECOND TIER FOUNDER MEMBERS

Ardwick
Bootle
Burslem Port Vale
Burton Swifts
Crewe
Darwen
Grimsby
Lincoln
Northwich Victoria
Sheffield United
Small Heath
Walsall Town Swifts

EAGLES SOAR DESPITE DRAWS

Crystal Palace set a new landmark in 1978/79 when they claimed the championship despite drawing 19 games. The Eagles drew more matches than any other team in the division that term, but they clinched the league crown by a point from runners-up Brighton and Stoke in third.

BLADES BLUNTED BY MISERABLE RUN

Sheffield United went 14 games without a win on their way to relegation from the npower Championship at the end of season 2010/11. The miserable run began with a 3–2 defeat at home to Hull on Boxing Day and the Blades didn't taste victory again until March 8, when they were surprise 2–1 winners against promotion-chasing Nottingham Forest. United's cause was not helped by 12 red cards – by far the most in the division. Both Shane Lowry and Lee Williamson were sent off twice.

⇢ Lee Williamson and his Sheffield United team-mates paid the price for a long winless run in 2010/11 as they dropped out of the npower Championship, racking up the most sendings off in the process.

TEAM RECORDS

SCORING BLUES FOR CITY

Birmingham failed to score in a record 24 of their 46 matches in 1988/89. Blues got the season off to a losing start when they were beaten 1–0 at Watford, and that set the tone as they went on to suffer relegation. The longest run of consecutive games they went without hitting the net was six.

⬇ Derby's only win of the 2007/08 Barclays Premier League season came against Newcastle in September. Rob Hulse was the Rams' match-winner when they ended their 36-game winless run against Sheffield United almost 12 months later.

SWANS MAKE IT THREE

Swansea became the third team in the division's history to draw eight games in a row following a run of stalemates in 2008/09. The sequence started with a 1–1 draw at Coventry, although the home side needed a late leveller from Daniel Fox to snatch a point. A goalless draw at Birmingham on December 28 was the last game of the run. Middlesbrough first set the record at the end of season 1970/71. Southampton also ac hieved the feat in 2005/06.

↑ Leon Britton missed part of Swansea's run of eight consecutive draws after he was red-carded against Cardiff on November 30 2008.

LONGEST UNBEATEN RUNS

33 games	Reading	2005/06
28 games	Liverpool	1893/94
27 games	Chelsea	1988/89

REDS ROMP TO TITLE

Liverpool managed to go through the whole of the 1893/94 season without losing a game. The Reds claimed the title by eight points from Small Heath – or Birmingham City as they are known today – with an impressive record of 22 wins and six draws. Two points were awarded for a victory in those days, with the Merseysiders collecting 50 from 28 games.

ROTTEN RUN FOR RAMS

Derby went 36 matches without a victory from September 22 2007 to September 13 2008, although the run actually started in the Barclays Premier League and ended in the second tier. The sequence began with a 5–0 loss at Arsenal, with Emmanuel Adebayor scoring a hat-trick, and continued for the remaining 31 league games until their relegation was confirmed. Four more second-tier games followed in 2008/09 before goals from Paul Green and Rob Hulse finally secured a 2–1 win against Sheffield United.

UNITED FALL SHORT

Mighty Manchester United were a second-tier team back in 1904/05 when they set a record for the most consecutive wins at that level. The Red Devils clocked up 14 straight victories, although that was still not enough to win them the title, as they finished third. Bristol City and Preston subsequently matched that record run, and unlike the Manchester giants, they went on to claim the championship. The Robins were almost unbeatable in season 1905/06, while North End achieved the feat in 1950/51.

HOME SWEET HOME

Liverpool and Sheffield Wednesday are the only teams to have won every home game during a second-tier season. The Reds completed that remarkable achievement during 1893/94, winning all 14 of their matches at Anfield as part of an unbeaten league campaign. Six years later, the Owls won all 17 of their home games on their way to clinching the championship by two points.

DONS DOWN AND OUT

Wimbledon suffered a record 33 defeats during the 2003/04 campaign on their way to finishing bottom of the second tier. The Londoners, who moved to Milton Keynes and reformed as MK Dons the following season, won just eight times all campaign and drew their other five games. They were beaten 4–0 by Watford, 5–0 by West Ham and 6–0 at Nottingham Forest during a season to forget.

NOT A BIG SQUAD FOR FOREST

For the second successive season in 2010/11, Nottingham Forest reached the second tier play-offs having used the fewest players throughout the campaign. Manager Billy Davies worked wonders with 25 players in 2009/10 and that increased by just five as Forest claimed a top-six place again 12 months later. Portsmouth also used a season-low squad of 30 as they secured a mid-table finish, while relegated Sheffield United had the least settled line-up, with 44 different players featuring at various points.

⋯⟶ *Nottingham Forest used just 30 players as they secured a place in the npower Championship Play-Offs in 2010/11, but defeat in the semi-finals cost manager Billy Davies his job. He was replaced by Steve McClaren.*

PROBLEMS CRYSTAL CLEAR FOR PALACE

Crystal Palace managed just one win away from home during the 2010/11 campaign – the worst record in the npower Championship. Their sole victory came at Norwich, who went on to secure automatic promotion, as goals from Julian Bennett and Anthony Gardner earned them a 2–1 win at Carrow Road in October. Luckily for the Eagles, their home form was impressive, as 11 victories and six draws from 23 games helped them to avoid relegation.

⋯⟶ *Crystal Palace's away-day blues almost cost them last term. A strike by Anthony Gardner (right) against Norwich gave them their only win on the road.*

PLAYER RECORDS

DANNY THE CHAMPION OF THE LEAGUE

Danny Graham was the second tier's top scorer in 2010/11 with a net-busting 24 goals from 45 appearances. The Watford hot-shot, who joined the Hornets from Carlisle on a free transfer in July 2009, bagged 14 league goals in his debut season at the club but bettered that tally by 10 in 2010/11. The feat was made all the more impressive by the fact that Watford finished 14th in the table. Norwich striker Grant Holt and Shane Long of Reading both scored 21 league goals.

TAARABT IS SHOT-ON FOR HOOPS

Queens Park Rangers star Adel Taarabt had more shots on target than any other player in the division in 2010/11. The Morocco international scored from 19 of his 88 goalbound attempts. When he wasn't scoring, the Hoops hitman was setting up goals for his team-mates, topping the assists chart with 16 in total.

SAVAGE BOWS OUT

One of English football's most colourful characters, Robbie Savage, retired at the end of the 2010/11 season with an unwanted record for the most bookings during the campaign. The midfielder, well known for his tough tackling, was shown 13 yellow cards while pulling the strings in the Derby County side. Bustling Norwich striker Grant Holt committed the most fouls, 103, but also won the most free-kicks, 111.

FRAZER'S FIRST

Frazer Richardson was the first player to score a goal in the newly-named Championship in 2004. Leeds, who had been relegated from the Premier League at the end of 2003/04, played Derby in an early kick-off on August 7, and full-back Richardson netted the game's only goal in the 72nd minute with a well-struck left-footed drive.

↑ *Frazer Richardson's goal made Leeds the first leaders of the newly-named Championship in 2004. United, however, won only 13 of their remaining 45 matches and ended the 2004/05 campaign in mid-table.*

⤏ *Adel Taarabt was the key man for QPR as they secured promotion from the npower Championship, firing in the most shots of any player in the division.*

MOVING ON UP

A number of players have made the jump from the second tier to the Premier League in recent seasons. Everton in particular have been quick to identify the talent available at this level, having signed Joleon Lescott, Phil Jagielka, Andrew Johnson and Jermaine Beckford from Wolves, Sheffield United, Crystal Palace and Leeds respectively. Tim Cahill also proved a shrewd buy for the Toffees when he joined the club for around £2million from Millwall in the summer of 2004. Other recent big-money moves between the two divisions include Theo Walcott and PFA Player of the Year Gareth Bale, who both left Southampton to join Arsenal and Tottenham respectively.

KEEPING UP APPEARANCES

Six npower Championship goalkeepers played every minute of every game for their clubs during the 2010/11 season. Luke Steele of Barnsley, Millwall shot-stopper David Forde, Nottingham Forest's Lee Camp and Jamie Ashdown of Portsmouth all completed 46 full games. Dorus De Vries of Swansea and Watford's Scott Loach both achieved the feat for the second straight season. Of the 16 players to feature in every match, Nottingham Forest (Camp and Wes Morgan), the Swans (De Vries and Ashley Williams) and Watford (Loach and Martin Taylor) all had two representatives in an impressive list.

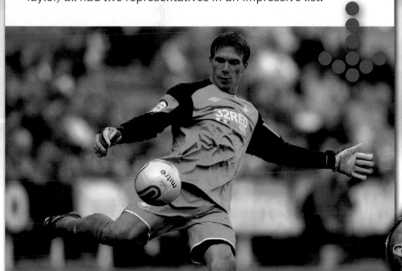

↑ Dorus De Vries was an ever-present for the second straight year in 2010/11, playing in all 46 regular-season games for Swansea, who won promotion from the npower Championship via the Play-Offs.

RICH FUTURE FOR LAZARUS

Reuben Noble-Lazarus is the youngest player ever to have featured in a Football League match. He made his debut for Barnsley aged 15 years and 45 days in a 3–0 Championship defeat at Ipswich on September 30 2008. Noble-Lazarus came off the bench in the 84th minute as a replacement for Martin Devaney. On the last day of the 2010/11 season the teen sensation scored his first goal for the Tykes to earn them a 1–0 win against Millwall.

LEAGUE OF NATIONS

The npower Championship's reputation as one of the most popular leagues in Europe is backed up by the fact that 56 different nationalities played in the division at some point during the most recent campaign. Apart from the home nations, Australia had the most representatives (12), with Holland not far behind (11). There were 10 Frenchmen, nine Spaniards and nine Argentinians in the list, including title-winner Alejandro Faurlin of QPR. Countries such as Guinea, Honduras and the Ivory Coast were also represented.

FORD MOTORS TO RECORD

Tony Ford made 931 league appearances – a Football League record for an outfield player – during a 26-year career that saw him play for eight different clubs. Grimsby-born Ford spent the most time with his home-town club in the second tier, featuring 355 times in his first spell with the Mariners between 1975 and 1986 and 68 on his return to Blundell Park from 1991 to 1994. Ford made over 100 league appearances for three other clubs – Stoke, West Brom and Mansfield.

⤍ Tony Ford was the epitome of an 'unsung hero', playing more than 1,000 matches in senior football. Originally a winger, he also scored more than 100 league goals.

BELLAMY LEAVES IT LATE

Welsh wizard Craig Bellamy left it late to snatch Cardiff a point in their 2–2 draw with Reading in February 2010. Bellamy, who was on loan at his home-town club from Manchester City, slammed in a free-kick after 96 minutes and 27 seconds – the latest goal to be scored in the second tier in that term. That strike came after the Royals had gone 2–1 ahead in the last minute, with Mathieu Manset poking home. Watford striker Danny Graham was responsible for the quickest goal of the campaign, scoring after just 17 seconds of a 3–1 win against his former club Middlesbrough in September 2010.

⤎ Cardiff City's Craig Bellamy celebrates after scoring a last-gasp equaliser against Reading. His goal went down as the last scored in the npower Championship last term.

GOALS

GOALS MAKE BIG DIFFERENCE

Reading's romp to the Championship title in 2005/06 saw the club break a host of records, including the second-tier mark for the best goal difference. The Royals scored a massive 99 goals and conceded only 32, giving them an incredible difference of +67. They won the title that year by 16 points from Sheffield United, who netted 76 times and let in 46 at the other end.

┄┄➤ *Prolific goalscorers and points-winners Reading celebrate their Championship title in May 2006. The Royals took their great form into their debut season in the top flight.*

BIGGEST WINS

Newcastle	13–0	Newport County	(1946)
Darwen	12–0	Walsall	(1896)
Arsenal	12–0	Loughborough	(1900)
Birmingham	12–0	Walsall	(1892)
Birmingham	12–0	Doncaster	(1903)
Port Vale	0–10	Sheffield United	(1892)

HAMMOND HITS TOP GEAR

Sheffield United recorded the biggest away win in the division's history when they hit 10 goals without reply past Port Vale in December 1892. Prolific forward Harry Hammond netted four times for the Blades as the South Yorkshire side ran riot.

DARWEN FAIL TO EVOLVE

Darwen hold the record for conceding the most league goals in a single season, having shipped 141 during the 1898/99 campaign. The Lancashire-based club were elected to The Football League in 1891 and lasted eight seasons. During their last term, Darwen suffered a record 18 consecutive defeats. Sunderland came close to equalling that run in 2003 when they lost 15 Premier League and two second-tier matches in a row.

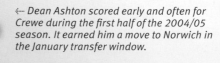

◄┄┄ *Dean Ashton scored early and often for Crewe during the first half of the 2004/05 season. It earned him a move to Norwich in the January transfer window.*

ASHTON QUICK OFF THE MARK

Dean Ashton was forced to retire through injury in December 2009 aged just 26, but he briefly held the distinction of having scored one of the fastest goals in the division's history. The former England forward took 10 seconds to open the scoring against Millwall in a 2–1 win for Crewe in 2004. Matt Fryatt shaved a second off that time when scoring for Leicester against Preston in 2006.

HORNETS LACK GOALSCORING SPARK

Watford found the back of the net just 24 times in 42 matches during the 1971/72 season to establish an unwanted league landmark for the fewest goals scored in a single campaign. The Hornets lost 28 times in total and finished the term at the bottom of the table with 19 points – 14 less than Charlton, who finished in 21st place and scored 31 more goals than their London rivals.

⋯ A young Brian Clough. He netted a hat-trick for Middlesbrough at Charlton, but both teams had to settle for a share of the points.

ADDICTED TO GOALS

Charlton and Middlesbrough played out an amazing 6–6 draw at The Valley in October 1960 – the highest-scoring draw ever seen in the division. Dennis Edwards scored a hat-trick for the Addicks, while Brian Clough also hit a treble for the visitors. It was 4–4 at half-time, with the free-scoring duo both bagging a brace. Middlesbrough took a 6–4 lead in the 63rd minute, but they were pegged back by Edwards' third and a last-gasp equaliser from Johnny Summers.

PRAT'S THE WAY TO DO IT!

Darren Pratley's goal for Swansea City against Nottingham Forest in May 2011 was scored from inside his own half, making it one of the longest-range strikes in Championship history. The midfielder, who left the Welsh club at the end of the season to join Bolton, took advantage after Forest goalkeeper Lee Camp had come up for a late corner. When the ball broke to him on the edge of his own box, Pratley ran to the half-way line before floating the ball into an empty net. That strike helped City into the npower Championship Play-Off Final.

OLD PROBLEMS FOR NEWPORT

Newport County endured a miserable campaign in 1946/47, conceding 133 goals and scoring 61 on their way to relegation to the third tier. They ended the season with a goal difference of -72, which still stands as the worst in the league's history. The South Wales club, who spent 68 years in The Football League, were hammered 13–0 by Newcastle, conceded seven against West Brom and were hit for six on three occasions that term.

LUCKY 13 FOR MAGPIES

Newcastle's 13–0 win against Newport County in October 1946 remains the biggest margin of victory in a second-tier game. Goalscoring legend Jackie Milburn scored twice for the Magpies, but he was outdone by Len Shackleton, who netted six times on his debut after signing from Bradford Park Avenue. Charlie Wayman added four more goals, with Roy Bentley also on target.

⋯⋯> Jackie Milburn was a Newcastle goalscoring legend. He played his part in the 13-goal haul against Newport.

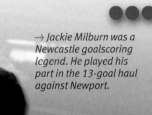

⋯⋯> Chris Nicholl earned a winners' medal with Aston Villa in the 1975 League Cup final. A year later, he managed to score all four goals in 2–2 draw with Leicester.

YOU WYNNE SOME...

Samuel Wynne scored four of the five goals in Oldham's 3–2 victory over Manchester United in October 1923. Wynne was the first player to score two for each side, with his goals at the right end coming from a free-kick and a penalty. Chris Nicholl equalled the feat for Aston Villa in a top-flight match at Leicester in March 1976, scoring all four in a 2–2 draw.

LEAGUE 1 ALL-TIME RECORDS

The third tier – npower League 1 – came into being in 1920 and was originally split into two leagues – north and south. That format remained in place until 1958 when regionalisation was abolished and the Third and Fourth Divisions were formed. Some big clubs have found themselves playing at this level, while the league has also provided the stage for some remarkable individual feats.

Brighton & Hove Albion celebrate success in 2010/11 after claiming the npower League 1 title.

Southampton duo Adam Lallana and Oscar Gobern helped the Saints march back into the second tier in 2010/11 as they secured automatic promotion.

CHAMPIONS, PARTICIPATION, UPS & DOWNS

A VALIANT EFFORT

Port Vale kept an impressive 30 clean sheets in 46 matches on their way to the title in 1953/54. The Valiants only conceded five goals at home during the whole campaign and 21 in total – another divisional record, which they share with Southampton. The Saints achieved the feat in 1921/22.

DOUBLE FOR DALE

Rochdale suffered relegation after managing just two wins from 46 matches during the 1973/74 campaign – the fewest ever recorded at this level. The Lancashire club unsurprisingly finished bottom of the table, seven points behind nearest rivals Southport and having conceded 94 goals. Dale's only wins came against Southend – 2–1 in September 1973 – and Shrewsbury – 3–2 the following January.

←··· Elliott Bennett's goal against Yeovil helped Brighton kick-start a winning run that led them to the title.

THIRD TIER TITLE WINS

Plymouth	4
Portsmouth	3
Swansea	3
Grimsby	3
Reading	3
Millwall	3
Lincoln	3
Hull	3

SEAGULLS SOAR TO TITLE

Brighton won eight games in a row as they romped to the npower League 1 title in 2010/11. The run spanned the whole of March, starting with a 1–0 win at Yeovil on the first day of the month – Elliott Bennett scoring the only goal. Seven more victories followed, including a thrilling 4–3 win at home to Carlisle, before Rochdale came from behind to snatch a point in a 2–2 draw at Spotland at the start of April.

ROVERS WIN BIG

Doncaster hold the league record for the most wins in a season. Rovers claimed 33 victories out of 42 matches on their way to the title in 1946/47. They drew six and lost the other three games. The South Yorkshire side posted some impressive wins along the way, putting nine past Carlisle and scoring eight goals without reply against Barrow.

BEES SOUNDLY BEATEN

Barnet suffered 10 straight defeats from the start of the 1993/94 season – the worst run by any third-tier side. The Bees went down that term after winning just five and losing 28 of their 46 matches.

↑ Having suffered the loss of key players following their 1993 promotion, it was little surprise that Brian Marwood and Barnet made an awful start to their first season in the third tier. They finished 25 points from safety.

BARNET'S RELEGATION RUN

v Hull	lost 2–1	(h)	14/08/1993
v Port Vale	lost 6–0	(a)	21/08/1993
v Swansea	lost 1–0	(h)	28/08/1993
v Reading	lost 4–1	(a)	01/09/1993
v Blackpool	lost 3–1	(a)	04/09/1993
v Bournemouth	lost 2–1	(h)	11/09/1993
v Fulham	lost 2–0	(h)	14/09/1993
v Leyton Orient	lost 4–2	(a)	18/09/1993
v Wrexham	lost 4–0	(a)	25/09/1993
v Bristol Rovers	lost 2–1	(h)	02/10/1993

READING ON A ROLL

Reading won the title in 1985/86 after making an incredible start to the season that saw them win their first 13 games – a record for the most consecutive victories at the beginning of a campaign. They started that term with 1–0 wins against Blackpool and Plymouth, who went on to finish as runners-up, before really hitting their stride. A narrow victory at Lincoln in October 1985 proved to be the last game of the winning sequence, with Wolves holding the Royals to a 2–2 draw at Elm Park a few days later.

SAINTS MARCH INTO CHAMPIONSHIP

Promoted Southampton ended the 2010/11 campaign with an impressive goal difference of +48. Under Nigel Adkins, Saints bagged 44 goals at St Mary's and conceded just 13, while their away record read 42 goals for and 25 against. Rickie Lambert was the club's leading scorer for the third successive season, netting 21 from an npower League 1-high 83 attempts on target. Saints struck the woodwork 19 times and collectively hit the target on 359 occasions, both of which were records.

RELEGATION ACADEMIC FOR CAMBRIDGE

Cambridge hold the unenviable record of having collected the least points in a third-tier season. The Us claimed just 21 on their way to relegation in 1984/85. They finished 25 points adrift of second-from-bottom Preston and a further point from safety. Cambridge were heavily beaten by eventual champions Bradford (4–0), Walsall (5–0) and York (4–0) during a campaign to forget.

↑ *Nigel Adkins' Southampton were hot shots in 2010/11, boasting the best goal difference in the division.*

LATICS LOVE LIFE ON THE ROAD

Wigan only conceded nine goals in 23 matches away from home during the 2002/03 campaign. The Latics' defence was breached just 25 times in total that term as they romped to the title with a 100-point haul – 14 more than second-place Crewe. Paul Jewell's side lost just two games on their travels and won 15 times.

↓ *Wigan's rise up England's football ladder gained pace with their third-tier title in 2003.*

TEAM RECORDS

LONG ROAD FOR ROVERS

Doncaster hold the league landmark for the most consecutive away wins, but it took them seven years to complete that achievement! Their impressive feat started with a 2–1 victory at Stockport on April 22 1939, with Rovers going on to win the last two away games of that season. The league was then interrupted by the Second World War, but on its resumption in 1946, the Yorkshire club claimed six more victories to create an overall record of nine straight wins on their travels.

PALACE STRETCH THEIR POINT

Crystal Palace played out the most home stalemates ever recorded in a row at this level. They made their point seven straight times during a run that spanned across two seasons – 1961/62 and 1962/63. The first game was a goalless draw against Bradford Park Avenue, which was followed by stalemates against Coventry, Port Vale and Bournemouth. The sequence continued into the following term before they finally snatched a 1–0 win against QPR.

POOLS RUN DRY

Hartlepool found goals hard to come by at the start of 1993, with the club failing to score in 11 straight matches. The north-east side had stunned top-flight Crystal Palace with a 1–0 win in the FA Cup on January 2 courtesy of Andy Saville's penalty, but that was the last time they scored for over two months. A goalless draw at Leyton Orient began the run, with Pools losing eight and drawing three games all without hitting the net before Saville was on target again at Blackpool in March to end the hoodoo.

⋯ Andy Saville failed to score at Brisbane Road on January 9 1993, and neither he, nor his Hartlepool team-mates, had a goal to celebrate for two months.

HORNETS HARD TO BEAT

The overall Football League record for the most successive draws away from home in a single campaign is held by Watford. The Hornets were playing in the third tier when they embarked on a nine-game run during 1996/97. Wayne Andrews opened the scoring in a 1–1 draw at Bury to start the sequence on October 19 1996, with the ninth game coming against Wycombe in February of the following year.

⋯ Wayne Andrews (right) in action for Watford. This FA Cup tie against Northampton in November 1996 was one of the few games that Watford didn't draw on their travels in 1996/97.

UNBEATABLE BEES

Brentford enjoyed a 100 per cent home record during the 1929/30 season. The Bees won all 21 of their games at Griffin Park that term, putting six past Merthyr Town and Walsall and scoring five goals against Brighton, Torquay, Watford and Fulham. It was not enough to win them the third-tier title, though, as they finished seven points behind champions Plymouth.

ELECTRIC AVENUE

Bradford Park Avenue hold the third-tier record for the most consecutive home wins. The 25-game sequence spanned across two seasons – 1926/27 and 1927/28. It began on October 9 1926 with a 2–0 victory against Ashington and continued for the rest of that campaign before a 4–0 win against Durham City kicked off the following season. The run went on until Bradford were finally beaten 2–0 by Doncaster in November 1927.

DRAW SPECIALISTS

Chesterfield equalled a league record when they drew eight consecutive matches during the 2005/06 campaign. The run started with a 1–1 draw against Blackpool at Saltergate in November – in which Sammy Clingan was on target – with the sequence continuing into the new year following a goalless draw against Barnsley on January 2. Birmingham (1990/91) and Torquay (1969/70) also achieved the same feat.

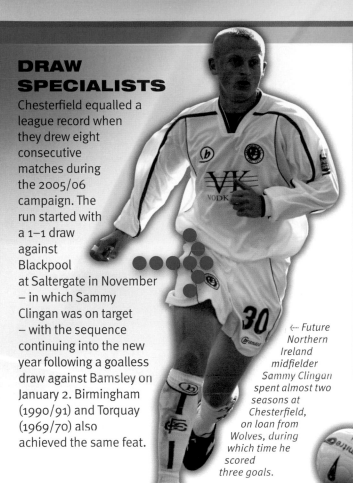

←⋯ Future Northern Ireland midfielder Sammy Clingan spent almost two seasons at Chesterfield, on loan from Wolves, during which time he scored three goals.

DALE'S UNWANTED DOUBLE

Rochdale set two unwanted records during the 1931/32 season. A 4–1 loss at Barrow in November 1931 sparked a poor run of results for the Lancashire club, who went on to suffer 17 consecutive defeats. That streak included 9–1 and 6–3 defeats against Tranmere. Dale also lost 13 home matches in a row that term and then started the following campaign with a 1–0 defeat at home to Carlisle to extend their slump.

PIRATES STEAL RECORD

Bristol Rovers went an amazing 32 games without defeat in the early 1970s. Don Megson's side claimed a 2–0 win over Scunthorpe at Glanford Park on April 7 1973 and then stayed unbeaten for the remaining four games of that campaign. They enjoyed a flying start to 1973/74 and played another 27 matches before finally losing 1–0 at Wrexham.

⋯→ Don Megson's Bristol Rovers finished a point behind third-tier champions Oldham in 1973/74, despite their amazing unbeaten start to the season.

MOST CLEAN SHEETS IN A SEASON

30	Port Vale	1953/54
27	Middlesbrough	1986/87
26	Aston Villa	1971/72
26	Southampton	1921/22
26	Rochdale	1923/24

DUO KEEP IT CLEAN

Millwall and York share the honour for the most consecutive clean sheets at third-tier level, with both managing 11. The Lions achieved the feat in 1925/26, drawing 0–0 with Gillingham before winning nine and drawing one of the following 10 matches without conceding. York, led by Scottish goalkeeper Graeme Crawford, equalled that in 1973/74, playing out six goalless draws in their 11 games.

↓ York City goalkeeper Graeme Crawford bravely dives at the feet of Chelsea's Micky Droy. The Minstermen's run of clean sheets in 1973/74 helped them to win promotion to England's second tier for the first and, to date, only time. They lasted only two seasons at that level.

PLAYER RECORDS

GOAL MACHINES

Ted Hartson scored a staggering 55 goals in a single season for Mansfield in 1936/37. And amazingly, the same feat was also achieved by Luton goal ace Joe Payne the same term! Hartson scored his hatful in Division Three North, while Payne matched that in the South. Hartson scored seven goals in a single game against Hartlepool on his way to the record.

TROLLOPE TOPS TABLE

John Trollope spent the majority of his career playing in the third tier on the way to establishing the record for the most Football League appearances for a single club. Trollope spent 20 years at Swindon between 1960 and 1980 and featured an amazing 770 times for the club. He made his debut aged just 17 against Halifax in August 1960 and broke Jimmy Dickinson's record in 1980/81. Trollope, who received an MBE for his achievements, went on to manage the Robins.

----> The epitome of the one-club man was Swindon left-back John Trollope, whose finest moment came in the 1969 League Cup final when the Robins beat Arsenal.

OLD-BOY McBAIN

Neil McBain was 51 years and 120 days old when he played for New Brighton against Hartlepool in March 1947 – making him the oldest player ever to feature in a Football League match. The Merseysiders played in the league from 1923 until 1951 and McBain was managing the club when he created the record, pulling on his goalkeeping gloves following an injury crisis. Unfortunately, he could not prevent New Brighton from slipping to a 3–0 defeat.

BELL RINGS TRUE

Harold Bell holds the overall Football League record for the most consecutive appearances, having played 401 games in a row for Tranmere between 1946 and 1955 while the club was in the third tier. Including FA Cup, Liverpool Senior Cup and Cheshire Bowl matches, Bell played in an incredible 459 unbroken games and made a club-record total of 633 appearances for Rovers. His run was finally ended in August 1955 when he was dropped.

JOSS BOSSES ROVERS MIDFIELD

Joss Labadie added bite to Tranmere's midfield in the 2010/11 campaign, committing the most fouls of any player in the division. The free-transfer arrival from West Brom was penalised 86 times in 29 starts, was booked on 13 occasions – the joint highest number of yellow cards of any player in the league – and was sent off at Notts County in November – a game Rovers managed to hold on to win 1–0.

<---- Tough-tackling Joss Labadie provided the steel in the Tranmere side last term. He took no prisoners, and was shown 13 yellow cards as a result.

ROCKET RONNIE DOWNS CANARIES

Ronnie Dix became the third tier's youngest goalscorer when he netted for Bristol Rovers against Norwich in March 1928 aged just 15 years and 180 days – a record that still stands. Rovers won the game 3–0 and Dix went on to score 33 league goals for the Pirates before moving to Blackburn. Dix won one full international cap for England, grabbing a goal on his debut against Norway.

EVER-PRESENTS 2010/11

(Players appearing in all 46 league games)

Jason Pearce   (Bournemouth)
Marcos Painter   (Brighton)
James Berrett   (Carlisle)
Frank Simek   (Carlisle)
Adam Collin   (Carlisle)
Romain Vincelot   (Dagenham)
Peter Clarke   (Huddersfield)
Marcus Holness   (Rochdale)
Kelvin Davis   (Southampton)
Matt Richards   (Walsall)

⤷ Midfielder James Berrett was one of three Carlisle players who appeared in every league game in 2010/11 as the Cumbrians finished 12th.

QUINTET SEE RED

Five players were sent off when Wigan took on Bristol Rovers in a third-tier clash in December 1997 – a record held jointly with Chesterfield and Plymouth, who had suffered the same fate 10 months previously. Rovers' David Pritchard was the first to go in first-half injury time for two bookable offences, and from the resulting free-kick, a melee broke out in the box that also resulted in Jason Perry, Andy Tillson and Wigan striker Graeme Jones seeing red. The visitors, who lost the game 3–0, were reduced to seven men in the 71st minute when Josh Low was shown a second yellow card.

PAYNE-FUL DAY FOR ROVERS

Joe Payne scored a remarkable 10 goals in a single game for Luton against Bristol Rovers in April 1936. The Hatters won the Division Three South match 12–0, with centre-forward Payne creating a Football League record with his scoring exploits. Robert 'Bunny' Bell had also been playing third-tier football when he bagged nine goals for Tranmere against Oldham a year previously on Boxing Day 1935. He also missed a penalty in his side's 13–4 victory!

↑ Bristol Rovers defender Andy Tillson was one of five players (four of them from Rovers) sent off during a tempestuous match against Wigan in 1997.

McCANN'S THE MAN

Grant McCann contributed 10 goals from midfield for Peterborough in season 2010/11, but it was assists where the Northern Ireland international really excelled. McCann topped the third-tier chart after setting up a hugely impressive 21 goals for his free-scoring team-mates, two more than nearest rival Dean Cox of Leyton Orient.

⤳ Grant McCann was Peterborough's playmaker-in-chief last season, setting up or scoring more than a quarter of his team's total npower League 1 goals.

GOALS

LIONS ON FIRE

Millwall hold the record for the most home league goals scored in a season. The Lions found the back of the net 87 times at The Den during the 1927/28 campaign on their way to the title. Notable results that term included 9–1 wins against Torquay and Coventry, a 7–1 victory against Walsall and putting six past Brighton, QPR and Gillingham.

HATTERS GO GOAL MAD

Stockport recorded the biggest victory in the division's history when they put 13 goals past Halifax without reply on January 6 1934. There were six different County goalscorers that day, with Joe Hill netting a hat-trick and Percy Downes going one better with four. The Hatters were only leading 2–0 at the break, but eight goals in a 16-minute spell early in the second half put the game well beyond their opponents. They went on to add three more in the last 10 minutes of a remarkable game.

TERRIFIC TRANMERE

The highest-scoring game ever played in the third tier came at Prenton Park on Boxing Day 1935 when Tranmere claimed an amazing 13–4 victory over Oldham! Rovers striker Robert 'Bunny' Bell scored nine goals in the game on his way to a total of 40 that season.

KNOCKOUT TOTAL FOR BANTAMS

Bradford scored 128 times during 1928/29 to break the record for the most goals in a third-tier season. The Bantams, who won the title by a point that year, cruised to an 11–1 win against Rotherham in the opening game and were 8–2 winners at Ashington in October. They also managed successive 8–0 victories against Tranmere and Barrow the following March. Millwall had previously held the record, having rattled in 127 goals the year before.

⋯⋯› Scunthorpe striker Billy Sharp celebrates after scoring against Huddersfield at Glanford Park, one of 30 goals he netted during the 2006/07 season, helping the Iron to the third-tier title.

⟵ Golden Boot winner Craig Mackail-Smith became hot property in npower League 1 after bagging an impressive 27 goals for Posh.

MACKAIL-SMITH TOPS CHARTS

Peterborough striker Craig Mackail-Smith finished season 2010/11 as the division's top goalscorer with 27, finally breaking Rickie Lambert's hold on the position. Mackail-Smith's impressive form also resulted in him making his international debut for Scotland against Brazil. Southampton hot-shot Lambert finished the season with 21 goals, nine less than the previous term when he claimed the Golden Boot for the second year running.

LEADING SCORERS SINCE 2005/06

2005/06	Billy Sharp (Scunthorpe)	23
	Freddy Eastwood (Southend)	
2006/07	Billy Sharp (Scunthorpe)	30
2007/08	Jason Scotland (Swansea)	24
2008/09	Rickie Lambert (Bristol Rovers)	29
	Simon Cox (Swindon)	
2009/10	Rickie Lambert (Southampton)	30
2010/11	Craig Mackail-Smith (Peterborough)	27

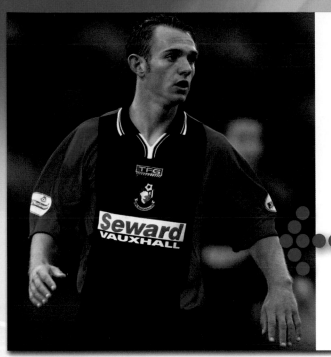

HASTY HAYTER

James Hayter made an instant impact when he scored the fastest hat-trick in Football League history in February 2004. The striker came off the bench for Bournemouth against Wrexham in the 84th minute and scored his first goal in the 86th. Two minutes and 20 seconds later, he was celebrating a treble! The Cherries ran out comfortable 6–0 winners.

⟵ How many goals might James Hayter have scored against Wrexham if he had started the match, rather than come off the bench? As it was, he grabbed three in the final six minutes of the game.

DUO'S FLYING START

Nick Barmby and Matt Fryatt share the distinction of having scored the fastest goals since the division became known as League 1. Barmby was first to achieve the feat, netting after seven seconds of Hull's 3–1 win at home to Walsall in November 2004 with a neat side-footed volley. Fryatt took the same length of time to open the scoring for Walsall in a home match against Bournemouth later that season. Unfortunately, the Saddlers went on to lose the game 2–1.

GOAL-CRAZY POSH

Peterborough went goal crazy during the 2010/11 campaign, scoring 106 times in 46 npower League 1 matches – easily the most by any club in the division. Posh netted 69 at London Road as they enjoyed some incredible wins, including 6–0 and 5–0 victories against Carlisle and Dagenham respectively, a 5–3 win over Sheffield Wednesday and a 5–4 success against Swindon. Darren Ferguson's men scored two or more goals in all but three of their home matches. Southampton were the second highest goalscorers with 86, while champions Brighton managed 85.

DERBY DELIGHT

Derby rivals Darlington and Hartlepool played out an amazing 5–5 draw at Feethams in November 1936 – the highest-scoring draw in the division's history. In March 2004, Chesterfield and Grimsby played out a 4–4 thriller at Saltergate, with David Reeves completing his hat-trick with a point-saving penalty for the home side.

⟵ No other team could match Peterborough's scoring feats in 2010/11. Darren Ferguson's team bagged 20 more goals than their nearest rivals as they secured promotion.

LEAGUE 2 ALL-TIME RECORDS

The fourth tier – currently known as npower League 2 – was introduced in time for the start of the 1958/59 season and was first made up of the sides who had finished in the bottom half of the last Division Three North and South tables. This bottom rung of The Football League ladder has featured big names such as David Beckham, Paul Gascoigne and Peter Beardsley.

Victory over Torquay in the 2010/11 Play-Off Final helped Stevenage write another chapter in their remarkable story as they secured a second successive promotion.

CHAMPIONS, PARTICIPATION, UPS & DOWNS

TITANIC TITLE TUSSLE

Wigan and Fulham were involved in the closest title race in fourth-tier history during the 1996/97 campaign. Both teams finished the season on 87 points, but the championship trophy went to Lancashire, despite the Cottagers having a better goal difference. The number of goals scored took precedence that term, and Wigan had netted 12 more than the Londoners.

CHAMPIONS SINCE 2001

2000/01	Brighton	92 points
2001/02	Plymouth	102 points
2002/03	Rushden & Diamonds	87 points
2003/04	Doncaster	92 points
2004/05	Yeovil	83 points
2005/06	Carlisle	86 points
2006/07	Walsall	89 points
2007/08	MK Dons	97 points
2008/09	Brentford	85 points
2009/10	Notts County	93 points
2010/11	Chesterfield	86 points

↑ *John Deehan kisses the trophy after Wigan had seen off Fulham on goals scored to win the fourth-tier championship in 1997.*

NO WORRIES FOR NORTH END

Preston drew 17 games but still managed to win the league in 1995/96. North End were held to a thrilling 3–3 draw by Cambridge in September 1995 and played out three consecutive 2–2 stalemates later that month. The Lancashire club won 23 games and lost six matches in all, but they clinched the championship by three points from Gillingham, who also drew 17 times.

BARKER BREEZES IN

When Alan Knill left Bury for Scunthorpe in March 2011, youth-team coach Richie Barker was handed the tricky task of trying to secure promotion to npower League 1. The former Rotherham, Mansfield and Hartlepool striker took to management with ease, winning six matches in a row – including an awesome 3–2 victory at leaders Chesterfield. That closed the gap on the Spireites, but defeat at Wycombe ended any chance of Bury snatching the title. They finished second to secure a place in the third tier for the first time since 2002.

↓ *Bury made light of losing their manager to clinch a place in the third tier in 2010/11.*

GREEN ARMY MARCH ON

Paul Sturrock led Plymouth to a place in the history books when they equalled a fourth-tier record for the most points in one season under the three-for-a-win system in 2001/02. Argyle claimed 102 points to clinch the championship by five from second-place Luton. Nobody else came close, with Mansfield finishing a massive 23 points behind in third. Swindon had previously managed the same total as Argyle in 1985/86.

←Paul Sturrock's Plymouth won 31 matches on their way to claiming the fourth-tier title in 2001/02 with a joint-record 102 points.

↓ Jim Stannard enjoyed a great season between the sticks for Gillingham in 1995/96, as they conceded only 20 league goals and won promotion to the third tier.

ROVERS' POOR RETURN

Doncaster hold the unwanted record for the most losses in a fourth-tier season. Rovers were beaten 34 times during the 1997/98 campaign, winning four games and drawing eight. They managed just 20 points, with a goal difference of -83 – both of which are also records. The Yorkshire side finished 15 points adrift of second-from-bottom Brighton and dropped out of The Football League.

GILLS SET DOUBLE RECORD

Gillingham gained promotion at the end of 1995/96 having kept a record 29 clean sheets. The Gills only conceded 20 goals that term – another fourth-tier landmark – although they also struggled to score, netting just 49 times. That total was less than any other side in the top 12. The Kent club finished as runners-up that year, three points behind champions Preston.

←... Matt Taylor and Luton had a fine 2001/02 season. In any other year this century, the Hatters' 97 points would have given them at least a share of the title. That season, however, Plymouth gained 102 points.

RE-ELECTION NOT RELEGATION

The bottom four clubs in the fourth tier had to apply for re-election to The Football League each season from the division's formation in 1958 up until the end of the 1986 campaign. In 1987, The Football League agreed that the team who finished bottom would be replaced by the champions of the Conference. Now the two bottom clubs are replaced by the two promoted sides from the Conference.

LUCKY LOSERS

Two teams share the landmark for the most defeats on the way to winning the division. Exeter lost 13 games – all away from home – during the 1989/90 season, while Brentford equalled that feat in 1998/99. The Grecians didn't lose a game in any competition at St James Park, but their form on their travels almost proved costly. Brentford claimed 26 victories overall in 1998/99 and drew seven games to finish four points ahead of Cambridge.

ROBINS ARE ROCKING

Swindon won the title by the biggest margin in history in 1985/86. The Robins finished 18 points ahead of second-place Chester, ending the campaign with a joint-record 102 points. The campaign had started badly for the Wiltshire club when they lost 1–0 at home to Wrexham and 4–1 away at Hereford in their first two league matches, but results soon picked up and Lou Macari's side scored four goals on six separate occasions as they cruised to the championship.

TEAM RECORDS

← Torquay's Chris Zebroksi celebrates finding the net against Port Vale in August 2010, but the Gulls were denied by the woodwork a record number of times during the rest of the campaign.

MINSTERMEN DRAW A BLANK

York failed to score in a record 11 of their 23 home matches during the 1990/91 season. The Minstermen's opening game was a 1–0 defeat to Maidstone at Bootham Crescent, and that was a sign of things to come. They ended the campaign in 21st place, with just eight wins to their name at home and only three on their travels.

ROYALS SEAL OF APPROVAL

Reading finished the 1978/79 season strongly, keeping 11 consecutive clean sheets in their final 11 games. A 4–0 victory against Grimsby started the sequence, with the Royals going on to win seven more matches while the other three ended goalless.

IMPS ROMP TO RECORD

Lincoln and Swindon jointly hold the record for the most wins ever recorded in a single season at this level. The Imps cruised to the fourth-tier title in 1975/76 after winning 32 of their 46 matches, drawing 10 and losing just four times. Ten years later, the Robins matched that impressive feat on their way to lifting the championship trophy under the management of Lou Macari.

↓ Swindon's rise up English football began under the management of Lou Macari and was continued by Glenn Hoddle. Less than 10 years after winning the fourth-tier title, the Robins were in the Premier League.

NO GOOD FORTUNE FOR GULLS

Torquay were officially the unluckiest team in the division during the 2010/11 season, striking the woodwork an incredible 30 times. It was also the most of any team in The Football League. The Gulls finished seventh to make the play-offs, but if the goal posts had been just a little wider and the crossbar a touch higher, who knows, they could have been celebrating automatic promotion!

→ *After Carlisle's horrendous losing run during 2003/04 – which began after Richie Foran converted a penalty to give his team the lead against Swansea – they couldn't produce enough results to stave off relgation.*

QUICK ON THE DRAW

Hartlepool and Cardiff both drew half of the 46 games they played during the 1997/98 season. Pools finished 17th in the table, despite losing just 11 games, while the Bluebirds were down in 21st place, with nine wins and 14 losses to add to their run of stalemates. Unsurprisingly, the pair played out a 1–1 draw when they met at Ninian Park that term. They share the fourth-tier record with Exeter, who managed the same number of draws back in 1986/87.

POSH'S DATE AT EIGHT

Peterborough hold the divisional record for the number of consecutive draws, having played out eight in a row in 1970/71. Posh's sequence began with a thrilling 3–3 clash against Exeter in December 1970 and ended following an equally watchable 4–4 stalemate against Lincoln at London Road two months later.

CARLISLE COME A CROPPER

Carlisle endured a miserable run during the 2003/04 campaign, losing 12 matches in a row on their way to relegation from The Football League. The sequence started with a 2–1 defeat at home to Swansea, despite Richie Foran opening the scoring for the Cumbrians from the penalty spot. Carlisle slipped to 11 more defeats, including a 4–1 loss at home to Scunthorpe, before they finally secured a long-overdue win when they beat Torquay 2–0 thanks to goals from Andy Preece and Paul Arnison.

NO LET-UP FOR NEWPORT

Newport County set two unfortunate records during the 1970/71 season. The Welsh club went 25 games without a win from the start of the campaign, with the opening 10 all ending in defeat. Their wretched start featured a 6–1 loss to Southport and a 4–1 home defeat against Oldham. They went on to finish the season in 22nd place, having lost 28 of their 46 games.

CLEAN SHEET KINGS SINCE 2005/06

2005/06	Northampton	23
2006/07	Bristol Rovers	22
	Hartlepool	
2007/08	Darlington	24
2008/09	Wycombe	21
2009/10	Notts County	26
2010/11	Wycombe	17
	Accrington	

→ *Accrington boss John Coleman made his side hard to beat at home in 2010/11 as they secured a play-off place.*

CROWN IS STANLEY'S JEWEL

Accrington turned their Crown Ground home into a fortress during the second half of the 2010/11 season to secure a play-off place. Stanley were unbeaten at home in 12 league matches from the start of February until the end of the regular season – a run which included a thumping 4–0 win against Hereford. John Coleman's men suffered just two defeats in total during that spell, losing 2–0 at Rotherham and 3–1 at Gillingham.

PLAYER RECORDS

BECKS IN AT THE DEEP END

Former England ace David Beckham played five games for Preston in the fourth tier during 1994/95. Beckham was on the fringes of the Manchester United first team at the time, and he was loaned to North End to gain some experience. He impressed at Deepdale, scoring two goals – one direct from a corner and the other a typically brilliant free-kick. An injury crisis at Old Trafford saw him recalled by Sir Alex Ferguson and as a result, Preston's promotion challenge faltered. They were beaten by Bury in the semi-finals of the play-offs that year.

NO-GO FOR TINO

Faustino Asprilla was on the verge of a sensational move to The Football League's basement division with Darlington in the summer of 2002. The former Newcastle and Colombia forward was pictured holding a Quakers shirt alongside the club's chairman at the time, George Reynolds, and he was even presented to the fans. However, he subsequently failed to turn up for a medical and the deal fell through.

⤳ Southend ace Ryan Hall provided plenty of ammunition for his team-mates with more assists than anyone else in the division last term.

⤳ Peter Beardsley played football for the love of it. At the age of 38 in 1999, he was still playing for Hartlepool in the fourth tier.

SWANSONGS FOR STARS

Some of England's finest internationals have enjoyed swansongs in the fourth tier. Peter Beardsley made 22 appearances for Hartlepool during the 1998/99 campaign, scoring on his debut against Cambridge. Chris Waddle turned out seven times for Torquay in 1998 while Paul Gascoigne played four league games for Boston United in 2004 and Darren Anderton was a Bournemouth player when he retired in December 2008.

MOST ASSISTS 2010/11

Ryan Hall	Southend	16
Nicky Law	Rotherham	12
Shaun Miller	Crewe	11
Mark Marshall	Barnet	10
Matt Harrold	Shrewsbury	10

DANGEROUS DAVIES

Craig Davies was a man on a goalscoring mission during Chesterfield's title-winning campaign of 2010/11. The Spireites striker ended the season with 23 goals – joint fourth in the overall charts – but he had the most attempts both on and off target in the division. Davies fired in 79 goalbound efforts but countered that with 84 that failed to trouble the goalkeeper. He also hit the woodwork five times.

DID YOU KNOW?

England cricket legend Sir Ian Botham played 11 Football League games for Scunthorpe in the early 1980s. Botham was a household name on the world cricket scene when he initially joined the Iron – at the time a fourth-tier club – apparently in a bid to get fit following an injury. He ended up training with the team during the winter months to maintain his fitness levels, and on occasion he played on a non-contract basis.

SHOCK MOVE FOR SOL

Sol Campbell stunned the footballing world in August 2009 when he signed for League 2 Notts County. However, the former England centre-back played just one game for the Magpies – a 2–1 defeat at Morecambe – before exiting the club. Campbell, who had been a free agent after leaving Portsmouth, moved back to the Barclays Premier League later in the season, rejoining former side Arsenal.

↑ *Former Scunthorpe players of the 1960s, 1970s and 1980s went on to captain England teams: Ray Clemence and Kevin Keegan at football and Ian Botham at cricket.*

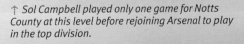

↑ *Sol Campbell played only one game for Notts County at this level before rejoining Arsenal to play in the top division.*

CURTIS BOXES CLEVER

Former Grimsby midfielder Curtis Woodhouse quit football to become a professional boxer in 2006. Woodhouse announced that he was hanging up his boots to concentrate on a career in the ring, playing his last match for the Mariners in the League 2 Play-Off Final against Cheltenham in May 2006. However, he returned to football in March 2007 with Conference side Rushden & Diamonds and signed for Eastwood Town in June 2011.

LOWE ON A HIGH

Bury striker Ryan Lowe scored in nine consecutive fourth-tier matches in 2010/11 to break a 53-year-old club record. Shakers legend John Willie Parker had set the benchmark after scoring in seven games in a row, but Lowe went two matches better and scored 10 goals in the process. The journeyman forward started the run by grabbing the only goal in a 1–0 victory against Shrewsbury at the end of January and he kept on scoring until two games into March. He finished the season with 27 goals.

GREAT SCOTT!

Scott McGleish was the first player to score in the newly-formed League 2 when he netted for Northampton at Swansea on August 7 2004. Summer signing McGleish didn't take long to open his account for the Cobblers, tapping in after three minutes of his league debut when a David Galbraith cross was deflected off the post and into his path. McGleish also tried to claim Northampton's second goal in the 2–0 win, but it went down as an own goal from Sam Ricketts.

⋯→ *Scott McGleish has scored goals everywhere he has played, averaging almost one in every three matches in a professional career that began in 1994. His first goal for Northampton was also the first in the rebranded League 2.*

GOALS

HATTERS BRING LITTLE TO PARTY

Stockport slipped out of The Football League in 2010/11 following their second successive relegation. The Hatters were not the lowest goalscorers at home but they were on their travels, netting just 17 times as they ended the season with a goal difference of -48. County managed just four wins at Edgeley Park, but one of those came against promoted Bury.

↑ *A lack of goals, particularly away from home, proved costly for Stockport as they were relegated out of the npower Football League in 2010/11.*

HIGHEST-SCORING GAMES

Accrington	7–4	Gillingham	(2010)
Hull	7–4	Swansea	(1997)
Burton	5–6	Cheltenham	(2010)
Barnet	1–9	Peterborough	(1998)
Rotherham	6–4	Cheltenham	(2010)
Chesterfield	5–5	Crewe	(2010)
Rochdale	5–4	York	(2002)
Crewe	8–1	Cheltenham	(2011)
Port Vale	7–2	Morecambe	(2011)
Bury	5–4	Gillingham	(2010)

GOAL TREAT FOR POSH

Peterborough fans were almost guaranteed to see goals during the 1960/61 campaign. The club established two notable landmarks on their way to winning the fourth-tier title that season, scoring in 33 consecutive matches and notching up a Football League-best 134 goals overall. Their run of consecutive strikes began on September 20 1960 with a 2–1 victory at Doncaster. Bradford Park Avenue stunned Jimmy Hagan's free-scoring side by claiming a 1–0 win on April 20 1961 to end the impressive sequence.

FRYATT'S FASTEST

Jim Fryatt scored what is believed to be the fastest goal in Football League history while playing for Bradford Park Avenue against Tranmere in April 1964. Fryatt's strike in the penultimate game of the 1963/64 season was recorded at four seconds and set the Yorkshire club on their way to a 4–2 victory. Fryatt made more than 100 appearances for Bradford, one of eight different English clubs he played for.

EARLY GOAL MAKES EASTWOOD'S DAY

Freddy Eastwood scored after just seven seconds of his Football League debut for Southend in a fourth-tier match against Swansea in October 2004. The Essex-born striker went on to mark the occasion with a hat-trick in a 4–2 victory at Roots Hall – one of three trebles he managed for the Blues during his three-year stay at the club.

← *Freddy Eastwood (left) scored after seven seconds of his Football League debut for Southend against Swansea, and he finished with a hat-trick. His first season ended with a goal in the 2005 Play-Off Final victory over Lincoln.*

← Adam Le Fondre was among the goals again for Rotherham last term. He finished with 23 – four of which came in an amazing game against Cheltenham.

IT'S RAINING GOALS!

The 2010/11 season witnessed some of the most amazing games in fourth-tier history. Crewe were involved in four of the highest-scoring clashes, drawing 5–5 with Chesterfield, putting eight past Cheltenham, seven past Barnet and losing 6–2 at Northampton! The most goals came at the Crown Ground as Accrington claimed a stunning 7–4 win against Gillingham. Adam Le Fondre scored four times for Rotherham in a thrilling 6–4 success at home to Cheltenham, while Louis Dodds and Justin Richards both scored hat-tricks in Port Vale's 7–2 demolition of Morecambe.

KEMPSON BAGS UNFORTUNATE BRACE

February 2010 was a bad month for Accrington's Darran Kempson, with the defender scoring two injury-time winners – both for the wrong team! His first gifted Lincoln a 2–1 victory at Sincil Bank, and he followed that two games later by finding the bottom corner of his own net against Torquay after he had attempted to take the ball away from striker Ashley Barnes. Perhaps the most famous fourth-tier own goal was scored by Bury's Chris Brass at Darlington in April 2006. He attempted an overhead clearance which cannoned off his face and rebounded into the back of the net!

⋯→ Chris Brass' own goal for Bury against Darlington in 2006 was a fine example of a good idea that went horribly wrong.

SHOT-SHY SHOTS

Aldershot had the fewest shots of any team in the division in 2010/11, but their goal return was enough to see them safely avoid the drop. Town fired in a combined total of 377 attempts – 15 less than Lincoln and a further eight less than Stockport, both of whom were relegated. Dean Holdsworth's men ended the season in 14th place with a goal difference of zero having scored and conceded 26 goals at home and 28 away.

CLAYTON PLAYS A BLINDER

Clayton Donaldson scored two hat-tricks for Crewe on his way to finishing the 2010/11 season as the league's leading marksman. The free-transfer signing from Scottish side Hibernian had only scored two goals at the start of October but ended the campaign with 28 to his name, one more than Bury's Ryan Lowe. Donaldson scored nine goals in his last seven games, only failing to find the target against Wycombe during that spell.

TORPEY TIMES IT RIGHT

Steve Torpey jointly holds the distinction of having scored one of the fastest goals in the division's history. Striker Torpey netted for Scunthorpe against Swansea with a neat header in December 2004 – a goal recorded at just seven seconds. It turned out to be the only goal of the game, although Iron winger Peter Beagrie had a penalty saved. Freddy Eastwood also scored for Southend after seven seconds.

⋯→ Steve Torpey scored regularly for Scunthorpe, but his goal after seven seconds against Swansea was the joint fastest since League 2 began.

CLUB RECORDS

There are 72 Football League clubs and 20 Premier League teams in England and Wales and each one has their own unique story to tell.

From Arsenal to Yeovil Town, every club, big or small, has had magical memories to savour and moments they would rather forget. Whether it's amazing games with incredible scorelines, record-breaking transfers, goalscoring legends or pop-star wannabes, English League football has had it all down the years.

Since the introduction of the Premier League there have been four different winners of the competition — Manchester United, Blackburn, Arsenal and Chelsea — and all of those successes went down in the history books for one reason or another.

There is much to get excited about for Football League clubs, too. One of the most exciting additions came in 1986/87 when the play-offs were introduced to give more teams in the second, third and fourth tiers the chance to achieve their promotion dreams.

Take the 2010/11 season. In the npower Championship, Swansea City clinched a promotion spot after winning a dramatic game against Reading at Wembley, while both the npower League 1 and League 2 matches threw up surprises. Peterborough United, who had finished eight points behind third-placed opponents Huddersfield Town in npower League 1, romped to a 3—0 victory at Old Trafford. And in the division below, sixth-placed Stevenage won through their semi-final clash to face seventh-placed Torquay United in the showpiece final, with Graham Westley's side holding on to reach the third tier for the first time in the club's history.

Some of the most talented players ever to grace the English leagues — from the likes of Sir Stanley Matthews, Billy Wright, Sir Tom Finney and George Best right through to modern-day greats such as Cristiano Ronaldo and Fernando Torres — are fondly remembered by fans of numerous clubs, along with the cult heroes who gave 100 per cent and went down in sporting folklore, sometimes for strange reasons!

At every club and at every level, English football has always captured the imagination of fans around the world. And the signs are that will continue to be the case for many years to come.

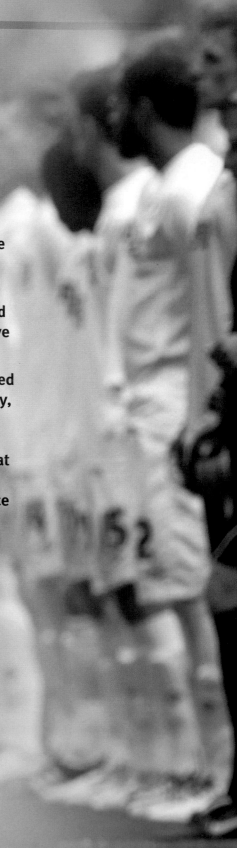

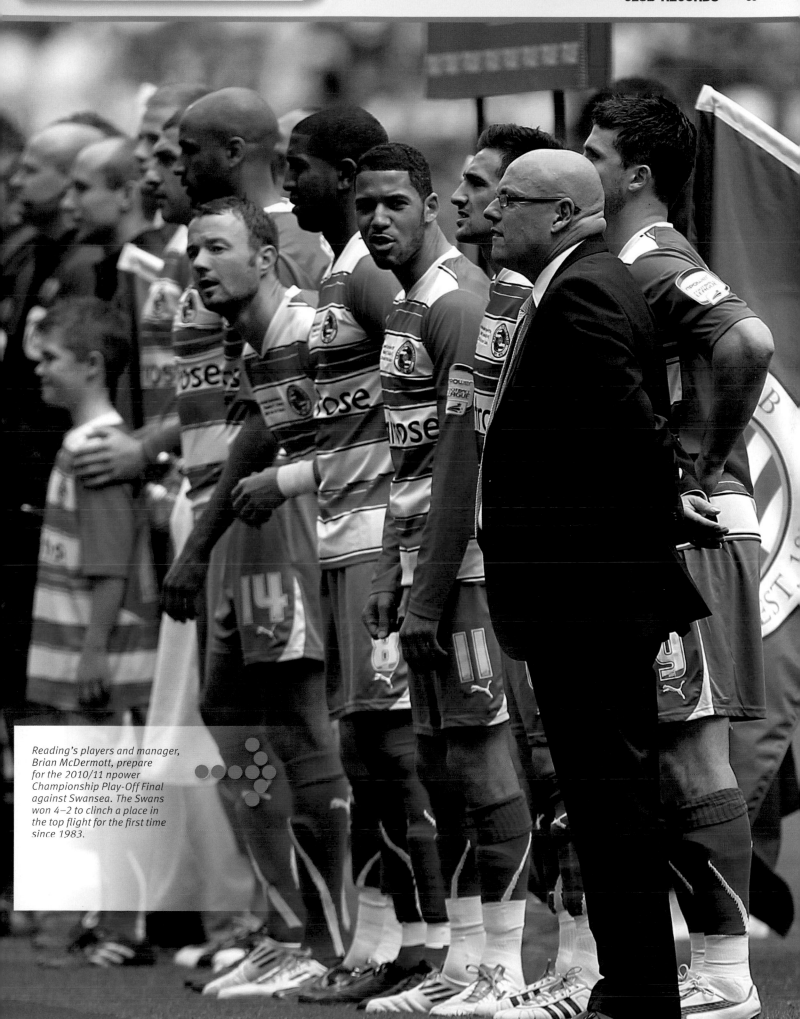

Reading's players and manager, Brian McDermott, prepare for the 2010/11 npower Championship Play-Off Final against Swansea. The Swans won 4–2 to clinch a place in the top flight for the first time since 1983.

BARCLAYS PREMIER LEAGUE CLUB RECORDS

The Barclays Premier League is widely regarded as one of the most exciting competitions in world football and has gone from strength to strength since the inaugural season in 1992. Attendances continue to grow, as do television viewing figures both in the UK and abroad, and it is easy to see why, with the league boasting some of the world's greatest players and biggest clubs.

Chelsea's Didier Drogba is one of the most prolific goalscorers in the Barclays Premier League, having netted an impressive 95 times in 202 top-flight games for the Blues.

Fans of the two Manchester clubs stand in tribute before City and United's clash in February 2008. They were remembering the Munich air crash of 1958 which decimated United's 'Busby Babes'.

ARSENAL

Arsenal are one of the most successful clubs in English football, having won 13 top-flight titles and 10 FA Cups during their illustrious history. The Gunners are also the only team to have completed a Premier League season without losing a game. That was in 2003/04 – the last time the London club lifted the league title.

HUMBLE BEGINNINGS

The Gunners may be one of the biggest clubs in the world but they have come a long way since they were founded in October 1886. They turned professional five years later and changed their name to Woolwich Arsenal, with their first competitive match taking place in 1893 – a 2–2 draw with Newcastle.

⤑ *In 2003/04, Arsenal emulated the inaugural champions, Preston North End, by going through a league season undefeated. They played 38 games (26 wins, 12 draws) compared to Preston's 22 (18 wins, 4 draws).*

THE INVINCIBLES

Arsenal wrote their name into modern football history in 2003/04 when they went through the entire league season unbeaten on their way to winning the Premier League title. 'The Invincibles', as they became known, were simply unstoppable and went on to stretch their streak to a record 49 games without defeat. It was well into the following season before the mammoth unbeaten run was finally brought to an end when, on October 24 2004, they were finally beaten by arch-rivals Manchester United, who triumphed 2–0 at Old Trafford. During that memorable title-winning season, Arsene Wenger's team failed to score on only four occasions, with Birmingham, Newcastle, Fulham and Manchester United the only teams able to hold them to 0–0.

⤑ *Although born in Spain, Cesc Fabregas is a product of the Arsenal Academy, having joined the club from Barcelona at the age of just 16.*

CESC MAGNIFIQUE

Cesc Fabregas is the youngest player to have pulled on an Arsenal shirt. He set that record in 2003 when he appeared in a League Cup clash with Rotherham aged 16 years and 177 days. Midfielder Jack Wilshere holds the record for being the youngest Gunner to have played in the Premier League, having made his debut aged 16 years and 256 days against Blackburn in September 2008.

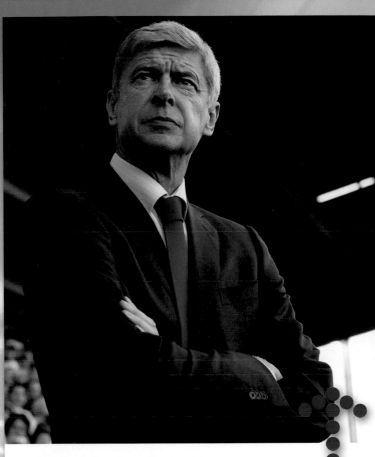

RECORD-BREAKING O'LEARY

David O'Leary is the Gunners' record appearance holder, having played 722 games in all competitions and 558 in the league between 1975 and 1993. The former Republic of Ireland international made his debut for the club in a goalless draw at Burnley in August 1975. Ray Parlour holds Arsenal's record for the most Premier League appearances with 333 – eight more than goalkeeper David Seaman.

·····> *David O'Leary was a more than dependable central defender. He won two league titles, two FA Cups and two League Cups at Highbury.*

↓ *Any questions about how Andrey Arshavin was settling in London were answered in April 2009 when he scored four times against Liverpool at Anfield in a pulsating 4–4 draw.*

THE PROFESSOR

Arsene Wenger is known as a real student of the game and has earned the nickname 'The Professor'. That reputation also comes in part from the fact that he is seen as one of the more intellectual managers in the Barclays Premier League. The Frenchman has a Masters degree in economics and is able to speak several languages. He is fluent in English, German, Spanish and Italian, as well as his native French. Wenger is the longest-serving manager in the club's history.

⇡ *Arsene Wenger's influence on Arsenal has been huge, both on and off the pitch. The trophies collected by the Gunners under his leadership bear testament to the Frenchman's football ideology.*

ARSENAL APPEARANCES

David O'Leary	722
Tony Adams	669
George Armstrong	621
Lee Dixon	619
Nigel Winterburn	584
David Seaman	564
Pat Rice	528
Peter Storey	501
John Radford	481
Peter Simpson	477

FROM RUSSIA WITH LOVE

Russian playmaker Andrey Arshavin scored all four Arsenal goals in an amazing 4–4 draw against Liverpool at Anfield in April 2009. He had scored two goals in seven Barclays Premier League appearances going into the game but really announced his arrival in English football that night with a stunning solo display. The £15million signing from Zenit St Petersburg had netted 22 top-flight goals for the Gunners by the end of season 2010/11.

ARSENAL'S LEADING GOALSCORERS

Thierry Henry	226
Ian Wright	185
Cliff Bastin	178
John Radford	149
Ted Drake	139
Jimmy Brain	139
Doug Lishman	137
Joe Hulme	125
David Jack	124
Dennis Bergkamp	120

ARSENAL

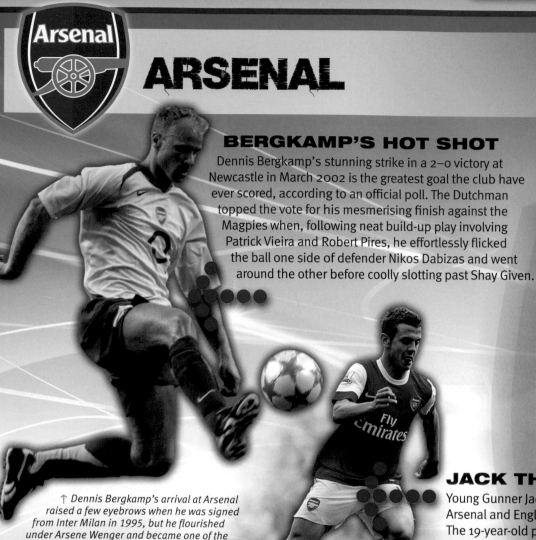

BERGKAMP'S HOT SHOT

Dennis Bergkamp's stunning strike in a 2–0 victory at Newcastle in March 2002 is the greatest goal the club have ever scored, according to an official poll. The Dutchman topped the vote for his mesmerising finish against the Magpies when, following neat build-up play involving Patrick Vieira and Robert Pires, he effortlessly flicked the ball one side of defender Nikos Dabizas and went around the other before coolly slotting past Shay Given.

↑ *Dennis Bergkamp's arrival at Arsenal raised a few eyebrows when he was signed from Inter Milan in 1995, but he flourished under Arsene Wenger and became one of the best players in Premier League history.*

⇢ *Jack Wilshere's status as one of the best young players in the country was cemented in 2010/11 as the Gunners midfielder broke into the England set-up.*

CANARIES TAKE FLIGHT

The Gunners began life in the Premier League with a surprise 4–2 defeat at home to Norwich. Arsenal had finished fourth in season 1991/92 and it was all going according to plan when Steve Bould opened the scoring and Kevin Campbell added a second before half-time. But the Canaries hit back, with Mark Robins scoring twice and David Phillips and Ruel Fox completing the turnaround. Norwich qualified for Europe by finishing third that term, while Arsenal were 10th.

JACK THE LAD

Young Gunner Jack Wilshere established himself as an Arsenal and England regular during the last campaign. The 19-year-old playmaker spent the second half of 2009/10 on loan at Bolton and was expected to go back there for a longer spell. But prolific Twitter user Wilshere instead broke into Arsenal's first team and featured in 54 games in total for club and country. His international coach, Fabio Capello, has described Wilshere as a 'real leader' and believes he is a future England captain.

THE GREATEST GUNNERS*

1	Thierry Henry
2	Dennis Bergkamp
3	Tony Adams
4	Ian Wright
5	Patrick Vieira
6	Robert Pires
7	David Seaman
8	Liam Brady
9	Charlie George
10	Pat Jennings

* As voted by Arsenal fans

⇢ *Thierry Henry came to epitomise the Arsenal flair under Arsene Wenger, scoring more than 200 goals, and most of them were beautiful.*

KING HENRY

Thierry Henry was named as Arsenal's greatest player in an official poll in 2008. The French forward is the club's all-time leading goalscorer, having netted 226 times in 380 appearances in all competitions between 1999 and 2007. Henry's most memorable strike came against Manchester United in October 2000 when he flicked the ball up, turned and lobbed a shot over Fabien Barthez. That strike came second in a list of Arsenal's top goals. Henry won two Premier League titles and two FA Cup winners' medals with the Gunners before leaving for Barcelona.

SUNDERLAND'S MEMORABLE MOMENT

Arsenal have won the FA Cup 10 times and have been involved in some of the most memorable cup final tussles. Perhaps their most dramatic victory came in 1979 against Manchester United. The Gunners were leading 2–0 at half-time through a Brian Talbot tap-in and Frank Stapleton's header. That was how it stayed until five minutes before the end, when United managed to haul themselves level. However, there was still time for another twist as, with only a few seconds remaining, Graham Rix sent over a cross which was misjudged by goalkeeper Gary Bailey and Alan Sunderland popped up at the far post to make it 3–2 to the Londoners.

← What had seemed set to be an unremarkable FA Cup final win for Arsenal against Manchester United in 1979 became memorable when United scored twice late on, only for Alan Sunderland (front) to snatch the trophy with a goal in the final seconds.

TOTTENHAM TUSSLES

Derby games between Arsenal and Tottenham are always good to watch, but there have been some titanic tussles between the two sides in recent years. In November 2004, the Gunners came from a goal behind to lead 3–1 and then 4–2, before finally winning 5–4 at White Hart Lane. It was a similar story in October 2008, although this time Spurs managed to snatch a point with two goals in the last two minutes making it 4–4 at the Emirates Stadium. Season 2010/11's clashes were equally epic, with Tottenham hitting back from two goals down to win 3–2 in November before drawing 3–3 having been 3–1 behind in the reverse fixture in April.

DRAKE'S SEVEN

Legendary striker Ted Drake scored seven goals in a single game for Arsenal in December 1935 – a club record. Aston Villa were the opposition and found themselves 3–0 down at the break, with Drake scoring a hat-trick. He had bagged six by the hour mark and completed his remarkable scoring feat in the last minute, having also hit the crossbar and had another effort well saved. The game finished 7–1 to the Gunners.

↑ Ted Drake was almost unstoppable against Aston Villa in 1935, scoring all seven goals in a 7–1 win at Villa Park.

SPIREITES' RECORD SHOT DOWN

Arsenal created an English record when they scored in 55 consecutive Premier League matches between May 19 2001 and December 7 2002. The run began in a 3–2 defeat at Southampton on the last day of the 2000/01 campaign and continued until 2002/03, as Juan Sebastian Veron and Paul Scholes scored the only goals of the game for Manchester United in a 2–0 win at Old Trafford. Chesterfield had previously held the record, scoring in 46 matches in a row in the third tier between 1929 and 1930.

GUNNERS' FA CUP FINAL WINS

1930	2–0 v Huddersfield
1936	1–0 v Sheffield United
1950	2–0 v Liverpool
1971	2–1 v Liverpool
1979	3–2 v Manchester United
1993	2–1 v Sheffield Wednesday
1998	2–0 v Newcastle United
2002	2–0 v Chelsea
2003	1–0 v Southampton
2005	0–0 v Manchester United (5–4 on penalties)

↓ Jens Lehmann (left) made the vital saves and skipper Patrick Vieira took the final kick as Arsenal won the 2005 FA Cup final in a penalty shootout.

AVFC
PREPARED

ASTON VILLA

Aston Villa were top-flight champions and kings of Europe back in the early 1980s, and they are re-emerging as a force again. The Birmingham-based club were founder members of both The Football League and the Premier League and have won the fourth highest total of major honours of any English team. They claimed their last major piece of silverware in 1996, winning the League Cup for the fifth time.

HOME-GROWN TALENT

Aston Villa were the last club to field an all-English starting line-up in a Premier League game. Coventry dampened the occasion by claiming a 4–1 win at Villa Park on February 27 1999. Michael Oakes started the game in goal for Villa, with Alan Wright, Gareth Southgate, Steve Watson and Riccardo Scimeca making up the defence. Ian Taylor, Paul Merson, Simon Grayson and Lee Hendrie were in midfield, while Dion Dublin and Julian Joachim began the game up front. Villa also used three English substitutes – Gareth Barry, Mark Draper and Stan Collymore.

CHAMPIONS OF EUROPE

Villa are one of four English clubs to have won the European Cup. Peter Withe scored the only goal of the game as the Midlands side beat German giants Bayern Munich in the final in May 1982. Villa had eased to victory against Valur Reykjavik in the first round and then edged past Dynamo Berlin before seeing off a strong Dynamo Kiev side in the last eight. A single Tony Morley goal separated the Villans and Anderlecht in a two-legged semi-final, and Villa survived the loss of goalkeeper Jimmy Rimmer to injury in the early stages of the final to snatch a 1–0 win.

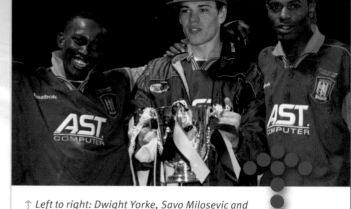

⬆ *Left to right: Dwight Yorke, Savo Milosevic and Ian Taylor, the Aston Villa goalscorers in the 3–0 1996 League Cup final victory over Leeds.*

VILLANS ARE CUP HEROES

The Villans have won the League Cup five times, with their last success coming in 1996. Savo Milosevic scored a superb opener in a 3–0 win against Leeds, with Ian Taylor adding a second and Dwight Yorke wrapping up the victory late on. Villa, who were the first club to win the competition when they beat Rotherham in 1961, were also victorious against Norwich in 1975, Everton after two replays in 1977 and Manchester United in 1994.

⬇ *Although experienced England international striker Peter Withe scored Aston Villa's match-winning goal in the 1982 European Cup final, substitute goalkeeper Nigel Spink came on for only his second first-team appearance.*

SEVENTH HEAVEN

Villa have won the top-flight title on seven occasions, although six of those successes came between 1894 and 1910. The last time the midlands club tasted championship glory was under Ron Saunders in season 1980/81, as they pipped Ipswich by four points.

← When Aston Villa won the league championship in 1981, it ended a 71-year drought. Captained by Dennis Mortimer (with the trophy) they used a record-low 14 players in the 42-game season.

BIG-TIME CHARLIE

Charlie Aitken holds the record for the most appearances in an Aston Villa shirt. He played 659 times in all competitions in a 16-year spell at the club between 1960 and 1976. Defender Aitken was a member of the Villa side that won the League Cup in 1975, having also been a losing finalist in the competition in 1971. The club were beaten 2–0 by Tottenham in the Wembley showpiece that year, with Martin Chivers scoring both goals for Spurs.

↓ Charlie Aitken was the most loyal Villan. His only league winners' medal came when Villa won the Division Three championship in 1972.

POINTS MEAN PRIZES

Villa's promotion-winning campaign of 1987/88 brought with it a club-record points haul. Graham Taylor's side finished as runners-up to Millwall in the second tier, having taken 78 points from 42 matches. The Lions topped the table on 82. The club's biggest total when two points were awarded for a win came in the 1971/72 campaign, as they claimed the third-tier title with 70 points and won 32 of their 46 games.

DR WHO?

Foreign bosses are common in English football these days, but Aston Villa were the first top-flight club to appoint a manager from outside Britain or Ireland in July 1990. Slovakian coach Dr Jozef Venglos didn't last long at Villa Park, though, stepping down after the club finished two places above the relegation zone in 1990/91. Venglos was the only foreigner to have managed the club until Gerard Houllier's appointment in September 2010.

DONS UNDONE BY JOHNSON

Villa's record Premier League victory came against Wimbledon at Villa Park on February 11 1995. An own goal from Dons defender Alan Reeves opened the floodgates and, after Tommy Johnson had helped himself to a hat-trick, Dean Saunders bagged a brace and Dwight Yorke completed a 7–1 victory with seven minutes remaining. Warren Barton netted a consolation for the visitors. The Villans' biggest away victory since the league's inception in 1992 was a 6–0 success at Derby in April 2008.

↑ Republic of Ireland defender Paul McGrath battled chronic knee trouble to help Aston Villa finish second in the inaugural Premier League season, and he won the PFA Player of the Year award.

ASTON VILLA APPEARANCES

Charlie Aitken	659
Billy Walker	531
Gordon Cowans	528
Joe Bache	474
Allan Evans	473
Gareth Barry	458
Nigel Spink	454
Tommy Smart	452
Johnny Dixon	430
Dennis Mortimer	405

AWARD-WINNING TRIO

Three Aston Villa players have been named the PFA Player of the Year, with Paul McGrath the last to scoop the prize in 1993. Defender McGrath won the award for his solid performances in a side that finished as runners-up to Manchester United. Andy Gray was the first Villa recipient in 1977, having ended the campaign as the top-flight's leading goalscorer, while David Platt also received the accolade in 1990.

AVFC
PREPARED

ASTON VILLA

YOUNG IS TRICKY CUSTOMER

Ashley Young proved just how tricky a customer he can be during the 2010/11 campaign, drawing the most fouls of any player in the Barclays Premier League. The England international, who won 89 free-kicks during the course of the season, said before the final game: 'I've got cuts, bumps, bruises, everything up and down my shins, but I've come to get used to it.' Villa team-mate Darren Bent was flagged offside 61 times last term, by far the most in the top flight.

↓ Opposition defences always find it hard to play against Ashley Young, who left Villa to join Manchester United at the end of the 2010/11 campaign.

MIDLANDS PRIDE

Villa finished the 2010/11 season as the highest-placed Midlands club in the Barclays Premier League, but the race went down to the wire as West Brom tried their best to snatch the bragging rights. Villa's 1—0 win at home to Liverpool on the last day proved enough, with the Baggies only managing a point in a 3—3 draw at Newcastle. The Villans finished ninth, West Brom were one point and two places behind while Wolves narrowly survived in 17th and Birmingham suffered relegation.

↑ Villa drew both of their Barclays Premier League games against arch-rivals Birmingham in 2010/11, but they still went on to claim bragging rights as the top club in the Midlands.

FLYING START

Villa managed a club-record run of 12 Premier League games unbeaten at the start of the 1998/99 season. The campaign began with a goalless draw at Everton, which was followed by four straight victories. After another stalemate with Leeds at Elland Road, Villa then won four of their next six matches. The run was finally brought to an end when Liverpool claimed a 4—2 victory at Villa Park, helped by a Robbie Fowler hat-trick.

BRAND NEW BADGE

A new club crest was revealed in May 2007, incorporating a star to represent Villa's European Cup success of 1982. The claret and blue stripes used in the previous shield were replaced by an all-blue background, although the traditional lion emblem remained in gold. Aston Villa was shortened to AVFC, but the club's motto, Prepared, remained at the foot of the badge.

A SUPER SHOW

Mighty Barcelona were beaten over two legs as Villa won the European Super Cup in 1982/83. The Catalan giants claimed a 1—0 victory at the Nou Camp in the first game, but a 3—0 extra-time victory in the second leg at Villa Park secured the hosts an aggregate success. Gary Shaw had levelled the tie late on, with a penalty from Gordon Cowans putting Villa ahead before Ken McNaught clinched victory.

HEALTH SCARE FOR HOULLIER

Gerard Houllier stepped down as Aston Villa manager for health reasons at the end of the 2010/11 season. The Frenchman, who had undergone heart surgery during his time in charge of Liverpool, was taken to hospital in April 2011 after suffering chest pains. It was felt it was too big a risk for him to return to work and his departure was announced on June 1. Football managers face the tricky task of keeping players, club owners, fans and even the media happy, making it a very stressful job.

PONGO ON SONG

Tom 'Pongo' Waring scored an amazing 49 goals in a single season for Aston Villa during the 1930/31 campaign. The Villans netted a club-record 128 times that term but finished runners-up to Arsenal in the top flight. Waring scored 159 league goals and 167 in total for Villa during a seven-year stay between 1928 and 1935, including 10 hat-tricks. He is the club's sixth highest goalscorer of all time.

--> *Tom Waring got his nickname 'Pongo' from a popular cartoon strip of the time. He was not a fan of training, but no one cared, because his goals were so important to the team.*

VILLA'S LEADING GOALSCORERS

Billy Walker	244
Harry Hampton	242
John Devey	186
Joe Bache	184
Eric Houghton	170
Tom Waring	167
Johnny Dixon	144
Peter McParland	120

<-- *Gerard Houllier shows the strain of being a manager during his time as Aston Villa boss. He left the club in June 2011 for health reasons.*

--> *Gabriel Agbonlahor completed the scoring as Aston Villa equalled their biggest top-division win over Birmingham City, 5–1, in 2008.*

HUNTER GATHERS RECORD

Archie Hunter was the first player to score in every round of the FA Cup when Aston Villa won the competition in 1887. He netted the opener in a 2–0 win against West Brom in the final to complete the feat. Hunter, who was the club's captain at the time, suffered a heart attack during a game against Everton in January 1890 and never played again. He died four years later aged just 35.

BEATING THE BLUES

The club secured their biggest league win over derby rivals Birmingham for 45 years when they claimed a 5–1 victory at Villa Park in April 2008. John Carew and Ashley Young both netted twice, with Gabriel Agbonlahor completing the scoring. Villa had been 4–0 winners in March 1963, while they have also enjoyed some other big victories against Blues over the years. In October 1960 they secured a 6–2 success, while in September 1895 they ran-out 7–3 winners!

BLACKBURN ROVERS

Blackburn enjoyed the high life in the early years of the Premier League, with the club following up a second-place finish in 1993/94 by winning the title in thrilling fashion the following season. The Lancashire side also have considerable cup pedigree and won the FA Cup five times in the space of seven years between 1884 and 1891.

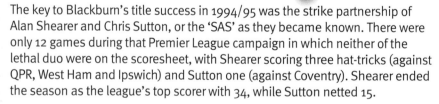

SIMON SAYS SCORE!

Simon Garner is the club's record league goalscorer. Garner netted 168 times in a 14-year spell between 1978 and 1992. Rovers earned promotion to the first-ever Premier League in Garner's final season, beating Leicester 1–0 in the Play-Off Final, with Mike Newell scoring a penalty.

↓ Simon Garner became a legend in Blackburn, helping Rovers climb into the Premier League.

SHEARER AND SUTTON

The key to Blackburn's title success in 1994/95 was the strike partnership of Alan Shearer and Chris Sutton, or the 'SAS' as they became known. There were only 12 games during that Premier League campaign in which neither of the lethal duo were on the scoresheet, with Shearer scoring three hat-tricks (against QPR, West Ham and Ipswich) and Sutton one (against Coventry). Shearer ended the season as the league's top scorer with 34, while Sutton netted 15.

↑ With almost 50 Premier League goals between them, Alan Shearer (left) and Chris Sutton were able to celebrate the title in 1995.

ROVERS MOTOR TO TITLE

Rovers won their first top-flight title since 1914 when they pipped Manchester United to be crowned Premier League champions in 1994/95. The race went down to the final day, but Kenny Dalglish's side were victorious, despite losing 2–1 at Liverpool. United failed to find the winner they needed at West Ham, with a 1–1 draw sending the title to Ewood Park.

WHAT'S THE POINT?

Blackburn's 91-point haul in the 2000/01 season is the highest total they have managed since three points for a win was introduced. Rovers gained promotion back to the Premier League that year, but they still finished the campaign as runners-up to Fulham, who broke the 100-point barrier under the management of Jean Tigana. When two points were awarded for a victory, the Lancashire club posted 60 points in the 1974/75 campaign to claim the third-tier title.

MIMMS KEEPS IT CLEAN

Goalkeeper Bobby Mimms and a Rovers rearguard featuring David May, Colin Hendry, Kevin Moran and Graeme Le Saux equalled a club record of 19 clean sheets in 1992/93. Blackburn had been promoted to the top flight the term before and they defied the critics by finishing fourth in the first-ever Premier League campaign. Jim Arnold was in goal when the club kept the same number of clean sheets in the third-tier campaign of 1979/80.

FRIEDEL IN FINE FORM

Rovers were League Cup winners for the one and only time in their history in 2002, beating Tottenham 2–1 at the Millennium Stadium. Matt Jansen opened the scoring for Blackburn in the 25th minute only for Christian Ziege to equalise shortly afterwards. Andrew Cole was the match-winner with just over 20 minutes remaining, taking advantage of hesitant defending to slot home. Rovers had goalkeeper Brad Friedel to thank for preserving their lead, as he pulled off a string of fine saves.

↑ Brad Friedel's heroics at the Millennium Stadium played a big part in Blackburn's first League Cup success in 2002, as they beat Tottenham 2–1.

ROVERS' MANAGERS SINCE 1995

Ray Harford	1995–1997
Roy Hodgson	1997–1998
Brian Kidd	1998–1999
Tony Parkes	1999–2000
Graeme Souness	2000–2004
Mark Hughes	2004–2008
Paul Ince	2008
Sam Allardyce	2008–2010
Steve Kean	2010–Present

←--- Andrew Cole repaid Blackburn's faith in him by scoring the winner in the 2002 League Cup final, two months after Rovers had paid Manchester United £8million for his services.

↑ Bobby Mimms played behind a solid Blackburn Rovers defence and kept 19 clean sheets in the club's debut season in the Premier League.

FANTASTIC FAZ

Derek Fazackerley is Rovers' record appearance holder, having featured in 596 league games for the club between 1970 and 1986. Fazackerley overtook Ronnie Clayton, who played in 529 games for the Ewood Park side. The defender only scored 23 league goals, but he is fondly remembered for his match-winner in a derby clash at Bolton in March 1973. He returned to Blackburn as a first-team coach under Ray Harford and Roy Hodgson.

BORO SOUNDLY BEATEN

Middlesbrough were on the receiving end as Blackburn hit nine goals without reply to rack up their record league victory in November 1954. Frank Mooney and Eddie Quigley scored hat-tricks, while Eddie Crossan bagged a brace in the emphatic victory. The club's record cup success came against Rossendale in the first round of the FA Cup in 1884, as they ran out 11–0 winners.

GOAL KING COLE

The Lancashire club broke their transfer record to sign striker Andrew Cole in December 2001. Cole had been a prolific goalscorer at Newcastle and Manchester United, and he scored four goals in his first six appearances for Rovers. He had netted 13 times in all competitions by the end of the 2001/02 campaign, scoring in five consecutive matches during the last two months of the season. He scored 37 goals in total for Blackburn before moving to Fulham.

BLACKBURN ROVERS

UNCLE JACK

Jack Walker invested millions of pounds into Blackburn to help the club realise their Premier League dream. Walker made his money in the steel and aviation industries. He took control of Rovers in 1991 and broke the British transfer record twice to sign Alan Shearer and later Chris Sutton. Walker oversaw the redevelopment of Ewood Park and has a stand named after him. 'Uncle Jack' died in August 2000. There is a memorial garden and statue in his honour outside Blackburn's stadium.

HIT FOR SIX

Rovers have won the FA Cup six times, although they last lifted the trophy in 1928. Blackburn were victorious for three years running between 1884 and 1886, and they also won the competition in 1890 and 1891. Rovers last reached the final in 1960, but they were beaten 3–0 by Wolves, with defender Mick McGrath putting through his own net to break the deadlock. They were also runners-up in 1882.

← Jack Walker's investment in Blackburn was not just on the pitch. He paid for the redevelopment of Ewood Park and his biggest reward came with the 1995 league title.

↑ Bryan Douglas is denied by Wolves goalkeeper Malcom Finlayson in the 1960 FA Cup final. It is now over 50 years since Blackburn have played in the showpiece final.

FOUNDER MEMBERS

Blackburn are one of only three clubs who were founder members of both The Football League and the Premier League. They share the honour with Everton and Aston Villa. Rovers finished fourth out of 12 teams in the first-ever league season of 1888, and they also ended the inaugural Premier League campaign in fourth place – three points behind runners-up Villa.

ROVER AT HALF-TIME

Blackburn would have been looking forward to UEFA Champions League football if games during the 2010/11 season had ended at half-time! Rovers were in a winning position at the break on 13 occasions, were on level terms in 20 games and were down at the interval in just five matches. That record would have given the Lancashire club a total of 59 points – 16 more than their actual total – and been good enough to secure fourth place. However, based on second-half performances alone, Blackburn would have been stranded at the bottom of the table, seven points adrift of West Ham.

EAGLES LAND AN OPENING POINT

Rovers enjoyed a memorable tussle in their first Premier League match in August 1992. Blackburn were eight minutes away from victory when Simon Osborn rescued Crystal Palace a point in a 3–3 draw at Selhurst Park. Stuart Ripley had cancelled out a Mark Bright opener to make it 1–1 and, after Gareth Southgate had restored the Eagles' advantage, Alan Shearer equalised again. The prolific striker then put Blackburn ahead for the first time in the 82nd minute, but they were denied by Osborn's last-gasp leveller.

⤙ Alan Shearer's acrobatics couldn't make Blackburn's Premier League debut a winning one, but he did score two of Rovers' goals in their 3–3 draw at Crystal Palace.

VENKY'S COUP FOR ROVERS

Indian company Venky's completed a multi-million pound takeover of Rovers in November 2010. They specialise in chicken meat processing and pharmaceutical products. The Rao family now own Rovers, with Venkatesh and Balaji Rao being greeted by fans at Ewood Park before the 2-0 win against Aston Villa. The new board made an announcement in December 2010, relieving Sam Allardyce of his duties as manager and promoting his assistant, Steve Kean, to the role.

BRIGGS SCORES SEVEN

Tommy Briggs scored a club-record seven goals in one game for Rovers in February 1955. Bristol Rovers were on the receiving end when Blackburn claimed an 8–3 victory at Ewood Park. Briggs was a prolific scorer for the Lancashire club between 1952 and 1957, netting 140 league goals in just 194 games.

⤳ New owners Venkatesh and Balaji Rao have big plans to make Blackburn one of the best teams in the Barclays Premier League.

FREE-SCORING ROVERS

Blackburn netted 114 goals during the 1954/55 season, but it was not enough to win them the title, or even gain them promotion. Rovers were the highest scorers in the second tier by some distance that term, netting 22 more than champions Birmingham. City claimed the title on goal difference from both Luton and Rotherham after all three had finished with 54 points. Rovers finished sixth.

⤓ Striker Jason Roberts continued a proud family tradition when he received an MBE at Buckingham Palace in 2010.

A SPORTING FAMILY

Jason Roberts is the third member of his family to be given an MBE. Two of the Blackburn striker's uncles – Ken Roberts and former West Brom and Coventry forward Cyrille Regis – had already received recognition from the Queen when Jason was awarded the honour for his services to sport in both Grenada and the UK in 2010. Roberts is also related to Olympic medallist John Regis, while David and Otis Roberts – both uncles – also played professional football.

ROVERS' PREMIER LEAGUE GOAL-SCORERS SINCE 2001

Season	Player	Goals
2001/02	Andrew Cole	13
2002/03	Damien Duff	9
2003/04	Andrew Cole	11
2004/05	Paul Dickov	9
2005/06	Craig Bellamy	13
2006/07	Benni McCarthy	18
2007/08	Roque Santa Cruz	19
2008/09	Benni McCarthy	10
2009/10	David Dunn	9
2010/11	Junior Hoilett/Nikola Kalinic/Jason Roberts	5

BOLTON WANDERERS

Bolton are now firmly established as a Barclays Premier League club, with the Lancashire side rejoining the top flight in 2001, having first gained promotion back in 1995. Wanderers have continued to build in recent years. They played in Europe for the first time in 2005/06, as well as qualifying again for the 2007/08 season.

BIG SAM HAS BOLTON SOARING

Sam Allardyce helped to make Bolton an established Premier League club. Allardyce, who now manages West Ham, led Wanderers back into the top flight in 2000/01 when they beat Preston 3-0 in the play-off final. The club battled successfully against relegation for the next two terms before an eighth-placed finish in 2003/04. A first-ever place in Europe was secured via a top-six finish in 2004/05 and, having narrowly missed out the following season, Bolton repeated the feat again in 2006/07, as they ended the campaign in seventh place.

↓ Sam Allardyce was a tough-tackling centre-half who played 198 league matches for Bolton in two spells before becoming the club's manager.

ROYALS RUMBLED

The 1995/96 season saw Bolton play in the Premier League for the first time. They secured their place with a thrilling play-off success against Reading at Wembley. Wanderers were 2–0 down after 15 minutes and things looked bleak when Reading were awarded a penalty before half-time. However, goalkeeper Keith Branagan saved the spot-kick and, after Owen Coyle and Fabian de Freitas had levelled, Mixu Paatelainen and De Freitas' second made it 4–2 in extra time. The Royals netted a consolation late on to make it 4–3.

↑ Bolton's players celebrate at Wembley in 1995 after their pulsating 4–3 victory over Reading, which gave the Trotters promotion to the Premier League for the first time.

THE WHITE HORSE FINAL

Bolton played in, and won, the first-ever game at Wembley Stadium – the 1923 FA Cup final. It is remembered as the 'White Horse Final' after mounted policemen, one on a light-coloured horse, had to be brought in to clear a huge crowd off the pitch. It was the defining image of the day. The official attendance for the game is recorded as 126,047, but it is estimated that close to 300,000 spectators turned up! People were lined up around the side of the pitch when the game began 45 minutes late, with goals from David Jack and Jack Smith earning Bolton a 2–0 win over West Ham.

↓ The only time a Wembley FA Cup final was not all-ticket was the first one, in 1923, when Bolton beat West Ham 2–0 in front of a crowd that has been estimated at 300,000.

GOODBYE TO BURNDEN PARK

Bolton ended their 102-year association with Burnden Park to move into the Reebok Stadium in 1997. The 27,879-capacity ground, named after the club's main sponsor, opened with two goalless draws. The first came against Everton on September 1 and the second against Manchester United later that month. Alan Thompson scored the first goal at the stadium – a penalty in a 1–1 draw with Tottenham.

NAT HITS LOFTY HEIGHTS

Nat Lofthouse is arguably the most famous name in Bolton's history, having spent his entire 15-year career at the club. He is Wanderers' record goalscorer with 285 in all competitions – 255 of those coming in the league – and has a stand named after him at the Reebok Stadium. Lofthouse, who played for the club between 1946 and 1961, scored both goals as the Trotters beat Manchester United to win the FA Cup in 1958. He also netted 30 goals in 33 appearances for England, putting him sixth in the all-time goalscorers' list for his country. Lofthouse died in January 2011 aged 85.

⤏ *Nat Lofthouse (with trophy) scored both goals in the 1958 FA Cup final, but his second is unlikely to have been allowed to stand in the modern game; he shoulder-charged Manchester United goalkeeper Harry Gregg into the net.*

FINAL WOE FOR WANDERERS

The Trotters have reached the final of the League Cup twice, but they were beaten 2–1 on both occasions. Steve McManaman had already scored twice for Liverpool when Alan Thompson's stunner gave Wanderers hope in 1995, while Middlesbrough were two goals up after seven minutes of the 2004 showpiece before Kevin Davies pulled one back for the Lancashire club.

BOLTON'S LEADING GOALSCORERS

Nat Lofthouse	285
Joe Smith	277
David Jack	161
Jack Milsom	153
Ray Westwood	144
Willie Moir	134
John Byrom	130
Harold Blackmore	122
Neil Whatmore	121
John McGinlay	118

CHELSEA LAND ANELKA

Nicolas Anelka spent two seasons at Bolton before Chelsea paid £11.5million to lure him to Stamford Bridge in January 2008 – a club-record transfer fee received. The Frenchman netted 21 goals in 53 league appearances for Wanderers after signing for £8million from Turkish side Fenerbahce. Swedish striker Johan Elmander cost the club a record £10million from Toulouse in July 2008, with Daniel Braaten moving to France as part of the deal.

WANDERER RETURNS

Current manager Owen Coyle played 78 times for Bolton between 1993 and 1995. Wanderers were the only English club Coyle played for, with the Republic of Ireland striker spending most of his career in Scotland. He was signed by the Trotters from Airdrie for £250,000 in the summer of 1993 and went on to score 23 goals in all competitions.

THE GIANTKILLERS

Bolton pulled off a stunning FA Cup victory at Liverpool in the third round of the competition in 1993 to start a remarkable spell of giantkillings. Wanderers were a third-tier side at the time but, after holding the Reds to a 2–2 draw at Burnden Park, goals from John McGinlay and Andy Walker secured a shock 2–0 win at Anfield. In 1994, a second-tier Wanderers side beat Everton at Goodison Park, knocked out holders Arsenal in a fourth-round replay and then edged past Aston Villa before losing to Oldham in the last eight.

⤏ *John McGinlay scores with a header in Bolton's surprise 2–0 FA Cup victory over Liverpool at Anfield in 1993.*

BOLTON WANDERERS

REMEMBER RICKETTS?

Michael Ricketts was a revelation in his first season with Bolton, scoring 24 goals and sealing promotion in the second tier Play-Off Final of 2001. His Premier League form – he scored 15 before the turn of the year – earned him an England call-up under Sven-Goran Eriksson, and he played 45 minutes of a friendly against the Netherlands in February 2002. It was his one and only appearance for his country and Ricketts left for Middlesbrough in January 2003.

† Michael Ricketts takes the ball around Manchester United goalkeeper Fabien Barthez on his way to snatching the Bolton winner at Old Trafford in October 2001.

TROPHY SUCCESS

Wanderers were Football League Trophy winners in 1989. Skipper Phil Brown lifted the cup following a 4–1 win against Torquay at Wembley. Julian Darby, Dean Crombie, Trevor Morgan and Jeff Chandler were the goalscorers that day. Bolton had suffered heartache in the same competition three years previously, losing 3–0 to Bristol City.

FOUL PLAY

Statistics show that Kevin Davies has conceded the most free-kicks since the Premier League began. The Bolton striker was penalised by referees 115 times during the 2010/11 campaign — 40 more than any other player — and had been hauled back 881 times in total up to the end of last term.

NEW RECORD AT OLD TRAFFORD

Bolton were the first club in Premier League history to come from behind to beat Manchester United at Old Trafford. The famous victory was achieved in 2001. Juan Sebastian Veron had curled home a stunning free-kick to put United ahead, but Kevin Nolan equalised with a thunderous drive. Goalkeeper Jussi Jaaskelainen played his part with a superb double save to deny Paul Scholes and then Andrew Cole before the break, with a fortunate ricochet allowing Michael Ricketts to snatch a 2–1 win six minutes from time.

† Bolton brought Nigerian glamour to the Premier League when they signed 'Jay-Jay' Okocha to partner French World Cup winner Youri Djorkaeff in attack.

WORLD-CLASS ARRIVALS

Bolton made the rest of the Premier League sit up and take notice when they signed internationally-renowned stars Jay-Jay Okocha and Youri Djorkaeff on free transfers in 2002. The duo enhanced Wanderers' top-flight reputation, while also helping them to avoid relegation in 2002/03. Both Nigeria ace Okocha, who later captained Wanderers, and Frenchman Djorkaeff scored seven Premier League goals that term. The club finished eighth the following season.

TROTTER THEORIES

It is not known exactly why Bolton are nicknamed the Trotters, although there are a couple of interesting theories to explain the name. In the early 1900s, Wanderers adopted a club mascot called Tommy Trotter, and around the same time the town became renowned for selling the delicacy of pigs feet – otherwise known as trotters.

---> *Daniel Sturridge proved a shrewd acquisition for Wanderers, with the on-loan striker scoring at rate of better than a goal every two games.*

LOAN STAR STURRIDGE

Daniel Sturridge's arrival on loan from Chelsea in the January 2011 transfer window proved an inspired piece of business by Owen Coyle. Hot-shot striker Sturridge featured in 12 Barclays Premier League matches for Wanderers and scored eight goals, with four of them coming in his first four appearances. He scored a last-minute winner on his debut against Wolves and a brace in a 3—0 win against West Ham.

STEADY EDDIE

Eddie Hopkinson is Bolton's record appearance holder, having turned out 578 times for the club in a 13-year spell between 1956 and 1969. Goalkeeper Hopkinson earned 14 caps for England from 1957 to 1959 and was part of the 1958 World Cup squad. Hopkinson, who made 519 league appearances, played his part in helping Wanderers to lift the FA Cup in 1958 – their last major piece of silverware.

BOLTON APPEARANCES

Eddie Hopkinson	578
Roy Greaves	575
Alex Finney	530
Warwick Rimmer	528
Bryan Edwards	518
Ted Vizard	512
Paul Jones	506
Nat Lofthouse	503
Roy Hartle	499
Joe Smith	492

↑ *Eddie Hopkinson was a Bolton regular for 13 years between 1956 and 1969, making a club-record 578 appearances.*

WANDERING AROUND EUROPE

Wanderers have been involved in two European campaigns, making it past the group stages of the UEFA Cup on both occasions. In 2005/06 they qualified behind eventual winners Sevilla and Zenit St Petersburg, before losing in the last 32 to Marseille. They fared better in 2007/08, progressing from a tough group having already drawn 2—2 with Bayern Munich in Germany. They then beat Atletico Madrid 1—0 on aggregate to make it to the round of 16, where they were knocked out by Sporting Lisbon.

---> *Bolton goalscorer Ricardo Gardner tries to get past Bayern Munich duo Marcell Jansen and Andreas Ottl during the 2—2 UEFA Cup Group F draw between the two clubs at the Allianz Arena in October 2007.*

CHELSEA

Chelsea have long been established as a top-flight club but it is only relatively recently that they have enjoyed a prolonged spell of success, having been transformed into a worldwide name by Russian owner Roman Abramovich. The Blues were crowned champions in 2009/10, their third title in the last seven seasons.

SEVEN UP FOR BLUES

Chelsea scored seven goals on three different occasions during 2009/10. Sunderland were the first to suffer, losing 7—2 at Stamford Bridge in January. Nicolas Anelka and Frank Lampard both netted twice in that game, while the latter hit four past Aston Villa in a 7—1 victory in March — the second time Lampard had achieved the feat in the Premier League. However, the Blues then hit seven past Stoke without reply a month later. Salomon Kalou scored a hat-trick, with Lampard grabbing two. The Londoners went one better on the final day of the season, beating Wigan 8—0 to claim the title in style.

THE SPECIAL ONE

Jose Mourinho brought Chelsea their first top-flight title in 50 years when he led the club to glory in his first season in charge in 2004/05. 'The Special One', as he was dubbed by the press, went on to make it back-to-back Barclays Premier League titles the following term and also guided the Blues to two Carling Cup triumphs – in 2005 and 2007 – and an FA Cup victory in 2007. They also reached the last four of the Champions League under the Portuguese boss. Mourinho left Stamford Bridge in September 2007 as the most successful manager in the club's history.

→ A 'Special' moment for Chelsea as (left to right) Frank Lampard, Jose Mourinho and John Terry celebrate the 2005 Barclays Premier League title.

← Frank Lampard has just scored the first of his four goals in Chelsea's 7—1 drubbing of Aston Villa at Stamford Bridge in March 2010.

LAMPS SHINES BRIGHT

Frank Lampard is third in the list of Chelsea's all-time goalscorers. Four goals against Aston Villa in March 2010 took the England midfielder above Roy Bentley and Peter Osgood, and by the end of the following season he had netted 170 times. Lampard still has some way to go to catch the top two, though, with second-placed Kerry Dixon having scored 193 in total and Bobby Tambling setting the benchmark with 202 goals.

A SCORE DRAW

Chelsea drew their first game in the Premier League on August 15 1992. Striker Mick Harford, a summer signing from Luton, had opened the scoring for the Blues in the home clash with Oldham, only for Nick Henry to net an equaliser following a mistake by goalkeeper Dave Beasant. The Londoners finished 11th that season.

MANAGERS UNDER ROMAN ABRAMOVICH

Claudio Ranieri	2000–2004
Jose Mourinho	2004–2007
Avram Grant	2007–2008
Luiz Felipe Scolari	2008–2009
Guus Hiddink	2009
Carlo Ancelotti	2009–2011
Andre Villas-Boas	2011–Present

⇢ *Andre Villas-Boas worked under Jose Mourinho during the latter's time in charge of Chelsea, and now he will be looking to emulate his former boss's success.*

FORTRESS STAMFORD BRIDGE

A 2–1 victory against Fulham at Stamford Bridge on March 20 2004 was the starting point for an amazing run of 86 home games in the league without defeat for the Londoners – a sequence that spanned four years! The 86th game was a 2–0 success against Aston Villa on October 5 2008, but Liverpool brought an end to their incredible run later that month, with Xabi Alonso's deflected strike, which went down as a Jose Bosingwa own goal, enough for the Reds to scrape a 1–0 win.

TORRES TAKES TIME

Fernando Torres took 732 minutes to score his first Chelsea goal following his stunning switch from Liverpool. The normally prolific striker was playing in his 14th game for the Blues against West Ham at a rain-soaked Stamford Bridge when he finally opened his account with a fine curling finish. After the game, Torres said: 'It was not the beginning I was expecting when I signed, but it's never easy when you arrive in January at a massive team like this. There's less pressure for me now. Now I can enjoy it.'

GOALS GALORE

The Blues were involved in some incredibly high-scoring games during the 1940s and 50s. They were beaten 7–4 by Liverpool in September 1946 and narrowly lost out 6–5 to Manchester United in their title-winning season of 1954/55, despite Seamus O'Connell netting a hat-trick on his debut. Chelsea also claimed a 7–4 win against Portsmouth in 1957, and the next season they beat Newcastle 6–5.

↑ *Fernando Torres struggled to adapt to life at Chelsea straight away but hopes to be now settled in.*

HARRIS CHOPS DOWN MARK

Ron 'Chopper' Harris is the Blues' record appearance maker, having turned out almost 800 times for the club between 1962 and 1980. Harris, who earned his nickname due to his uncompromising style, played 795 games for Chelsea in all competitions, 66 more than goalkeeper Peter Bonetti, who is second in the list. The tough-tackling centre-back captained the Londoners to FA Cup glory against Leeds in 1970 and was also skipper for the Cup Winners' Cup victory over Real Madrid a year later.

⇠ *Ron Harris was one of football's hard men in an era when tough tackling was acceptable, and he gave Chelsea fantastic service.*

CUP QUARTET

The Blues have won the League Cup four times. The 1965 final against Leicester was played over two legs, with a 3–2 win in the first clash at Stamford Bridge enough for the Blues to claim the trophy. It wasn't until 1998 that Chelsea next tasted glory in the competition, beating Middlesbrough 2–0, but they were winners again in 2005 with a 3–2 success over Liverpool after extra time. Didier Drogba scored both goals as Arsenal were beaten 2–1 at the Millennium Stadium two years later.

CHELSEA

EURO GLORY

The Londoners may still be searching for an elusive first Champions League trophy, but they have tasted victory in the European Cup Winners' Cup on two occasions. Their first success came back in 1971 when they played Spanish giants Real Madrid in the final in Athens. They drew 1–1 in the first game before claiming a 2–1 win in the replay at the same venue two days later, with Peter Osgood scoring in both matches. A stunning volley from Gianfranco Zola was enough to earn them the trophy again when they beat German side Stuttgart in Stockholm in 1998.

←·· Chelsea captain Dennis Wise lifts the European Cup Winners' Cup in Stockholm in 1998, as the Blues became England's last winners of the trophy before the competition was discontinued in 1999.

THE CREST OF TIMES

The Blues have had five different club badges throughout their history, with the current crest introduced in November 2004. It is based on the design from the 1950s and shows a blue lion holding a staff. The club's first badge featured a Chelsea pensioner, but it was never worn on a shirt, while the second had the Londoners' initials housed inside a shield. The club adopted their fourth badge in 1986. That depicted a lion draped over the letters 'CFC'. It was used for almost 19 years until the current emblem was unveiled.

PLAYER OF THE YEAR SINCE 2001

2001	John Terry
2002	Carlo Cudicini
2003	Gianfranco Zola
2004	Frank Lampard
2005	John Terry
2006	John Terry
2007	Michael Essien
2008	Joe Cole
2009	Frank Lampard
2010	Didier Drogba
2011	Petr Cech

⤓ Didier Drogba (scoring against Arsenal in November 2009) claimed the 2009/10 Barclays Premier League Golden Boot with a hat-trick on the final matchday.

LEADING BLUES GOALSCORERS

Bobby Tambling	202
Kerry Dixon	193
Frank Lampard	170
Roy Bentley	150
Peter Osgood	150
Didier Drogba	144
Jimmy Greaves	132
George Mills	125
George Hilsdon	108
Barry Bridges	93

GOAL-DEN DROGBA

Didier Drogba has won the Premier League's Golden Boot award twice. He finished the 2009/10 campaign as top scorer with 29 goals. The Ivory Coast international won the prize for the first time in 2006/07 after scoring 20 goals. Drogba was the Blues' sixth highest all-time goalscorer at the end of last season, having netted 144 times in all competitions since arriving at the club from Marseille in July 2004.

← A stunned Old Trafford crowd looks on as Joe Cole (second left) is congratulated by (left to right) Frank Lampard, Paulo Ferreira and Nicolas Anelka.

BIG FOUR BEATEN

Chelsea's emergence in recent years as one of the most dominant forces in English football was underlined in 2009/10 by the fact that they took a maximum 18 points off the rest of the perceived 'Big Four'. Manchester United were beaten 1–0 at Stamford Bridge and 2–1 at Old Trafford, with Joe Cole scoring an audacious backheel in the latter game. Didier Drogba proved the scourge of Arsenal by scoring twice in both wins against the Gunners – 2–0 at home and 3–0 at the Emirates Stadium. And Liverpool could not stop the rampant Blues, who won 2–0 at home and 2–0 at Anfield – a result that all-but sealed the title. Manchester City, who finished fifth, did manage to beat the Londoners both home and away.

ZOLA'S THE BEST

Gianfranco Zola was voted as Chelsea's greatest player in an official poll held in 2003. The diminutive Italian spent seven seasons at Stamford Bridge between 1996 and 2003, scoring 80 goals in 312 games. Perhaps his most memorable strike came in an FA Cup replay against Norwich in January 2002 when he scored with a spectacular mid-air backheel.

NEW BLUES BENCHMARKS

Chelsea set new Premier League records for the most goals scored in a single season and the biggest goal difference on their way to winning the title in 2009/10. The Blues netted 103 times as they secured a fourth top-flight crown, with big wins over Blackburn (5–0), Sunderland (7–2), Portsmouth (5–0), Aston Villa (7–1), Stoke (7–0) and Wigan (8–0) among the highlights. They kept it tight at the other end of the pitch too, conceding just 32 goals in their 38 league matches to end the campaign with an impressive goal difference of +71.

↑ Former Italy international Gianfranco Zola may be the finest player not to claim a Premier League winners' medal.

ARRIVEDERCI ANCELOTTI

↓ Carlo Ancelotti has won 12 trophies as a manager, but failing to claim any silverware with Chelsea in 2010/11 cost the Italian his job.

Carlo Ancelotti's reign as Chelsea coach came to an end in May 2011. The Londoners finished nine points behind champions Manchester United in the Barclays Premier League, with third-place Manchester City ending the campaign on the same number of points. Ancelotti, who had led the Blues to a memorable double in 2009/10, saw his side knocked out of the Carling Cup by Newcastle, the FA Cup on penalties by Everton and the UEFA Champions League by Manchester United to make it a trophyless season.

HIT FOR SIX

The FA Cup final victory against Portsmouth in 2010 was the sixth time the club have won the competition. The Blues lifted the trophy for the second successive year following their 2–1 win against Everton 12 months previously. They first tasted victory in the competition in 1970 when they beat Leeds 2–1 in a replay, but it was another 27 years before they won it again. Roberto Di Matteo scored after 42 seconds of the 1997 final to set Chelsea on their way to a 2–0 win against Middlesbrough. The Italian also netted the only goal as Aston Villa were beaten in 2000, and Didier Drogba was the hero in a 1–0 win against Manchester United in 2007.

EVERTON

Everton

Everton have won the top-flight title on nine occasions, with their last success coming in 1986/87. The 1980s were a hugely successful decade for the club, both domestically and in Europe. The last major trophy the Toffees won came in 1995 when they lifted the FA Cup, but they have made steady progress in recent years under boss David Moyes.

BEACON SHINES ON SHIRT

The motto 'Nil Satis, Nisi Optimum', which can be found underneath the Everton crest, means 'Nothing but the best is good enough'. The tower that features on the club badge is known as The Beacon and is located on Netherfield Road in the Everton area of Liverpool, while the laurels used either side were associated with winners in classical times. The shield design with the Latin text was not used on Everton's shirts until 1980.

EVERTON APPEARANCES

Neville Southall	750
Brian Labone	534
Dave Watson	528
Ted Sagar	497
Kevin Ratcliffe	493

⋯⟩ Neville Southall was a binman, a waiter and a hod carrier before he turned professional. He rose to become one of the world's best goalkeepers in the 1980s.

⋯⟩ Gary Lineker's 1985/86 season at Everton was very successful on a personal level, but the Toffees were pipped to the league title and FA Cup by neighbours Liverpool. His goals in the 1986 World Cup then earned him a move to Barcelona.

ONE-SEASON WONDER

Gary Lineker may have only spent one season at Goodison Park, but he still managed to score 40 goals in all competitions and finished the 1985/86 campaign as the top flight's leading scorer. Unfortunately, Everton finished as runners-up to Liverpool in both the league and the FA Cup that year. Lineker won the Golden Boot at the 1986 World Cup after scoring six times for England. He moved to Barcelona that summer.

CHAMPIONS LEAGUE WOE

Everton finished the 2004/05 season in fourth place in the Barclays Premier League and qualified for the Champions League for the first time. Sadly for the Toffees, they missed out on the group stages after they were beaten 4–2 over two legs by Spanish side Villarreal in the third qualifying round. They dropped into the UEFA Cup, as it was then known, but lost at the first hurdle to Romanian side Dinamo Bucharest.

LAST-DAY DRAMA

The Toffees have escaped relegation on the last day of the season twice since the Premier League began. They did it the hard way in season 1993/94, falling 2–0 behind against Wimbledon at Goodison Park before a screamer from Barry Horne and two goals from Graham Stuart snatched a 3–2 victory to keep them up. Gareth Farrelly was the unlikely hero four years later, scoring early as Everton held on to draw 1–1 with Coventry and claim the point they needed to survive on goal difference.

EVERTON'S LEADING GOALSCORERS

Dixie Dean	383
Graeme Sharp	159
Bob Latchford	138
Alex Young	125
Joe Royle	119

···→ William Ralph Dean did not like being called Dixie and how he got the nickname is lost in time. His goalscoring feats, however, are the stuff of legend and record.

···→ Few players have ever made as big an impact at such a young age as Wayne Rooney. After his stunning goal to beat Arsenal in 2002, veteran striker Kevin Campbell gave him a piggy-back ride.

REMEMBER THE NAME!

Wayne Rooney announced his arrival on the big stage with a stunning goal to earn Everton a 2–1 win against Arsenal in October 2002. Debutant Rooney was just 16 when, in the dying seconds of the Goodison Park clash, he expertly controlled a high ball, turned and curled a superb shot into the top corner past the despairing dive of David Seaman. The wonder strike also ended the Gunners' 30-match unbeaten run. Rooney moved to Manchester United for a club-record fee – reported to be £27million – in August 2004.

DIXIE IS GOODISON GREAT

William Ralph Dean, or Dixie Dean as he was more popularly known, was a goalscoring hero for Everton between 1925 and 1937. The hot-shot striker still holds the Football League record for the most goals in a single season, having netted an incredible 60 times in the club's top-flight campaign of 1927/28. He is also the Merseysiders' all-time top goalscorer with 383 in all competitions – 224 more than Graeme Sharp. There is a statue of Dean standing outside Goodison Park.

TOTTENHAM TORN APART

One of the most memorable matches in Everton's recent history came against Tottenham in the semi-finals of the FA Cup in 1995. Spurs started as strong favourites, but they were blown away by a stunning Toffees display. The game is best remembered for striker Daniel Amokachi bringing himself on as a substitute while Paul Rideout was receiving treatment. Manager Joe Royle was furious but later said: 'It was the best substitution I never made!' as the Nigerian went on to secure a 4–1 victory with two goals. Everton shocked Manchester United in the final – the last time they lifted the trophy.

EVERTON ON TOP

Everton were a dominant force in the 1980s, tasting success both at home and in Europe. With a team featuring club legends such as Kevin Ratcliffe, Peter Reid and Graeme Sharp, the Toffees scooped a host of major trophies. They won the top-flight title in 1984/85 and again in 1986/87, finishing as runners-up in between. They edged past Watford to win the FA Cup in 1984 but were beaten finalists in 1985, 1986 and 1989. They also reached the final of the League Cup in 1984, before enjoying their finest hour a year later when they won the European Cup Winners' Cup, setting a then English record of seven successive clean sheets in European competition.

←··· Andy Gray runs away after scoring in the 1984 FA Cup final against Watford. It was the first of many trophies Everton won during Howard Kendall's first spell in charge during the 1980s.

EVERTON

A SWEET TRADITION

The club's nickname, the Toffees, is thought to have been adopted after a sweet shop called Mother Noblett's, situated in the Everton area of Liverpool, started selling Everton Mints. The Merseysiders have a tradition at Goodison Park where a Toffee Lady walks around the side of the pitch on a matchdays throwing Everton Mints into the crowd.

TOFFEES COME UNSTUCK

Barry Horne scored on his debut as Everton drew 1—1 with Sheffield Wednesday in their first Premier League game on August 15 1992. The Toffees fell behind to a goal from Nigel Pearson after quarter of an hour before Horne equalised just short of half-time. Midfielder Horne scored a famous volley against Wimbledon to help the club survive relegation in 1994 but only managed one other goal, on February 3 1996, when he scored against his former club Southampton in a 2—2 draw at The Dell.

···› Duncan Ferguson joined Everton from Rangers in 1994 and quickly became a fan favourite at Goodison Park. He played more than 250 times for the Toffees in two spells and scored more than 60 goals.

RED AND WHITE DELIGHT

Everton have been 7—1 winners in the Premier League on two occasions – their biggest victories since the competition began. Gary Speed scored a hat-trick and Andrei Kanchelskis bagged a brace as the Toffees beat Southampton at Goodison Park in November 1996. They managed the same scoreline in November 2007 against another team playing in red and white stripes, this time securing victory against Sunderland. Ayegbeni Yakubu and Tim Cahill both netted two goals each, with Steven Pienaar, Andrew Johnson and Leon Osman also on target.

↑ Welsh midfielder Gary Speed was Everton's unlikely hat-trick hero when they beat Southampton 7–1 at Goodison Park in 1996.

EVERTON'S BIGGEST LEAGUE WINS

9–1	v	Manchester City	(September 3 1906)
8–0	v	Stoke	(November 2 1889)
8–0	v	Southampton	(November 20 1971)
9–2	v	Leicester	(November 28 1931)
8–1	v	Darwen	(October 21 1893)

BIG DUNC

Duncan Ferguson became a cult hero at Goodison Park during two spells at the club between 1994 and 2006. The fiery Scottish striker arrived on an initial three-month loan deal from Rangers and, after scoring a towering header against Liverpool to set up a famous 2–0 derby victory, he made a permanent £4million switch. 'Big Dunc', who has an Everton-related number nine tattoo on his arm, left for Newcastle in November 1998 but returned to Merseyside in 2000 to spend another six years with the Toffees before retiring.

TIM IS HEAD BOY

Tim Cahill is officially the best header of the ball in Barclays Premier League history. A list was released in October 2010, shortly after the Australian had nodded in a late goal at Birmingham, which had him top with 27 goals in 170 top-flight matches. By the end of the season that figure had increased to 31 in 182 games — that's one in every 5.87 matches. Duncan Ferguson was third in the list.

RECORD TOTAL

The Merseyside giants claimed their biggest points total under two points for a win in season 1969/70. Everton finished their title-winning top-flight campaign on 66 points, nine ahead of nearest challengers Leeds. Joe Royle was their top scorer that term with 23 goals, with Alan Whittle adding 11 and Alan Ball netting 10. The Toffees were league winners again in 1984/85 with a 90-point haul, which is a club record since three points for a win was introduced.

GOODNIGHT VIENNA

Everton won the European Cup Winners' Cup in 1985 with a 3–1 win against Rapid Vienna. A strong line-up, which included club greats such as Neville Southall and Peter Reid, secured victory thanks to goals from Andy Gray, Trevor Steven and Kevin Sheedy. Unfortunately, Everton were denied the chance to play in the European Cup the following season due to a ban imposed on all English clubs following the Heysel stadium tragedy.

A START TO FORGET

The club suffered their worst start to a season in 1994/95 when they went 12 games without a win under manager Mike Walker. A 1–0 victory at home to West Ham in November ended the sequence, but the run cost Walker his job, with Joe Royle coming in to replace him. Everton's Premier League safety was assured at the end of April that term, while they went on to win the FA Cup, with Paul Rideout scoring the only goal of the final against Manchester United.

↑ Joe Royle scored 102 league goals for Everton in only 231 appearances – a great strike rate in the defensive-minded era of the 1960s and 70s.

THE HOLY TRINITY

Alan Ball, Colin Harvey and Howard Kendall were a formidable midfield trio at Goodison Park in the late 1960s and early 1970s. Known as 'The Holy Trinity', the stylish triumvirate helped the club reach the FA Cup final in 1968 — where they were beaten by West Brom. They won the top-flight title in emphatic fashion in season 1969/70, with a superb solo goal from Harvey clinching the championship following a 2–0 home win against the Baggies.

↑ Colin Harvey was nicknamed 'The White Pele', but he wasn't given a real chance to shine on the international stage, making just one appearance for England.

← Alan Ball joined Everton from Blackpool in the summer of 1966. All three members of 'The Holy Trinity' became managers, but only Ball didn't manage Everton.

FULHAM

Fulham are relative newcomers to the Barclays Premier League, having gained their place among the elite in time for the start of the 2001/02 campaign. The London club enjoyed their highest league finish in 2008/09, and the following term was one of the most memorable in their history as they reached the Europa League final.

SAHA SO GOOD

It proved to be a transfer masterstroke when the club signed Louis Saha in 2000. The French striker arrived in a £2.1million deal from Metz, having played on loan at Newcastle in 1999. He scored 27 league goals and 32 in all competitions in his first season as the Cottagers achieved their aim of Premier League football. After two relatively quiet top-flight campaigns, a run of 13 goals in 21 league games at the start of the 2003/04 season then prompted Manchester United to spend around £12million to sign him – a Fulham record.

↑ Louis Saha's 53 goals in 117 league games for Fulham resulted in a club-record £12million transfer deal with Manchester United.

⇢ Owner Mohamed Al Fayed let football people run his club and Fulham rose from the fourth tier in 1996/97 to the Premier League in 2001/02.

THAT WINNING FEELING

The west Londoners managed a club-record run of 12 straight league victories in 2000. The last game of the 1999/2000 season started the sequence, with Fulham claiming a 3–0 win at home to Huddersfield. A 2–0 success against Crewe on the opening day of the following campaign continued the streak, and big wins followed against Stockport and Barnsley. The Cottagers were held to a goalless draw by Wolves on October 2 – that stalemate starting a three-game winless run.

CUP OF PLENTY

The Cottagers were one of three Intertoto Cup winners in 2002, earning a place in the UEFA Cup. Now defunct, the summer knockout competition was made up of a series of two-legged matches involving the highest-ranked applicants from Europe's many leagues. Fulham beat Finnish side FC Haka, Greek club Egaleo and Sochaux of France to set up a final clash with Italians Bologna. Junichi Inamoto scored a hat-trick in a 3–1 home win to secure a 5–3 aggregate victory. They lost to Hertha Berlin in the third round of the UEFA Cup.

AL FAYED FULFILS PREMIER LEAGUE DREAM

Mohamed Al Fayed, the former owner of London department store Harrods, transformed the club when he took over in 1997. The ambitious Egyptian brought in Kevin Keegan and Ray Wilkins to replace Micky Adams, who had achieved promotion to the third tier in season 1996/97. The Cottagers reached the play-offs in 1997/98 before Wilkins left and Keegan oversaw an incredible title-winning campaign the following term. He also departed soon after to concentrate on the England job, paving the way for Jean Tigana to help realise Al Fayed's Premier League dream in 2000/01.

HERO HAYNES

Johnny Haynes is the player to have made the most appearances for the club, having pulled on the Fulham shirt 657 times during an 18-year stay at Craven Cottage. Inside-forward Haynes, who was the first player in Britain to earn £100 a week, captained England in 22 of the 56 games he played for his country, securing him another record as Fulham's most capped player. Having made his debut for the club in 1952, he left for South Africa in 1970 at the age of 35, joining Durban City.

⋯⋯> *Johnny Haynes (with ball) was Fulham captain for almost a decade and, but for a knee injury that ended his international career in 1962, might have been the England skipper when they won the 1966 World Cup.*

A LEG UP

Graham Leggat scored one of the fastest hat-tricks in history – three in three minutes – when Fulham recorded their biggest league victory, against Ipswich on Boxing Day 1963. Former Scotland international Leggat scored four times and Bobby Howfield, who went on to play American football in the NFL as a kicker for the Denver Broncos and New York Jets, hit a treble in a 10–1 win.

POINTS MEAN PRIZES

A number of club records were broken on the way to achieving a place in the top flight, with Kevin Keegan's 1998/99 side setting a new points record of 101 to claim the third-tier title. However, Frenchman Jean Tigana equalled that feat in 2000/01 when the Cottagers gained promotion to the Premier League in emphatic style.

SEVENTH HEAVEN

Fulham secured their best-ever Barclays Premier League finish in 2008/09, ending the campaign in seventh spot and qualifying for the Europa League. Roy Hodgson's men, who had escaped relegation on goal difference the season before, finished above two of the top flight's big spenders in Tottenham and Manchester City. Notable results that term included a 1–0 win against Arsenal and a 2–0 victory at home to Manchester United.

A FINAL TOO FAR

Fulham were beaten FA Cup finalists in 1975 – the closest they have come to winning the competition. A side including club legends such as Bobby Moore and skipper Alan Mullery lost 2–0 to London rivals West Ham, with Alan Taylor scoring both goals. Fulham had endured some epic battles on the way to Wembley, playing Hull three times and Nottingham Forest four times before winning through.

⋯⋯> *Alan Mullery began and ended his league career with Fulham. He led out the team at Wembley in 1975, with World Cup-winning skipper Bobby Moore behind him.*

↑ *Roy Hodgson performed miracles in transforming Fulham from relegation favourites in 2007 to one of the most respected teams in the top flight and 2010 UEFA Europa League finalists. He moved to Liverpool for the start of the 2010/11 season.*

FULHAM'S RECENT MANAGERS

Paul Bracewell	1999–2000
Jean Tigana	2000–2003
Chris Coleman	2003–2007
Lawrie Sanchez	2007
Roy Hodgson	2007–2010
Mark Hughes	2010–2011
Martin Jol	2011–Present

FULHAM

COTTAGERS ARE SPOT ON

Fulham only conceded one penalty during season 2010/11 — and that was missed! The solitary spot-kick was awarded to Manchester United during the Cottagers' first home game of the season, but goalkeeper David Stockdale kept out Nani's effort. It was 2–1 to United at the time, with defender Brede Hangeland going on to snatch a last-gasp leveller for Fulham in a 2–2 draw. Everton conceded just two penalties throughout the campaign, while Arsenal gave away the most with nine.

↓ Fulham goalkeeper David Stockdale played for York City and Darlington before making the step up to the Barclays Premier League.

RECORD CLIPS CANARIES' WINGS

Fulham's record Premier League victory came against Norwich on the final day of the 2004/05 campaign – a result that relegated the Canaries. Brian McBride opened the scoring in the 10th minute, with Papa Bouba Diop doubling their advantage before the break. Zat Knight made it three and Steed Malbranque added a fourth, with McBride's second and a late Andrew Cole strike completing a 6–0 victory. Fulham also hit West Brom for six in February 2006, although the Baggies scored a late consolation.

↑ Fulham's hopes of escaping relegation in 2007/08 stayed alive when Diomansy Kamara (right) scored a stoppage-time match-winner against Manchester City at Eastlands. Clint Dempsey is also pictured.

A GREAT ESCAPE

Former manager Roy Hodgson masterminded a great escape in season 2007/08, with Fulham winning four of their last five games to stay up. The amazing run began with an away victory at Reading, although they were then beaten 2–0 by Liverpool. The Cottagers looked to be heading for relegation when they fell 2–0 behind at Manchester City in their next game, but Diomansy Kamara snatched an injury-time winner as they hit back to win 3–2. The Londoners then won a tense relegation clash against Birmingham, and safety was secured with a 1–0 win against Portsmouth on the final day.

SWANS SUNK

The Cottagers' record cup victory came in November 1995 when they scored seven without reply against Swansea. Mike Conroy bagged a hat-trick in the FA Cup first-round tie at Craven Cottage, with Paul Brooker, Nick Cusak, Duncan Jupp and Martin Thomas also getting in on the act. Fulham were in the fourth tier at the time, with the Swans in the division above.

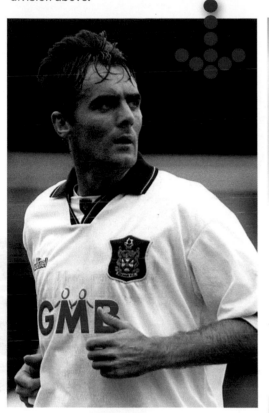

←— Mike Conroy scored only three FA Cup goals in his three seasons with Fulham and all came in the record 7–0 victory over Swansea on November 11 1995.

BY GEORGE

World Cup winner George Cohen is regarded as one of Fulham's greatest players, having spent his entire 13-year career at Craven Cottage. Full-back Cohen made 459 appearances for the club and helped them into the top flight in 1958/59. He was a regular for his country, with the pinnacle of his career coming in 1966 when he was in the England team that beat West Germany to lift the World Cup. Cohen was described by Sir Alf Ramsey as 'England's greatest right-back'.

--→ George Cohen's career was cut short by injury in 1969. His nephew, Ben Cohen, was also a World Cup winner with England, at rugby in 2003.

FLASH GORDON

Gordon Davies scored 178 goals for Fulham in two spells between 1978 and 1991, making him the club's all-time top goalscorer. The Welsh striker, who bagged two goals in 18 appearances for his country, left Craven Cottage for Chelsea in October 1984 but returned two years later via Manchester City to carry on scoring and move to the top of the Cottagers' goal charts.

BEST OF TIMES

George Best played 42 games for Fulham in the late 1970s. The legendary winger, who made his name at Manchester United, scored eight goals for the Cottagers — one of those coming 71 seconds into his debut. Northern Irishman Best had lost some of his pace by the time he moved to Craven Cottage, but he still wowed the crowds alongside the likes of Rodney Marsh and Bobby Moore.

BINGO FOR BONZO

Frank Newton holds the club record for the most league goals scored in a single season. Newton, affectionately known as 'Bonzo', netted 43 times in 39 games during the 1931/32 campaign to help the Cottagers secure the first promotion in their history by winning the third tier title. He scored his 50th goal for the club in only his 42nd game and ended his first spell at Craven Cottage with 72 in 74 matches.

WORLD OF PAIN FOR ZAMORA

Bobby Zamora made his England debut in August 2010 but saw his World Cup dream shattered by injury. After scoring 19 goals for Fulham in 2009/10, Zamora won a first cap for his country in a 2–1 friendly win against Hungary. He was expected to make Fabio Capello's provisional squad for the World Cup in South Africa, only for an Achilles injury to rule him out. The unlucky striker suffered a broken leg against Wolves in September 2010 but came back to earn a recall to the England squad for the Euro 2012 qualifier against Switzerland.

←— After much of his 2010/11 season was wrecked by injury, striker Bobby Zamora will be hoping to get back among the goals for both club and country in 2011/12.

FULHAM'S LEADING GOALSCORERS

Gordon Davies	178
Johnny Haynes	158
Bedford Jezzard	154
Jim Hammond	150
Graham Leggat	134
Arthur Stevens	124
Steve Earle	108

LIVERPOOL

The Reds are one of England's most successful clubs, having claimed a total of 18 top-flight titles, seven FA Cups, seven League Cups, three UEFA Cups and five European Cups. However, they have yet to win the Premier League, with their last championship success coming back in 1989/90.

LIVERPOOL'S LEADING GOALSCORERS

Ian Rush	346
Roger Hunt	286
Gordon Hodgson	241
Billy Liddell	228
Robbie Fowler	176
Kenny Dalglish	172
Michael Owen	158
Harry Chambers	151
Jack Parkinson	130
Sam Raybould	128

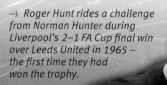

⇢ Roger Hunt rides a challenge from Norman Hunter during Liverpool's 2–1 FA Cup final win over Leeds United in 1965 – the first time they had won the trophy.

GOAL RUSH

Ian Rush is Liverpool's record goalscorer in all competitions, having netted 346 times in two spells between December 1980 and May 1996. The Welsh striker scored 39 FA Cup and 48 League Cup goals, which are both club records. Season 1983/84 was the most productive for Rush – he bagged 47 goals as the Reds claimed the top-flight title, the League Cup and the European Cup. Rush scored five in one game against Luton during that campaign – a feat managed by three other Liverpool players, including Robbie Fowler.

⇠ Ian Rush runs away in celebration after giving Liverpool the lead in the 1986 FA Cup final against Everton.

IN THE HUNT

Roger Hunt is one of the few men to have rivalled Ian Rush in terms of goalscoring for the Reds. Hunt, who played for Liverpool for 10 years between 1959 and 1969, netted on his debut against Scunthorpe and went on to score 245 league goals for the club – a Reds record. Striker Hunt, who grabbed three goals for England during the tournament as they won the World Cup in 1966, also holds the record for the most league goals in a single season for the club, scoring 41 times – including five hat-tricks – as Liverpool claimed the second-tier title in 1961/62.

PFA PRIDE

Five Liverpool players have been awarded the PFA Player of the Year trophy. Steven Gerrard was the last Reds recipient, claiming the prize in 2006. Terry McDermott was the first in 1980, with the club's dominance of English football during that decade also resulting in Kenny Dalglish (1983), Ian Rush (1984) and John Barnes (1988) winning the accolade.

MEIRELES MAGIC

Raul Meireles scooped Liverpool's Goal of the Season award in 2010/11 for a stunning strike in a 3–0 win against Wolves at Molineux. Christophe Berra's defensive header fell kindly for the Portuguese midfielder and he smashed a dipping 25-yard volley into the top corner. It was Kenny Dalglish's first win since returning as Reds manager. Luis Suarez took second place for his superb solo effort against Sunderland, with Dirk Kuyt's opener against Manchester United — made by Suarez's brilliant skill — completing the top three.

BRUCE ALMIGHTY FOR REDS

The Reds' European Cup success of 1983/84 is best remembered for the antics of goalkeeper Bruce Grobbelaar. They had played out a 1–1 draw with Italian side Roma after extra time, meaning the game went to a penalty shootout. Grobbelaar was all smiles as he prepared for Bruno Conti to take his kick, biting the back of the net in front of a mass of photographers. Conti blazed his effort high and wide. The Liverpool goalkeeper then tried to distract Francesco Graziani by wobbling his legs on the goal-line. He succeeded and Graziani also missed, with the Merseysiders claiming a 4–2 shootout win.

REINA IS RESOLUTE

Goalkeeper Pepe Reina and a stubborn Liverpool defence set a club record of 11 games without conceding a goal between October and December 2005. The run started with a 2–0 win at home to West Ham on October 29, with Xabi Alonso and Boudewijn Zenden scoring. After seven Barclays Premier League matches and three Champions League games without being beaten, Reina kept an 11th shut-out in the FIFA Club World Championship clash with Saprissa on December 15.

GUNNERS TAKE AIM

The club's record League Cup defeat came in January 2007 when Arsenal claimed a thrilling 6–3 victory at Anfield. A young Gunners side were 5–1 up at one stage, with Brazilian forward Julio Baptista scoring four of the Londoners' goals. Robbie Fowler, Steven Gerrard and Sami Hyypia were the Reds' goalscorers.

↑ Bruce Grobbelaar looks behind him as Francesco Graziani's penalty flies high over the crossbar to give Liverpool their fourth European Cup victory in 1984.

↓ Phil Neal was the first signing made by Bob Paisley after he had replaced Bill Shankly as Liverpool boss. The full-back won almost every honour available.

← Pepe Reina isn't celebrating another clean sheet. He's actually got an assist after setting up a goal for Albert Riera against Aston Villa at Anfield in 2009.

RELIABLE RED

Phil Neal made an incredible 365 consecutive league appearances for Liverpool between December 1974 and September 1983. The dependable right-back held down a first-team spot for almost a decade before he was sidelined through injury and Steve Nicol stepped in. Neal claimed a club-record 20 medals during those nine ever-present seasons and played in five European Cup finals. He was a winner on four occasions.

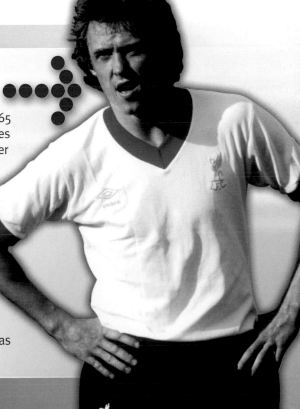

MERSEY PARADISE

Liverpool have played, and beaten, Merseyside rivals Everton in two FA Cup finals. The first, in 1986, saw Gary Lineker put the Toffees ahead, but Ian Rush (2) and Craig Johnston were on target to secure a 3–1 victory for Liverpool. An early goal from John Aldridge looked to have won it three years later, only for Everton midfielder Stuart McCall to snatch an equaliser in the 89th minute to send the game to extra time. Rush restored the Reds' advantage and, after McCall had levelled again, the Welsh striker grabbed the winner.

LIVERPOOL

CALLAGHAN A TRUE RED

No one has played for Liverpool more times than Ian Callaghan. The legendary midfielder featured 857 times in an 18-year spell with the club between 1960 and 1978. He made his debut against Bristol Rovers in April 1960 aged 17 and played his part in the club's progression from a second-tier side to the champions of Europe. Callaghan was named the Football Writers' Player of the Year in 1974 and was awarded an MBE for his services to football before leaving for Swansea in 1978.

⇢ *Ian Callaghan gave Liverpool great service over 18 years and enjoyed many glorious moments at Anfield. He was also in the England 1966 World Cup squad.*

JACK THE LAD

Jack Robinson became the youngest player to have pulled on a Liverpool shirt when he was brought on as a substitute at Hull on the final day of the 2009/10 season. Robinson, who had not even played for the reserves at the time, was 16 years and 250 days old when he entered the action in the 88th minute of the 0–0 draw. The defender smashed Max Thompson's record of 17 years and 129 days set in 1974. After the game, Robinson said: 'Sitting on the bench would have been good enough but it became even better to get on.'

MOLBY IS SPOT ON

Midfielder Jan Molby scored a club-record 42 penalties during his Liverpool career. The former Denmark international, who spent 11 years at Anfield between 1984 and 1995, was prolific from the spot. Molby only missed three penalties, two coming in 1985/86 against Sheffield Wednesday and QPR and the other against Chelsea in 1989/90. He scored a hat-trick of spot-kicks in a League Cup replay against Coventry in 1986.

REINA'S GOLDEN GLOVES

Pepe Reina has won the Golden Glove award for the best goalkeeper in three of the last six Barclays Premier League seasons. The Spanish shot-stopper, who was an ever-present in the top flight for the fourth consecutive season in 2010/11, missed out on the honour to Manchester City's Joe Hart (18) and Petr Cech of Chelsea (15) last term. Reina kept 14 clean sheets.

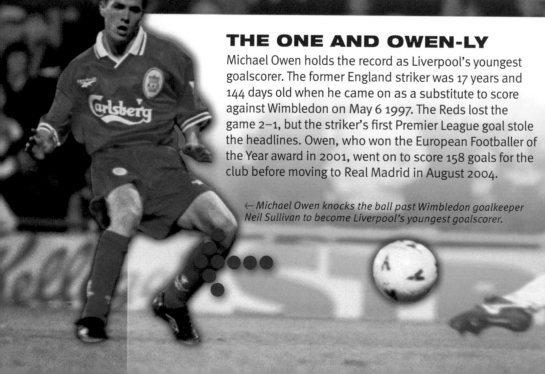

THE ONE AND OWEN-LY

Michael Owen holds the record as Liverpool's youngest goalscorer. The former England striker was 17 years and 144 days old when he came on as a substitute to score against Wimbledon on May 6 1997. The Reds lost the game 2–1, but the striker's first Premier League goal stole the headlines. Owen, who won the European Footballer of the Year award in 2001, went on to score 158 goals for the club before moving to Real Madrid in August 2004.

⇠ *Michael Owen knocks the ball past Wimbledon goalkeeper Neil Sullivan to become Liverpool's youngest goalscorer.*

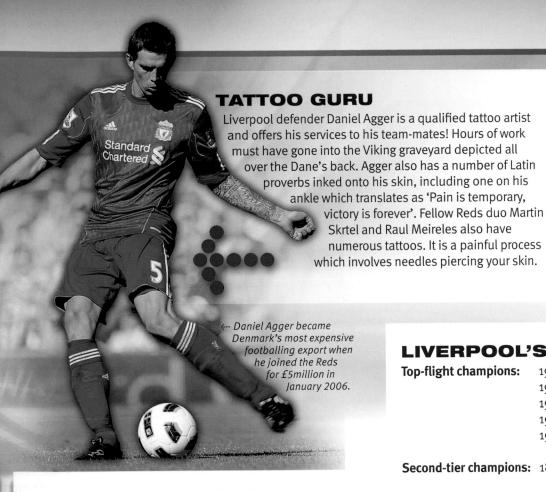

TATTOO GURU

Liverpool defender Daniel Agger is a qualified tattoo artist and offers his services to his team-mates! Hours of work must have gone into the Viking graveyard depicted all over the Dane's back. Agger also has a number of Latin proverbs inked onto his skin, including one on his ankle which translates as 'Pain is temporary, victory is forever'. Fellow Reds duo Martin Skrtel and Raul Meireles also have numerous tattoos. It is a painful process which involves needles piercing your skin.

Daniel Agger became Denmark's most expensive footballing export when he joined the Reds for £5million in January 2006.

EURO AGONY

Liverpool's seventh-place finish in 2009/10 was their lowest in the top flight for 11 years. The Reds missed out on Champions League qualification, instead having to settle for a place in the Europa League. The Merseysiders suffered 19 defeats in all competitions – the most they have lost since the first Premier League season back in 1992/93.

LIVERPOOL'S HONOURS TABLE

Top-flight champions:	1900/01, 1905/06, 1921/22, 1922/23, 1946/47, 1963/64, 1965/66, 1972/73, 1975/76, 1976/77, 1978/79, 1979/80, 1981/82, 1982/83, 1983/84, 1985/86, 1987/88, 1989/90
Second-tier champions:	1893/94, 1895/96, 1904/05, 1961/62
European Cup winners:	1976/77, 1977/78, 1980/81, 1983/84, 2004/05
FA Cup winners:	1964/65, 1973/74, 1985/86, 1988/89, 1991/92, 2000/01, 2005/06
League Cup winners:	1980/81, 1981/82, 1982/83, 1983/84, 1994/95, 2000/01, 2002/03
UEFA Cup winners:	1972/73, 1975/76, 2000/01

THE MIRACLE OF ISTANBUL

Liverpool were involved in one of the greatest European finals in history in 2005 when they came from behind to beat AC Milan on penalties after extra time. The Italian giants were leading 3-0 at half-time in Istanbul, only for Liverpool to score three goals in six minutes through Steven Gerrard, Vladimir Smicer and Xabi Alonso to haul themselves level. With no further goals, the game went to penalties and goalkeeper Jerzy Dudek saved from Andriy Shevchenko to seal an amazing victory for the Reds.

Jerzy Dudek's outstretched legs block Andriy Shevchenko's penalty to give Liverpool their unlikely 2005 UEFA Champions League triumph over AC Milan in Istanbul.

PAISLEY IS TROPHY KING

Bob Paisley is the club's most successful manager. He won six top-flight titles, the League Cup on three occasions, the UEFA Cup once and the Charity Shield five times. However, the biggest achievements of his nine-year stay at Anfield were the three European Cup victories of 1977, 1978 and 1981. Other hugely successful Reds bosses include Bill Shankly and Kenny Dalglish, who both won three top-flight titles and two FA Cup finals. Dalglish is now back in charge at Anfield for a second spell. Joe Fagan (1984) and Rafael Benitez (2005) have both led the club to European Cup glory.

Bob Paisley with the European Cup in 1977, after the Reds had won the trophy for the first time.

MANCHESTER CITY

City are now one of the best clubs in the top flight. Italian Roberto Mancini and his squad claimed the blue half of Manchester some long-overdue silverware as they celebrated their first trophy since 1976 by winning the FA Cup in May 2011. They suffered relegation twice in three years during the 1990s but have now established themselves back in the Barclays Premier League, finishing third in 2010/11.

PRIDE IN BATTLE

A new club badge was unveiled in 1997. The crest is based on the coat of arms of the city of Manchester. The shield standing in front of a golden eagle features a ship in the upper half, which represents the Manchester Ship Canal, and three diagonal stripes in the lower half, which symbolise the city's three rivers. Club motto 'Superbia in Proelio' translates from Latin as 'Pride in Battle'.

MAINE MOVE

City left Maine Road, their home of 80 years, to move into the City of Manchester Stadium, or the Etihad Stadium as it is now known, in 2003. Built for the Commonwealth Games of 2002, it was later converted into a football stadium which can hold 47,715 spectators. Barcelona were the Blues' opponents for the first football match to be played at the ground, with Nicolas Anelka scoring the opening goal as City claimed a 2–1 win.

CITY'S GROUNDS

1880	Clowes Street
1881	Kirkmanshulme Cricket Ground
1882	Queens Road
1884	Pink Bank Lane
1887	Hyde Road
1923	Maine Road
2003	City of Manchester Stadium

⋯➤ The 1999 third-tier play-off trophy is in safe hands as Manchester City goalkeeper Nicky Weaver celebrates his team's dramatic victory over Gillingham.

⋖⋯ Paul Stewart was one of the three hat-trick heroes in Manchester City's 10–1 destruction of Huddersfield Town in 1987.

HAT-TRICK HEROES

The Blues' record league victory came against Huddersfield in the second tier in November 1987. Three players scored hat-tricks that day as City raced to a 10–1 win at Maine Road. David White, Tony Adcock and Paul Stewart netted nine of the goals between them, with Neil McNab the other goalscorer. Bobby Marshall scored five goals when City recorded their biggest cup victory – also 10–1 – against Swindon in 1930.

BACK TO THE PREMIER LEAGUE

Back-to-back promotions in 1998/99 and 1999/00 secured City a return to the Premier League. Goalkeeper Nicky Weaver was the hero against Gillingham in the third-tier Play-Off Final, saving two penalties in a shootout to send City up. The following term, Joe Royle led the club back to the top flight via a runners-up finish in the second tier behind Charlton. Unfortunately, the Blues' stay in the Premier League was shortlived. They finished third from bottom and were relegated back down 12 months later.

↑ Sven-Goran Eriksson made Eastlands a fortress in 2007/08 as Manchester City won their first nine home Barclays Premier League games.

UNITED RED-FACED

Manchester City recorded the biggest home derby victory in their history in 1989 when Manchester United were beaten 5–1 at Maine Road. Mel Machin's side had started the season with one win in six league games, but they ran riot against their fierce rivals. They were 3–0 up at half-time, with David Oldfield, Trevor Morley and Ian Bishop on target. Mark Hughes, who later managed City, pulled a goal back for United with a stunning scissor-kick, but Oldfield's second and a superb header from Andy Hinchcliffe wrapped up the victory.

CUP DOUBLE

City won the European Cup Winners' Cup in 1970, beating Polish side Gornik Zabrze in the final in Vienna. Goals from Neil Young and Francis Lee earned them a 2–1 victory and completed a cup double, following their League Cup success of a few weeks earlier. Joe Mercer was in charge as City knocked out Athletic Bilbao, Belgian club Lierse, Academica Coimbra of Portugal and Schalke on the way to the final.

CITY GO UP IN STYLE

City's title-winning campaign of 2001/02 in the second tier saw the club finish with a record-breaking total of 99 points. They also equalled a 75-year-old club goalscoring record, as Kevin Keegan's men netted 108 times on their way to the title. Notable results that season came against Crewe (5–2), Sheffield Wednesday (6–2), Burnley (5–1) and Barnsley (5–1). Hot-shot striker Shaun Goater scored 28 league goals and Darren Huckerby added 20 more, with Ali Benarbia pulling the strings in midfield.

↓ Kevin Keegan's attacking tactics brought Manchester City great success in the 2001/02 promotion season. He managed the club until 2005.

ON THE RUN

Manchester City created a club record when they won the first nine home games of the 2007/08 campaign under Sven-Goran Eriksson. Michael Johnson set the ball rolling by scoring the only goal of the game against Derby, and Manchester United were beaten 1–0 four days later when Brazilian Geovanni snatched the winner. The last victory of the sequence came against Bolton on December 15, with the Blues coming back from 2–1 down to win 4–2. City were held to a 2–2 draw by Blackburn on December 27.

A TOUCH OF GRASS

If a footballer was going to be allergic to anything, then grass would probably be the worst thing possible! Manchester City striker Mario Balotelli had to be substituted after suffering a reaction on the pitch in Kiev during a Europa League game in March 2011. He was constantly rubbing his face, and after it began to swell he was taken off. It turns out Balotelli is allergic to certain types of grass!

⇢ Mario Balotelli's unusual allergy didn't stop him banging in the goals for City in 2010/11, as he netted six times in 12 Barclays Premier League starts.

MANCHESTER CITY

PENALTY KINGS

City won more penalties during the 2010/11 season than any other Barclays Premier League team. Roberto Mancini's men were awarded nine in total and successfully converted eight of them, with one being missed by Carlos Tevez – his first spot-kick blunder since arriving at Eastlands. The Argentinian did score five times from the spot, including two in one game against West Brom as he bagged a hat-trick. Mario Balotelli also managed that feat as he netted a treble in a 4–0 win against Aston Villa on December 28 2010.

⌁ Alan Oakes won a second League Cup winners' medal in his final season with Manchester City – a 2–1 defeat of Newcastle in 1976.

FA CUP SUCCESS

City won the FA Cup for the fifth time in their history in 2011. Yaya Toure scored the only goal of the final, 16 minutes from time to snatch a 1–0 win against Stoke at Wembley. It was 1969 when the club had previously lifted the trophy, beating Leicester by a single strike from Neil Young. Their first success in the competition came in 1904 when Bolton were beaten 1–0. They claimed a 2–1 win against Portsmouth 30 years later and enjoyed a 3–1 victory against Birmingham in 1956.

⌁ Tony Book, the Manchester City captain and co-winner of that season's Footballer of the Year award, shows off the FA Cup in 1969.

SIMPLY THE BEST

City enjoyed their highest Premier League finish in season 2010/11 and their best in the top flight for 34 years. Roberto Mancini's side finished third — two places higher than their previous best in 2009/10 — to claim a much-coveted Champions League spot. An impressive run of five wins from their last six games saw City finish level on points with runners-up Chelsea and three points ahead of Arsenal.

FAMILY TIES

Alan Oakes made a club-record 565 league appearances for Manchester City in a 17-year spell between 1959 and 1976. He made his debut in a 1–1 draw with Chelsea in November 1959, with his last game coming as a substitute against derby rivals Manchester United in May 1976. Oakes' cousin, Glyn Pardoe, is the Blues' youngest-ever player. He was just 15 years and 314 days old when he made his debut in April 1962.

CITY'S LEADING LEAGUE GOALSCORERS

Eric Brook	158
Tommy Johnson	158
Billy Meredith	145
Joe Hayes	142
Billy Gillespie	126
Tommy Browell	122
Colin Bell	117
Frank Roberts	116
Francis Lee	112
Fred Tilson	110

JOHNSON'S JOY

Tommy Johnson shares the record for scoring the most league goals for the club, having netted 158 times between 1919 and 1930. The forward scored 38 goals in 39 games in the top-flight campaign of 1928/29 – still the most by any Blues player in a single season. Johnson is also one of four players to have scored five times in a game for the club. He stole the show in a 6–2 win against Everton at Goodison Park on September 15 1928. Eric Brook also bagged 158 league goals and 178 in total – 12 more than Johnson.

FIRST-ROUND EXIT

Manchester City were briefly involved in the European Cup in season 1968/69. Joe Mercer's men secured their place in the competition by winning the top-flight title in 1968, but they failed to get past the first round. City played out a goalless draw in the first leg of their clash with Turkish side Fenerbahce at Maine Road, but they lost the away leg 2–1.

ROBINHO MOVES ON

City may have splashed millions of pounds on a string of world-class players in recent years, but Samba star Robinho remains their club-record signing. The Brazilian cost a cool £32.5million — a British transfer record at the time — when he arrived at the club from Real Madrid in September 2008. Unfortunately Robinho failed to settle in Manchester, and after scoring 14 Barclays Premier League goals in season 2008/09, faded from view and returned home to Santos on loan in January 2010. He now plays for AC Milan.

Despite the huge hype that surrounded his record transfer fee, Brazilian ace Robinho left England in 2010.

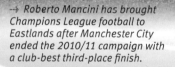

Roberto Mancini has brought Champions League football to Eastlands after Manchester City ended the 2010/11 campaign with a club-best third-place finish.

BERT PUTS HIS NECK ON THE LINE

Legendary Manchester City goalkeeper Bert Trautmann played the last 15 minutes of the 1956 FA Cup final with a broken neck! The German was knocked out when he collided with Birmingham's Peter Murphy. Trautmann was in obvious discomfort when he came around, but there were no substitutes in those days, so he stayed on. He made a string of fine saves to preserve City's 3–1 lead. An X-ray three days after the game revealed he had dislocated five vertebrae in his neck, one of which was cracked in two!

MANCINI TAKES CHARGE

Roberto Mancini was appointed manager of Manchester City on December 19 2009 following the departure of Mark Hughes. The Italian won his first game in charge against Stoke, and that was followed by a first away victory in two months at Wolves. He masterminded a 4–2 success at Chelsea and oversaw big wins against Burnley (6–1) and Birmingham (5–1). In 2010/11 Mancini managed 21 Barclays Premier League victories and eight draws as he led City to a Champions League spot with a third-place finish and also scooped the FA Cup.

Bert Trautmann is helped from the field by team-mates Dave Ewing (left) and Bill Leivers after Manchester City's 3–1 victory over Birmingham City in the 1956 FA Cup final. Trautmann had played on despite suffering a broken neck.

MANCHESTER UNITED

United rank as one of the biggest and most widely-supported clubs in world football. They have won 19 top-flight titles, a record 11 FA Cups, four League Cups and three European Cups, among a host of other trophies. Manager Sir Alex Ferguson is the most successful boss in their history, while record appearance holder Ryan Giggs is still turning out for the club.

THE BUSBY BABES

The 'Busby Babes' were a group of young and talented players who progressed through Manchester United's youth system to win the top-flight title under the management of Sir Matt Busby in 1955/56 and 1956/57. Tragically, in February 1958, eight members of the squad – including Duncan Edwards and Tommy Taylor – were killed when the passenger plane they were travelling on crashed on the runway at Munich Airport. The team had been returning from a European Cup match in Belgrade.

NEWTON HEATH

Manchester United were formed as Newton Heath in 1878. The club were elected to The Football League in 1892 and were renamed in 1902 by a group of businessmen who had saved them from bankruptcy. United released a green and yellow third shirt in 1992 to celebrate 100 years since Newton Heath's election.

↑ As Manchester United boss, Sir Matt Busby created three outstanding teams: the 1948 FA Cup-winning side, the 'Busby Babes' of the 1950s and finally the 1968 European champions.

UNITED'S LEADING LEAGUE GOALSCORERS

Bobby Charlton	199
Jack Rowley	182
Denis Law	171
Dennis Viollet	159
Joe Spence	158
George Best	137
Stan Pearson	128
Mark Hughes	120
David Herd	114
Tommy Taylor	112

⋯→ Arguably England's greatest ever player, Bobby Charlton is both Manchester United's and his country's all-time leading goalscorer.

WEMBLEY WONDERS

The Red Devils became the first English club to win the European Cup in 1968 when they claimed a 4–1 win against Portuguese side Benfica at Wembley. United took the lead through a Bobby Charlton header, but Benfica equalised to take the game into extra time. George Best went around the goalkeeper and slotted home to make it 2–1, before Brian Kidd and another Charlton strike secured a famous victory.

CHARLTON'S DOUBLE LANDMARK

Bobby Charlton is Manchester United and England's record goalscorer. Charlton netted 249 times in all competitions for the Red Devils – 199 in the league – and hit 49 for England. Gary Lineker was one goal away from equalling his international record when he retired. Charlton survived the Munich air disaster of 1958, and having already played a part in the title-winning season of 1956/57, he went on to win the FA Cup, two more top-flight titles, the World Cup and the European Cup in a glittering career for both club and country.

GREY DAY FOR UNITED

United famously changed their grey away shirts at half-time during a 3–1 defeat at Southampton in April 1996. Sir Alex Ferguson claimed that his players were struggling to pick each other out due to the colour of the kit, with United 3–0 down at the time. They appeared for the second half sporting a blue-and-white-striped shirt and managed to pull a goal back. The Red Devils lost four and drew one of the five games they played in the grey shirt. It was retired from use two days after the Dell defeat.

THE BABY-FACED ASSASSIN

Ole Gunnar Solskjaer wrote his name into United's history books when he scored the winning goal in the dying seconds of the 1999 European Cup final. The 'Baby-Faced Assassin', as he was affectionately known due to his boyish looks and finishing ability, stabbed the ball home in injury time to snatch United a 2–1 win against Bayern Munich. United had been 1–0 down going into time added on. The Norwegian striker scored 91 league goals in 235 appearances for United. Four of those came as a substitute in the last 10 minutes of an 8–1 win at Nottingham Forest in February 1999.

‑‑> Ole Gunnar Solskjaer scores Manchester United's dramatic winner in the 1999 UEFA Champions League final.

POST-WAR UNITED MANAGERS

Matt Busby	1945–1969
Wilf McGuinness	1969–1970
Matt Busby	1970–1971
Frank O'Farrell	1971–1972
Tommy Docherty	1972–1977
Dave Sexton	1977–1981
Ron Atkinson	1981–1986
Alex Ferguson	1986–Present

A FAMOUS FIRST

Manchester United were the inaugural winners of the Premier League in 1992/93 – their first top-flight title for 26 years. They finished the season 10 points ahead of Aston Villa in second, but things had not started well when they lost their first game of the newly-formed competition at Sheffield United. Brian Deane scored twice for the Blades – the opener creating history as the first-ever Premier League goal – before Mark Hughes pulled one back just after the hour.

↑ Brian Kidd had celebrated his 19th birthday by winning the European Cup in 1968. As assistant manager, Kidd (left) helped 'Fergie's Fledglings' to the 1996 Premier League title.

FERGIE'S FLEDGLINGS

'Fergie's Fledglings' were the modern-day equivalent of the 'Busby Babes', with Sir Alex Ferguson nurturing talents such as David Beckham, Ryan Giggs, Gary Neville and Nicky Butt. When a new-look Manchester United side lost 3–1 at Aston Villa on the opening day of the 1995/96 season, TV pundit Alan Hansen famously said: 'You'll never win anything with kids.' How wrong he was. The youngsters clawed back Newcastle's 14-point lead at the top of the Premier League to claim the title by four points. They also won the FA Cup that year to secure the double.

←‑‑ Steve Bruce (left) and Bryan Robson with the Premiership trophy at the end of the first season of the new competition, Manchester United's first top-tier title for 26 years.

MANCHESTER UNITED

EDWIN THE UNBEATABLE

Goalkeeper Edwin van der Sar and the Manchester United defence went a record-breaking 1,311 minutes without conceding a league goal in the 2008/09 season. They beat a Premier League benchmark set by Chelsea's Petr Cech in the 2004/05 campaign and then surpassed Steve Death's English league record of 1,103 minutes without conceding four days later. The British top-flight record fell against West Ham on February 8 2009 and the world record was broken on February 18. The Dutchman was finally beaten by Newcastle forward Peter Lovenkrands on March 4.

TRAVEL SICKNESS

United won the title in 2010/11 despite picking up just 25 points away from Old Trafford – the lowest total by any Premier League winner. Thankfully for Sir Alex Ferguson, his side were unstoppable at home, equalling Chelsea's record from 2005/06 of taking 55 points from their 19 matches. They claimed 18 wins and drew once against West Brom – a game they had been winning 2–0!

LUCKY NUMBER SEVEN

The number seven shirt has become iconic at Manchester United. Some of the club's greatest players have worn it, with George Best starting the tradition in the 1960s. 'Captain Marvel' Bryan Robson also had the honour, before Eric Cantona took over. David Beckham was next to be handed the shirt, with Cristiano Ronaldo taking it on when the England talisman left for Real Madrid. Michael Owen currently has the squad number, having been handed it following his arrival at the club in July 2009.

······> George Best was the first superstar footballer. With Denis Law and Bobby Charlton, he was part of the most entertaining and lethal strike force in England in the 1960s.

OOH AAH CANTONA!

Eric Cantona was voted as the greatest Manchester United player of all time in an official poll in 2001. He helped Sir Alex Ferguson's men to two Premier League titles and an FA Cup in his first two seasons at Old Trafford. Arguably his finest hour came in the 1995/96 season, as he returned from a nine-month suspension to almost single-handedly win the club another double and scored eight goals in United's last 11 games, including a late winner against Liverpool in the FA Cup final. 'King Eric' retired the following year after another title success.

<······ Eric Cantona celebrates a derby goal for Manchester United against City in 1993, in his first season with the Reds.

UNITED'S GREATEST PLAYERS*

1   Eric Cantona
2   George Best
3   Ryan Giggs
4   Bobby Charlton
5   Peter Schmeichel
6   Bryan Robson
7   Roy Keane
8   David Beckham
9   Duncan Edwards
10   Denis Law

* As voted by the club's fans in 2001

EURO DOMINATION

The Manchester giants hold the record for the longest unbeaten run in the Champions League – a staggering 25 matches without defeat. That sequence started with a 1–0 win at Sporting Lisbon in their opening group game of the 2007/08 campaign, with a 3–1 success at Arsenal in the semi-finals of the 2008/09 competition completing the run. Their streak came to an end when they were beaten 2–0 by Barcelona in the final. Dutch outfit Ajax had previously held the record with a run of 20 unbeaten matches.

DUO HANG UP BOOTS

Two Manchester United legends retired in 2011. Gary Neville, who is England's most capped right-back, announced his decision to quit in February after almost 20 years at the club. His final first-team appearance came at West Brom in a 2–1 win on New Year's Day. Classy midfielder Paul Scholes called time on his playing career 24 hours after he was part of a trophy parade to mark United's record 19th top-flight title and his 10th. They were both 36. The duo have since taken up coaching roles at Old Trafford.

⇢ Wayne Rooney celebrates his goal in the 2011 UEFA Champions League final, but it was not enough for United to beat mighty Barcelona.

OWN GOAL RECORD

Manchester United benefited from a record 11 own goals in 2009/10. Arsenal put through their own net in both fixtures against the Red Devils, with Abou Diaby helping United to a 2–1 win at Old Trafford in August and goalkeeper Manuel Almunia scooping a cross from Nani into his own net as the Gunners were beaten 3–1 at the Emirates Stadium in January. Portsmouth scored two own goals in a single game in February to help United to a 5–0 win.

⬆ Midfielder Paul Scholes went on to complete 676 appearances for the Red Devils after making his debut against Port Vale in 1994.

BARCA THE BEST

The Red Devils met their match in the 2011 Champions League final at Wembley as Barcelona proved too strong for Sir Alex Ferguson's side. It was United's third final appearance in the last four seasons. Wayne Rooney grabbed an equaliser just before half-time to offer hope, but the Catalan giants stepped it up after the break to ease to a 3–1 win. After the game, a gracious Ferguson admitted Barcelona were the best side he had ever faced in 25 years. 'No one has given us a hiding like that,' he said.

CRISTIANO IS THE RON

Cristiano Ronaldo is the only player in Manchester United's history to have won the FIFA World Player of the Year award. The Portuguese forward claimed the prize in 2008 following a memorable campaign. He scored 42 goals in all competitions as United won the Barclays Premier League title and also lifted the European Cup. Ronaldo headed the opener against Chelsea in the Champions League final, with Sir Alex Ferguson's men going on to win the trophy on penalties. The Portuguese also claimed the Ballon d'Or, the European Golden Shoe and the UEFA Footballer of the Year trophies that season.

⇢ Cristiano Ronaldo was the catalyst for Manchester United's championship runs of 2007–09. In the 2007/08 season he scored 42 goals in all competitions, mainly from midfield.

NEWCASTLE UNITED

Newcastle spent 16 years in the Premier League before they were relegated at the end of 2008/09, challenging for the title for two consecutive seasons in the mid-1990s. Their stay in the second tier was shortlived as they claimed the Championship title in style in 2009/10 and then finished comfortably in mid-table last term.

MAGPIES NUTTY OVER BRAZILIAN

Mirandinha became the first Brazilian to play in English football when he signed for Newcastle in 1987. The forward, who cost the Magpies £575,000 from Palmeiras, had hit the headlines with a goal for his country against England in the Rous Cup earlier that year. He failed to settle in the north-east and moved back to his former club in Brazil in 1989 having scored 33 goals – although he has since revealed that the Magpies tried to sign him again during Kevin Keegan's first spell as manager.

↑ Andrew Cole scores one of his two goals against West Ham in Newcastle's 2–0 victory at St James' Park in September 1993.

↑ Mirandinha (right) was the first Brazilian to play in English football, but he only stayed with the Magpies for two seasons.

RED-HOT COLE

Andrew Cole has the best strike rate of any post-war Newcastle player with 81 per cent. Cole scored an impressive 68 goals in 84 matches for the Magpies between 1993 and 1995, 41 of those coming in a single season (1993/94) – a club record that also earned him the PFA Young Player of the Year prize. Alan Shearer had a 51 per cent strike rate, having scored 206 goals in 404 matches, while Les Ferdinand netted 50 goals in 83 games – a strike rate of 60 per cent.

TEENAGE KICKS

Steve Watson is the youngest player to have featured in a league game for Newcastle at 16 years and 223 days old. The defender made his debut as a substitute in the Magpies' 2–1 defeat at Wolves in November 1990. He went on to make over 200 appearances for the club in an eight-year spell before being sold to Aston Villa for £4million in October 1998. Striker Andy Carroll became the club's youngest European debutant when he featured in the 1–0 UEFA Cup win in Palermo in November 2006.

SHEAR MAGIC

Alan Shearer scored 206 goals for Newcastle – 131 of those at St James' Park – in a 10-year spell with the club between 1996 and 2006, making him the Magpies' all-time leading goalscorer and a true club legend. Shearer scored 49 headers, 45 penalties, five free-kicks and four hat-tricks in the famous black and white shirt. In season 1996/97, the former England hot-shot netted in an amazing seven consecutive matches, including a memorable goal in Newcastle's stunning 5–0 win against Manchester United.

⇢ Alan Shearer wheels away in celebration with his trademark raised arm after scoring against Southampton in September 1998 in a 4–0 win.

NEWCASTLE'S LEADING ALL-TIME GOALSCORERS

Alan Shearer	206
Jackie Milburn	200
Len White	153
Hughie Gallacher	143
Malcolm MacDonald	121
Peter Beardsley	119
Bobby Mitchell	113
Tom McDonald	113
Neil Harris	101
Bryan Robson	97

BARCELONA BEATEN

Newcastle have been involved in the Champions League on three occasions, with mixed results. Faustino Asprilla scored a stunning hat-trick as Barcelona were beaten 3–2 in the group stages in 1997/98, but the Magpies failed to progress. They made history as the first club to lose their opening three group games and still finish in the top two places in 2002/03, only to be knocked out at the now defunct second group stage. And the following season saw them fail to get past the qualifying round as they lost on penalties to Partizan Belgrade.

JURASSIC JONAS!

Jonas Gutierrez has an unusual hobby away from football – he loves dinosaurs! Newcastle's Argentinian winger has been fascinated by fossils and the Jurassic period since he was a child and still likes nothing more than reading books and visiting exhibitions to increase his knowledge of the creatures. 'It is a subject that fascinates me and always has done,' he enthused.

⸱⸱⸱⸱▸ Jonas Gutierrez has earned a reputation as one of the fun characters in football. During his time at former club Real Mallorca he used to celebrate scoring by donning a Spider-Man mask.

RED AND WHITE ARMY

Newcastle's home shirts once featured red and white stripes – the colours now worn by rivals Sunderland. That was one of a number of different coloured kits worn by the Magpies' founding club, Newcastle East End. It is thought that the black-and-white-striped jerseys now associated with the Tynesiders were introduced in a bid to stop frequent colour clashes that were occurring in the league at the time, although there are also a number of other interesting theories.

NOLAN IN THE MOOD FOR SCORING

Kevin Nolan enjoyed his best goalscoring season in the top flight in 2010/11, reaching double figures for the first time. Nolan ended the campaign with 12 Barclays Premier League goals, which included a hat-trick in Newcastle's crushing 5–1 win against rivals Sunderland. Nolan had managed nine goals for Bolton in 2003/04 and again in 2005/06, while he went goal crazy in Newcastle's second-tier title-winning campaign of 2009/10, netting an 17 league goals. He was named the Championship's Player of the Year that term. He has since moved to West Ham.

⸱⸱⸱⸱▸ The Magpies will miss Kevin Nolan's goals in 2011/12. He had another fine season last term with 12 league strikes in all.

CARROLL CASH

A blistering start to the 2010/11 season resulted in Andy Carroll leaving Newcastle for Liverpool in January. The hot-shot Magpies striker had netted 11 goals in the first 19 games to lead the way at the top of the Barclays Premier League scoring charts. That prompted Liverpool to smash their transfer record to sign the bustling forward, who was injured at the time, and he went on to score two more top-flight goals. He also opened his account for England in a 1–1 draw with Ghana at Wembley.

NEWCASTLE UNITED

LOYAL FOLLOWING

St James' Park has a capacity of 52,339, making it the third largest club stadium in English football. Newcastle were relegated from the Premier League at the end of the 2008/09 season, but they still played in front of crowds of over 40,000 in 16 of their 23 home games in the second tier. The club's highest attendance during the 2010/11 campaign came against Sunderland in October when 51,988 spectators watched the Magpies ease to a 5–1 victory.

MIXED MAGPIES

Only Barclays Premier League champions Manchester United scored more goals than Newcastle at home during the 2010/11 season. Sir Alex Ferguson's men bagged 49 goals on their way to the title, while the Magpies netted 41 times. They hit Aston Villa for six without reply in their opening home game, thrashed Sunderland 5–1 in the Tyne-Wear derby and thumped West Ham 5–0, with Leon Best grabbing a hat-trick. However, nobody scored fewer than Newcastle on the road, where both they and Stoke managed just 15 apiece.

GEORDIE HEROES

Two of England's best-ever playmakers shot to prominence at Newcastle. Both Paul 'Gazza' Gascoigne and Peter Beardsley were born in the area and lit up St James' Park in the 1980s and 90s. Gazza played for the club between 1985 and 1988, making just over 100 appearances in all competitions and scoring 25 goals. He was named Young Player of the Year in season 1987/88. Beardsley, who enjoyed two spells at the club, was famed for scoring spectacular goals and his ability to pick a pass but he also conceded three times as a stand-in goalkeeper during an 8–1 defeat to West Ham in April 1986!

↑ Paul Gascoigne became a cult hero with the Toon Army, Newcastle's legion of fans, before going on to make his name as one of the best players of his generation.

⟵ Shola (pictured) and Sammy Ameobi actually have another brother who plays football too, although Tommi – who splits them in age – plies his trade with BI/Bolungarvik in Iceland.

THERE'S ONLY TWO AMEOBIS!

Shola and Sammy Ameobi became the first brothers to play together in a league game for Newcastle since George and Ted Robledo in 1952 when they both featured in the 2–2 draw at Chelsea on May 15 2011. Striker Shola played the whole 90 minutes, while Sammy, 19, came on as a substitute alongside him with seven minutes remaining. Fans changed a favourite chant from 'There's only one Ameobi' to 'There's only two Ameobis'!

↑ *Alan Pardew became the club's 12th permanent manager in the last 19 years when he was appointed in December 2010.*

⋯→ *'Wor Jackie' is arguably Newcastle's most famous son and is second only to Alan Shearer in the club's all-time goalscorers list.*

NEWCASTLE MANAGERS SINCE 1992

Kevin Keegan	1992–1997
Kenny Dalglish	1997–1998
Ruud Gullit	1998–1999
Bobby Robson	1999–2004
Graeme Souness	2004–2006
Glenn Roeder	2006–2007
Sam Allardyce	2007–2008
Kevin Keegan	2008
Joe Kinnear	2008–2009
Alan Shearer	2009
Chris Hughton	2009–2010
Alan Pardew	2010–Present

WOR JACKIE

Jackie Milburn is a Newcastle legend. Still fondly remembered by fans as 'Wor' Jackie, powerful centre-forward Milburn scored 200 goals for the Magpies between 1943 and 1957. He wore the club's number nine shirt with great distinction, helping them to FA Cup glory in 1951, 1952 and 1955, when he found the net after 45 seconds in a 3–1 win against Manchester City. Milburn has a stand named after him at St James' Park and there are two statues of him, in Newcastle and his birthplace of Ashington.

CUP SAGA

Stevenage stunned Newcastle by claiming a 3–1 victory in the third round of the FA Cup in January 2011. The then-npower League 2 side were already 2–0 up through a Mike Williamson own goal and Michael Bostwick strike when Cheik Tiote saw red for a wild tackle on Jon Ashton. Joey Barton pulled one back for the Magpies in injury time, but there was still time for Peter Winn to break away and cap an impressive display with a third. Newcastle were famously knocked out of the competition by Hereford – then a non-League side – in 1972.

REDS TAKEN APART

Arguably Newcastle's most memorable result of the Premier League era came in 1996/97 when they dismantled Manchester United 5–0 at St James' Park. Defender Darren Peacock headed in an early opener and David Ginola added a second before half-time with a stunning effort into the top corner. Les Ferdinand netted the third from a trademark header and Alan Shearer got in on the act with a close-range fourth. The best was saved for last, though, as centre-back Philippe Albert chipped Peter Schmeichel from 25 yards. Kevin Keegan claimed afterwards that it was 'the most enjoyable day' of his managerial career.

TOON ARE FAIR GAME

Newcastle were Fairs Cup winners in 1969, beating Hungarian side Ujpest in a two-legged final. It was the first time the club had competed in European competition. The Inter-Cities Fairs Cup was the predecessor to the UEFA Cup, or Europa League as it is now known. The tournament was initially only open to teams from cities that hosted trade fairs. Bobby Moncur was the hero for the Magpies, scoring twice in the first leg at home and again in the return as Newcastle claimed a 6–2 aggregate victory.

⋯→ *A goalscoring rate of almost one every 2.5 games for the Magpies earned Andy Carroll a move to Liverpool in January 2011.*

MAGPIES STEAL GOALS

Kevin Nolan and Andy Carroll shared top spot in the goalscoring stakes for Newcastle as the Magpies netted 90 times on their way to the Championship title in 2009/10. The goals were spread throughout the team, with midfielder Nolan and striker Carroll both grabbing 17 apiece in the league and fellow forward Peter Lovenkrands hitting 13.

NORWICH CITY

Norwich are back in the top flight for the first time since 2004/05. The Canaries were the surprise package of the first Premier League season in 1992/93 when they finished third. Under Paul Lambert, they have achieved back-to-back promotions and are now looking to establish themselves back in the big time.

LAMBERT WALKS TO CITY

The Canaries suffered the heaviest home defeat in their history on the opening day of the 2009/10 campaign when they were beaten 7–1 by Colchester. Club legend Bryan Gunn, in charge of Norwich at the time, parted company with the club soon after and was replaced by Paul Lambert – the man who had been in the Colchester dug-out for that game!

CANARIES FLYING HIGH

Norwich secured their highest-ever league finish under manager Mike Walker in 1992/93. They ended what was the first Premier League campaign in third place, two points behind Aston Villa and 12 behind champions Manchester United.

←·· Mike Walker guided Norwich to their best-ever league finish in 1993. The Canaries then enjoyed a UEFA Cup run that included a victory over Bayern Munich.

ASHTON UNDER THE HAMMER

Norwich made a tidy profit from the sale of Dean Ashton to West Ham in January 2006. The £3million paid by the Canaries to Crewe for the striker in January 2005 was a club record, but when he left for Upton Park in a £7.25million switch a year later he broke the record for the biggest transfer fee received by the Carrow Road club. An ankle injury forced Ashton to retire in December 2009, aged just 26.

···→ Dean Ashton seemed destined for great things when Norwich paid Crewe £3million for his signature in 2005 and collected a club-record fee of £7.25million from West Ham a year later, but injuries ensured it wasn't to be.

FIVE-STAR CITY

Bizarrely, Norwich had four shots on target in their derby clash at Ipswich in April 2011 but managed to win the game 5–1! It was an own goal from Town defender Gareth McAuley that brought about the unusual statistic as he glanced in a David Fox corner. Andrew Surman had opened the scoring, with further goals from Simeon Jackson, Russ Martin and Daniel Pacheco completing the rout. The victory meant that the Canaries achieved their first double over their fierce rivals since the 2003/04 season.

THRILLING FINISH FOR JACKSON

Simeon Jackson had scored just four times going into City's npower Championship clash with Scunthorpe at Carrow Road in April 2011. The Canada international found himself on the bench for that game but he was introduced into the action with 20 minutes remaining. Within a matter of seconds, the striker had scored his first goal of the game and Norwich's fourth. He went on to complete a hat-trick as the Canaries claimed a 6–0 victory. That sparked an incredible run of form as Jackson managed nine goals in his last eight games, including another treble against Derby as City secured promotion.

←·· Simeon Jackson had plenty to celebrate in 2010/11, as his goals helped fire the Canaries back into the Barclays Premier League.

···→ The 2011/12 campaign will mark the first time that Paul Lambert has managed in the top-flight, but he has certainly acquitted himself well during his career so far.

GERMAN GIANTS STUNNED

Norwich stunned the footballing world when they knocked mighty Bayern Munich out of the UEFA Cup in 1993 in one of the biggest upsets in European football history. The Canaries had qualified for Europe for the first time by finishing third in the Premier League the previous season. Jeremy Goss struck a stunning volley to open the scoring in the Olympic Stadium before Mark Bowen headed in a second. The first leg finished 2–1 to City and another strike from Goss in the return leg at Carrow Road sent them through 3–2 on aggregate. They were beaten by eventual winners Inter Milan in the next round.

CITY'S TOP SCORERS SINCE 2002/03

2002/03	Paul McVeigh	14
2003/04	Darren Huckerby	13
2004/05	Leon McKenzie	7
	Dean Ashton	
	Damien Francis	
2005/06	Dean Ashton	10
2006/07	Robert Earnshaw	19
2007/08	Jamie Cureton	12
2008/09	Leroy Lita	7
2009/10	Grant Holt	24
2010/11	Grant Holt	21

↑ *The volley that Jeremy Goss scored against Bayern Munich in 1993 is rated by many Canaries' fans as the best goal ever by a Norwich player.*

HARD TO BEAT HOLT

Grant Holt has finished as Norwich's top scorer for each of the last two seasons, scooping back-to-back Player of the Year trophies at the same time. Holt grabbed 24 goals in the club's title-winning League 1 campaign of 2009/10 and the step up to the npower Championship didn't faze the bustling striker, as he slammed in another 21 last term. He has scored 53 goals in total since signing from Shrewsbury in July 2009.

↓ *The contribution of powerful striker Grant Holt is likely to be key to City's campaign in the 2011/12 Barclays Premier League.*

CANARY YELLOW

Norwich's nickname is thought to originate from the city's links with nurturing canaries and further connections to Flemish weavers who used to import the birds. Originally the club were known as The Citizens – or 'Cits' for short – and played in light blue and white halved shirts. But to match their new nickname, City started playing in yellow shirts with green trim – the colours they still use today.

ALL TOO EASY FOR PAUL

Paul Lambert is the first manager since Joe Royle 11 years ago to win back-to-back promotions to reach the top flight. The Scot took charge at Carrow Road in August 2009 and led the club to the League 1 title in emphatic style as they finished with 95 points – nine ahead of second-place Leeds. City took that momentum into their npower Championship campaign, amassing 84 points to finish as runners-up to QPR and secure a place in the top flight for the first time since 2004/05.

NORWICH CITY

THREE IS MAGIC NUMBER

It was a case of third time lucky for City in the League Cup final of 1985. Having lost narrowly to Tottenham in 1973 and again to Aston Villa two years later, the Canaries finally lifted the trophy at Wembley following a 1–0 win against Sunderland. Asa Hartford's goal – which took a wicked deflection off Sunderland defender David Corner – was enough for Norwich, who enjoyed another slice of good fortune when Clive Walker fired wide from the penalty spot.

ON THE BALL CITY

As well as Stephen Fry and Delia Smith, Prince Andrew is reported to be one of the club's biggest celebrity fans.

Popular terrace chant 'On The Ball City' is said to be the oldest football song in the world still in use today. It is thought to have been written for either Norwich Teachers or Caley's FC in the 1890s and then adopted by the Canaries. The part of the chant commonly heard pre-match and throughout Norwich games is: 'Kick it off, throw it in, have a little scrimmage. Keep it low, a splendid rush, bravo, win or die. On the ball, City, never mind the danger. Steady on, now's your chance. Hurrah! We've scored a goal. City! City! City!'

Norwich enjoyed one of their most successful periods in the mid-1980s. As well as winning the second-tier title, they also lifted the League Cup in 1985.

FRY ON BOARD

City now have two celebrities on their board after comedian, actor, writer and presenter Stephen Fry became an ambassador for the club in August 2010. Fry, who hosts popular BBC panel show QI, is a lifelong Norwich fan and is often seen at Carrow Road. TV chef Delia Smith has been a joint majority shareholder of the Norfolk club for many years.

LAST-FOUR MISERY

Norwich have made it to the semi-finals of the FA Cup on three occasions, only to miss out each time. City were a top-flight side the last time they reached the last four in 1992 and were favourites to see off Sunderland, who had finished in the lower reaches of the second tier. But, such is the magic of the FA Cup, the underdog triumphed, with a single goal from John Byrne settling the tie. The Canaries were beaten 1–0 by Everton in the semi-final of 1989 having also missed out in 1959 to Luton following a replay.

TOP-10 CANARIES

A club-record run of 10 consecutive league wins helped Norwich to the second-tier title in season 1985/86. The sequence began with a 3–2 victory against Grimsby on November 23 1985, while the stand-out result came against Millwall, who were brushed aside 6–1 at Carrow Road. The run came to an end at Barnsley on February 1, although City did take a point in a 2–2 draw. They finished seven points clear of Charlton that term, while striker Kevin Drinkell finished as the league's top scorer with 22 goals.

DOZEN MAKE A DIFFERENCE

Norwich managed to score an incredible 12 goals in the 90th minute of matches or the injury time that followed in their promotion-winning season of 2010/11. The first game of the campaign against Watford set the tone, although Michael Nelson's strike mattered little as City slipped to a 3–2 defeat. However, last-gasp goals helped Paul Lambert's side to claim an extra 29 points during the course of the season. The most dramatic was Simeon Jackson's effort that snatched a 3–2 win against Derby in April that put Norwich firmly in charge of second place.

┈➔ This goal from Simeon Jackson (centre) against Derby proved crucial in Norwich's promotion push in 2010/11. It was one several late strikes scored by the Canaries last term.

NORWICH'S 10-YEAR LEAGUE RECORD

2001/02 (second tier)	6th
2002/03 (second tier)	8th
2003/04 (second tier)	1st
2004/05 (Premier League)	19th
2005/06 (second tier)	9th
2006/07 (second tier)	16th
2007/08 (second tier)	17th
2008/09 (second tier)	22nd
2009/10 (third tier)	1st
2010/11 (second tier)	2nd

LAST-GASP GOALS 2010/11

Michael Nelson v Watford	Lost 3–2
Grant Holt v Scunthorpe	Won 1–0
Simeon Jackson v Swansea	Won 2–0
Andrew Crofts v Burnley	Drew 2–2
Wes Hoolahan v Sheff Utd	Won 4–2
Russ Martin v Cardiff	Drew 1–1
Henri Lansbury v Millwall	Won 2–1
Grant Holt v Reading	Won 2–1
Andrew Surman v Bristol City	Won 3–1
Simeon Jackson v Scunthorpe	Won 6–0
Daniel Pacheco v Ipswich	Won 5–1
Simeon Jackson v Derby	Won 3–2

(all 90 minutes or later)

CARROW ROAD

Carrow Road has been City's home since 1935. The stadium took 82 days to build – just under three months. The club's record attendance stands at 43,984 for an FA Cup game against Leicester in 1963, but that was before all-seater stadiums. A fire in 1984 partially destroyed one of the stands, meaning it had to be demolished and rebuilt. Carrow Road's current capacity is 27,033, with a season-high 26,532 turning up to watch the derby clash with Ipswich in November 2010.

┈ Even arch-rivals Ipswich couldn't halt Norwich's march in 2010/11. The Tractor Boys were on the wrong end of a 5–1 thumping in April.

TOP-FLIGHT RETURN

Norwich secured a place in the Premier League in style in 2003/04. The Canaries claimed a club-record 28 victories in total, losing just two games at Carrow Road all season. They rattled up 94 points to finish eight ahead of runners-up West Brom. Club legend Darren Huckerby finished the campaign as the club's leading scorer with 13 league goals. Unfortunately for City, they could only muster a record low points haul of 33 the following term as they came straight back down, going 13 games without a win at the start of the season.

QUEENS PARK RANGERS

QPR can count themselves among the oldest clubs in English football, and they are now back in the Barclays Premier League for the first time since 1996. The west London club initially moved to their Loftus Road ground in 1917 but did not settle there permanently until 1963.

RAY OF LIGHT

Ray Wilkins is the oldest player to have featured in the Premier League for QPR aged 39 years and 352 days. Wilkins, who was assistant manager of Chelsea, made his last appearance for the Hoops on September 1 1996 – a 2–1 defeat at home to Bolton.

⋯⋯➤ *Ray Wilkins made 208 appearances for the Loftus Road club towards the latter end of his distinguished 24-year playing career.*

SO CLOSE FOR SEXTON

Dave Sexton had QPR pushing hard for the top-flight title in 1975/76. Unfortunately for the Hoops, they finished a point behind champions Liverpool. Bizarrely, a strong Rangers side, which included the likes of Gerry Francis, Stan Bowles and Frank McLintock, had finished their season 10 days before the Reds and watched on TV as the Merseysiders claimed a 3–1 win against Wolves to pip them to the championship. Liverpool's involvement in the UEFA Cup had delayed their final match. It was still the Rs' highest-ever finish and meant they qualified for the UEFA Cup.

HOOPS HIT GOAL TON

QPR scored an amazing 111 league goals during the 1961/62 season – but only finished fourth in the third tier. That total was 24 more than champions Portsmouth, but Alec Stock's men finished six points behind the south-coast club. The Hoops ended the season having scored 129 goals in 52 matches in all competitions, with Brian Bedford netting 39 times, including six hat-tricks and four in a 5–3 win against Southend.

ARISE SIR LES

Les Ferdinand went for QPR's biggest-ever transfer fee when he joined Newcastle for £6million in 1995. Former England striker Ferdinand scored a total of 91 goals in 183 games for the Hoops – an average strike rate of almost a goal every other game. 'Sir Les', as he was known by fans throughout his career, was awarded an MBE by the Queen in 2005. His big-money switch to St James' Park proved a huge success as he scored 50 times in 83 games for the Magpies.

⋯⋯➤ *Les Ferdinand spent eight seasons at Loftus Road before Newcastle paid QPR a club-record £6million for his services in 1995.*

HOT ROD

Rodney Marsh scored 44 goals in all competitions as QPR claimed the title in the third tier and won the League Cup in 1966/67. Striker Marsh fired 30 goals in the league – seven shy of George Goddard's club record – three in the FA Cup and 11 on the way to the League Cup triumph. Marsh, who went on to become a TV pundit after he finished playing, scored Rangers' equaliser in the cup final against West Brom as they came from two goals down to win 3–2.

REPLAY WOE

The closest QPR have ever come to winning the FA Cup was in 1982 when they were beaten 1–0 in a final replay by London rivals Tottenham. The Hoops were underdogs having finished fifth in the second tier, while Spurs had ended their top-flight campaign in fourth. Young goalkeeper Peter Hucker put in a man-of-the-match display in the first game, with Terry Fenwick heading a last-gasp equaliser in extra time to make it 1–1. Plucky Rangers were undone by an early Glenn Hoddle penalty in the replay, with John Gregory hitting the crossbar.

BRILLIANT BAILEY DESTROYS UNITED

Dennis Bailey wrote himself into QPR folklore when he scored a hat-trick against Manchester United at Old Trafford on New Year's Day 1992 – the last player to achieve that feat domestically against the Red Devils on their own ground. United topped the table at the time, but they were stunned 4–1 by a rampant Rangers side. Andy Sinton had opened the scoring before Bailey took over, with Brian McClair pulling a goal back for the home side. Since Bailey, only one other player has scored a hat-trick against United at Old Trafford – Ronaldo, who bagged a treble for Real Madrid in the Champions League in 2003.

⤑ *Manchester United don't concede many goals, especially at home, but they couldn't handle Dennis Bailey in 1992.*

KENNY KEEPS IT CLEAN

Paddy Kenny kept a record-breaking 24 clean sheets during the Hoops' title-winning season of 2010/11. That total was three more than Swansea shot-stopper Dorus De Vries and a whopping 13 more than John Ruddy, whose Norwich side also gained automatic promotion. Kenny broke the previous club record of 22 clean sheets set by Phil Parkes during the 1971/72 campaign. Speaking about his achievement, Kenny said: 'I think the most clean sheets I've ever kept in one season was 21 during my Sheffield United days, so it's a personal record too.'

⤑ *Goalkeeper Paddy Kenny was virtually unbeatable for the Hoops in 2010/11, and played a huge part in the club's title success.*

RANGERS' UNBEATEN RUN

Rangers enjoyed a 19-game unbeaten run at the start of the 2010/11 season, falling one game shy of equalling a 38-year-old club record. The Hoops began the season in style, winning seven of their opening eight matches and keeping clean sheets in all of those victories. They drew four games in a row during October and remained unbeaten until December 10 when Watford pulled off a shock 3–1 win at Loftus Road. In 1972, QPR went 20 league games undefeated, with the run starting towards the end of the 1971/72 season and continuing into the early part of the following term.

⟵ *Rodney Marsh's time at QPR helped him break into the England set-up, as well as earning him plenty of plaudits from the club's fans.*

RANGERS' ALL-TIME XI*

GK	Phil Parkes
DEF	Dave Clement
DEF	Alan McDonald
DEF	Paul Parker
DEF	Ian Gillard
MID	Trevor Sinclair
MID	Stan Bowles
MID	Gerry Francis
MID	Dave Thomas
ATT	Les Ferdinand
ATT	Rodney Marsh

*As voted by QPR fans

QUEENS PARK RANGERS

DROOP STREET

The old boys of Droop Street Board School may sound like something you would read in a Beano comic, but without them QPR may never have been formed! They were all members of the St Jude's Institute which merged with a team called Christchurch Rangers in 1886. They called themselves Queens Park Rangers as most of the players were from the district of Queens Park.

↧ Heidar Helguson was dependable for the Hoops last season, scoring five times from penalties to take his overall goal tally to 13 in the league.

STAN BOWLS THEM OVER

Stan Bowles made his mark on the UEFA Cup in 1976/77, scoring 11 goals as QPR made it to the last eight on their first European adventure. Norwegian club Brann Bergen were glad to see the back of him as he scored hat-tricks in both legs of their first-round tie – 4–0 and 7–0 victories. Bowles then netted twice in a 3–3 draw against Slovan Bratislava, with the the Hoops winning the home leg. Stan was the man again in a third-round win against FC Koln as Rangers progressed on away goals, and he also bagged in the quarter-final first leg against AEK Athens, only for an injury-hit side to lose on penalties.

←⋯ One of the game's great mavericks, Stan Bowles spent just over seven years at QPR and was part of arguably their best-ever side.

TAKE YOUR KICK

The Rs scored more penalties than any other npower Championship side in 2010/11. Neil Warnock's title winners converted 12 spot-kicks, with three different players taking them throughout the course of the campaign. Adel Taarabt and Heidar Helguson were the regular takers, netting six and five respectively, with both on the scoresheet in a 4–0 first-day win against Barnsley. Tommy Smith kept his cool to snatch a point at the death against his former club Portsmouth in a 1–1 draw in November 2010. Helguson was out and Taarabt had been substituted.

HIGHBURY HOME

QPR were forced to play their home matches at Arsenal when they made it into the UEFA Cup for a second time in 1984/85. The governing body would not sanction games to be played on artificial pitches, so the Hoops had to borrow Highbury from their London rivals. Rangers, who won both games they played at the Gunners' ground, had a plastic pitch at Loftus Road for seven years between 1981 and 1988 until new rules were put in place and grass had to be laid.

---> A spell at Loftus Road helped Terry Venables become one of the country's best managers. As well as Barcelona, he went on to boss England.

GOING GREEN

Did you know that for almost 35 years QPR played home games in green-and-white-hooped shirts? They adopted the colours in 1892 and won The West London Observer Cup in their first season sporting the colours. The blue and white hoops worn by Neil Warnock's men today were not introduced until the 1926/27 campaign. Rangers' third shirt for the 2010/11 season was green and white hoops, as a nod to the club's history.

LEAGUE AND CUP DOUBLE

QPR were a third-tier side when they won the League Cup for the only time in their history in 1967. Alec Stock's men were champions that season, finishing 12 points ahead of Middlesbrough, but they were not fancied to get the better of top-flight West Brom at Wembley. The Baggies were 2–0 up and coasting at half-time, but an amazing second-half turnaround saw goals from Roger Morgan, Rodney Marsh and Mark Lazarus snatch victory for the underdogs.

QPR MANAGERS SINCE 2001

Ian Holloway	2001–06
Gary Waddock	2006
John Gregory	2006–07
Luigi Di Canio	2007–08
Iain Dowie	2008
Paulo Sousa	2008–09
Jim Magilton	2009
Paul Hart	2009–10
Neil Warnock	2010–Present

EL TEL REIGNS IN SPAIN

Terry Venables' success as manager of QPR in the early 1980s saw him leave to coach the mighty Barcelona. Venables had led the Hoops to the FA Cup final and back to the top flight by the end of the 1982/83 campaign. The following season saw Rangers finish fifth – still their highest placing since 1976 – and qualify for the UEFA Cup. That prompted Barca to make a move, and in his three seasons at the Nou Camp, 'El Tel' scooped the Spanish league title and led the club to the European Cup final.

TAARABT STANDARD

Adel Taarabt obviously sets himself very high standards. During a goalless draw at Hull in January 2011, the Morocco international asked to be substituted as he was struggling to get into the game. Boss Neil Warnock refused to take his star player out of the action and he went on to complete the full 90 minutes. After the game, the Hoops manager revealed: 'Adel wasn't injured, it was just his pride. He can't play to the level he wants to every game.' Taarabt's 19-goal haul in 2010/11 was the best total by any QPR player since 2001/02.

QPR'S TOP SCORERS SINCE 2001/02

2001–02	Andy Thomson	21
2002–03	Paul Furlong	13
	Kevin Gallen	
2003–04	Kevin Gallen	17
2004–05	Paul Furlong	18
2005–06	Gareth Ainsworth	9
	Marc Nygaard	
2006–07	Dexter Blackstock	13
2007–08	Akos Buzsaky	10
2008–09	Dexter Blackstock	11
2009–10	Jay Simpson	12
2010–11	Adel Taarabt	19

---> Hot-shot Adel Taarabt slots home against Bristol City, one of 19 goals he netted for the Hoops in 2010/11.

STOKE CITY

Stoke, who were founded in 1863, are the oldest club in the Barclays Premier League and are thought to be the second oldest professional club in the world after Notts County. The Potters regained their top-flight status in 2008 and have finished in creditable mid-table positions in their three seasons back there so far.

BRITANNIA RULES

Stoke's first season at the Britannia Stadium ended in disappointment when they were relegated to the third tier. The Potters finished second from bottom in the second tier in season 1997/98, with Reading at the foot and Manchester City also going down. The club had played their home games at the Victoria Ground since 1878, but moved to their new 27,500-capacity ground in 1997. Graham Kavanagh scored the first goal at the stadium in a League Cup clash against Rochdale.

↑ Terry Conroy (arm raised) scores in the 1972 League Cup final. It was only the second domestic honour won by Stoke keeper Gordon Banks.

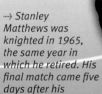

⇢ Stanley Matthews was knighted in 1965, the same year in which he retired. His final match came five days after his 50th birthday.

A FIRST POT

The Potters scooped their first major trophy in 1972 when they beat Chelsea to win the League Cup. Stoke, who had finished 17th in the top flight that season, were underdogs going into the game at Wembley, but goals from Terry Conroy and veteran forward George Eastham earned them a 2–1 victory. Tony Waddington was in charge as City also reached the semi-finals of the FA Cup that year, losing out to Arsenal in a replay. Stoke reached the final in 2010/11, but were beaten by Manchester City.

MATTHEWS HONOURED

Sir Stanley Matthews' ashes are buried under the centre circle of the Britannia Stadium pitch. There are also three nine-foot statues showing the forward at different stages of his career standing outside the ground. Matthews is a Potters legend, having scored 51 league goals in 259 appearances for the club.

DEFENCE TO ATTACK

An impressive 22 per cent of Stoke's goals were scored by defenders in 2010/11. That figure was the highest in the Barclays Premier League. Robert Huth led the way with six, just three less than top scorer Kenwyne Jones. Huth bagged two late goals to earn the Potters a 3–2 win against Sunderland in February. Danny Higginbotham and Rory Delap both netted twice, while Abdoulaye Faye, Ryan Shawcross and Marc Wilson also got their names on the scoresheet.

THE HUMAN SLING

Stoke unleashed their secret weapon on the Barclays Premier League in 2008 courtesy of Rory Delap's long throw-ins. The midfielder's missiles are said to be more accurate than a corner, and they set up nine goals in his debut season in the league – including both of his side's efforts in a 3–2 defeat at home to Everton in September and another brace in a 2–1 win against Arsenal two months later. In 2010/11, the Potters took 570 long throws – an incredible 282 more than Bolton, who were second on the list – and scored four goals as a result of them.

STEIN MAKES MARK

Stoke have won the Football League Trophy on two occasions. The first came in season 1991/92 when Mark Stein scored the only goal to see off Stockport at Wembley. County gained revenge in the play-offs, though, beating the Potters over two legs at the semi-final stage. Diminutive forward Stein netted five goals in the Trophy that season and 17 in the third tier. City were winners of the competition for the second time in 2000 when Graham Kavanagh and Peter Thorne were on target in a 2–1 victory against Bristol City.

↑ A string of rock-solid defensive performances earned Robert Huth the player of the year honour last term.

SUPER SUB SOULEYMANE

Souleymane Oulare may have only played 80 minutes in two substitute appearances for Stoke, but he is fondly remembered for his part in the club's promotion to the second tier in 2002. Following his debut against Northampton in January 2002, Oulare was diagnosed as having a blood clot on his lung and was told he would not play again that season. However, the striker came off the bench against Cardiff in the semi-final of the play-offs to score the winning goal via his backside in extra time!

THORNE IN THE SIDE

Peter Thorne scored 20 goals in the last 17 games of the 1999/00 season as Stoke narrowly missed out on promotion but won the Football League Trophy. Having started the campaign with three goals in his first three matches, the striker had only netted 10 when Chesterfield arrived at the Britannia Stadium on March 4 2000. However, Thorne scored four times in a 5–1 win to spark an incredible run of form. He bagged a hat-trick against Bristol Rovers and the winner against Bristol City in the Football League Trophy final.

⇢ Peter Thorne stretches to knock the ball into an unguarded goal to give Stoke a 2–1 victory over Bristol City in the 2000 Football League Trophy final at Wembley.

STOKE'S PLAYER OF THE YEAR SINCE 2002

2002	Wayne Thomas
2003	Sergei Shtaniuk
2004	Ade Akinbiyi
2005	Clint Hill
2006	Carl Hoefkens
2007	Danny Higginbotham
2008	Liam Lawrence
2009	Abdoulaye Faye
2010	Matthew Etherington
2011	Robert Huth

⚓ Tony Pulis masterminded Stoke's return to English football's top flight in 2008 and defied the odds by keeping the club in the Barclays Premier League.

PULIS IS PREMIER CLASS

Tony Pulis led Stoke to the Barclays Premier League in season 2007/08. The Potters finished second in the Championship – two points behind West Brom – to gain automatic promotion. Ricardo Fuller finished as the club's top scorer with 15 league goals, while midfielder Liam Lawrence netted 14 – his best goalscoring season since 2003/04.

STOKE CITY

VALE RIVALRY

Port Vale are Stoke's traditional rivals, but the clubs have not faced each other in competitive action since the third-tier campaign of 2001/02. The Valiants, who are currently in The Football League's bottom division, were 1–0 winners at the Britannia Stadium the last time the two sides met, with Michael Cummins scoring the only goal of the game. The two Potteries teams have played each other 44 times in the league, with Stoke edging the number of wins 16 to 13, while 15 games have been drawn.

↑ Ricardo Fuller's goal against Bolton was the first of 11 he scored in 34 appearances in the league for Stoke in 2008/09.

SHERON'S SEVEN

Mike Sheron scored in a club-record seven consecutive matches for Stoke in 1995/96. Striker Sheron joined the club from Norwich in November 1995 and netted 15 goals in 28 appearances as the club reached the play-offs the following year. His impressive goalscoring run started in City's 2–1 defeat at Charlton on March 23 1996 and ended against the same opposition at the Victoria Ground on April 17. Sheron scored a total of 34 league goals in 69 matches for the club before leaving for QPR.

⋯➤ Mike Sheron (left), trying to get the better of Wolves' Eric Young, was a prolific goalscorer throughout his career, averaging a goal every three starts. His best strike rate came at Stoke.

FULLER IS FIRST UP

Jamaican striker Ricardo Fuller scored the club's first goal in the Barclays Premier League, but it was only a consolation strike as Stoke went down 3–1 at Bolton. Goals from Gretar Steinsson, Kevin Davies and Johan Elmander had put Wanderers firmly in control of the game in August 2008, with Fuller's injury-time header proving too little, too late.

SEMI STUNNER

Stoke produced a scintillating display to stun Bolton 5–0 in the semi-finals of the FA Cup in 2011. The Wembley clash was expected to be a tight affair, but the Potters were having none of it, racing into a three-goal lead after just half an hour with goals from Matthew Etherington, Robert Huth and Kenwyne Jones. Jonathan Walters stole the show after the break, scoring the goal of the game with a fine solo effort to make it four before tapping in a fifth late on. Stoke were beaten 1–0 by Manchester City in the final.

POTTERS SINK GREENS

Stoke scored nine goals without reply against Plymouth in December 1960 – the biggest winning margin in the club's history. Johnny King grabbed a hat-trick that day, while Bill Asprey and Don Ratcliffe both got their name on the scoresheet twice. A Dennis Wilshaw strike and an own goal from Gordon Fincham completed the scoring as City ran riot. The Potters finished 18th in the second tier that season.

CITY KEEP IT CLEAN

The Potters set a club record when they went seven games without conceding a goal during the 2006/07 campaign. A 1–0 win against Coventry at the Britannia Stadium on November 6 kicked off the run, with their seventh clean sheet coming just over a month later in a 1–0 victory against QPR. Goalkeeper Steve Simonsen went a total of 658 minutes without being beaten during that streak.

→ *Steve Simonsen made only eight Barclays Premier League appearances for Stoke in their first two seasons in the top flight, but he did play in nine cup ties.*

STOKE'S LEADING GOALSCORERS

Tommy Sale	282
Freddie Steele	240
Frank Bowyer	205
John Ritchie	171
Charlie Wilson	118
Johnny King	113
Harry Oscroft	108
Harry Davies	101
Jimmy Greenhoff	97
Bobby Liddle	96

HENRY IS SUPER SUB

Karl Henry has made the most substitute appearances for Stoke, having come off the bench 60 times in his five years at the club between 2001 and 2006. Midfielder Henry went on to join Wolves for an initial £100,000 fee and has since captained the midlands side on numerous occasions. Jon Parkin holds the record for the most sub appearances in a single season for the Potters. The striker was brought on 26 times in 2007/08.

✝ *As well as his 61 substitute appearances for Stoke, Karl Henry started 75 times, though he scored just one goal. At Wolves, however, he has come off the bench only five times and been in the starting line-up for 193 matches.*

DEBUT DELIGHT FOR SHAWCROSS

Ryan Shawcross was the last player to score on his Stoke debut, netting the only goal of the game at Cardiff on the opening day of the 2007/08 season. It took the defender just 27 minutes of his first professional start in English football to get his name on the scoresheet. Shawcross was on loan from Manchester United at the time and signed a permanent deal with City in January 2008.

EARLY AND LATE

Jonathan Walters scored Stoke's fastest and latest goals of the 2010/11 campaign. The £2.75million signing from Ipswich, who netted 12 goals in all competitions, opened the scoring after seven minutes and 24 seconds against Chelsea in April 2011. The game finished 1–1. Earlier in the season, Walters scored two late goals to secure a 3–0 win at West Brom, with his second strike coming in the third minute of injury time.

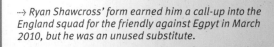

→ *Ryan Shawcross' form earned him a call-up into the England squad for the friendly against Egypt in March 2010, but he was an unused substitute.*

SUNDERLAND

Sunderland are enjoying a fifth successive season in the Barclays Premier League having secured their highest finish in a decade in the 2010/11 campaign. The Black Cats have won the top-flight title on six occasions, although the last time was in 1936. They have also won the FA Cup twice, in 1937 and 1973.

A NEW LOW...TWICE!

Sunderland have held the record for the lowest points total in a Premier League season twice – but they no longer have that unfortunate mark against their name. The Black Cats won just four games as they were relegated with 19 points in season 2002/03, but they broke their own record in the 2005/06 campaign, winning three times as they posted a total of 15 points. Derby's 11-point season of 2007/08 is the current low.

NEIGHBOURHOOD WATCH

Sunderland's record league victory came against derby rivals Newcastle at St James' Park in December 1908. Billy Hogg and George Holley scored hat-tricks and Arthur Bridgett netted twice as the visitors romped to a 9–1 win. Gary Rowell was the hero when the Black Cats got the better of their near-neighbours in another memorable Tyne-Wear battle in February 1979, scoring a hat-trick in a superb 4–1 away win.

BOB STOKES CUP FIRE

Bob Stokoe led the club to FA Cup glory in 1973 – the second time Sunderland had won the competition. Ian Porterfield's first-half strike was enough to snatch a shock 1–0 victory for the then second-tier side against Leeds, although goalkeeper Jimmy Montgomery played a starring role, pulling off a string of superb saves. The club's first FA Cup success had come in 1937 with a 3–1 win against Preston.

⤏ John Byrne's 1992 FA Cup run ended when Sunderland faced Liverpool in the final. For the first time in that season's competition, Byrne didn't score.

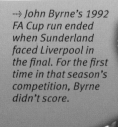

BYRNE MISSES OUT

John Byrne had scored in every round of the FA Cup when he lined up for Sunderland against Liverpool in the 1992 final. The former Republic of Ireland striker was on target against second-tier rivals Port Vale and Oxford before moving on to top-flight opposition. Byrne's run continued with goals against West Ham and Chelsea, while he netted the only goal of the game to see off Norwich in the last four. He spurned a golden chance in the final but could not complete a remarkable feat as Sunderland lost 2–0.

↑ Sunderland's Bobby Kerr sits on the shoulders of Dennis Tueart after captaining the team to their shock victory in the 1973 FA Cup final.

SUNDERLAND'S PREMIER LEAGUE RECORD

1996/97	19th	40 points
1999/00	7th	58 points
2000/01	7th	57 points
2001/02	17th	40 points
2002/03	20th	19 points
2005/06	20th	15 points
2007/08	15th	39 points
2008/09	16th	36 points
2009/10	13th	44 points
2010/11	10th	47 points

FANS VOTE FOR NEW NAME

Sunderland changed their nickname to the Black Cats after leaving Roker Park, with supporters having the final say. There have been a number of historical links between the club and black cats, with one appearing on a team photograph and another turning up at the old ground to be fed and watered. A kitten owned by young fan Billy Morris was said to have brought the Wearsiders luck when it sat in his pocket during the 1937 FA Cup final.

MONTY IS THE DON

Legendary goalkeeper Jimmy Montgomery is Sunderland's record appearance holder, having featured in 537 league games for the club between 1962 and 1977. He is best remembered for a stunning double save in the 1973 FA Cup final against Leeds when he kept out Trevor Cherry and then Peter Lorimer. Montgomery moved to Birmingham in 1977 after 15 years on Wearside.

‑‑‑› *Jimmy Montgomery's first and last games for Sunderland were in the League Cup, 15 years and two days apart, against Walsall and Manchester United respectively.*

↑ The North Stand at Sunderland's Stadium of Light is behind the goal where the home fans sit. The slogan is common to fans of most clubs in the north-east.

SUNDERLAND LEAGUE APPEARANCES

Jimmy Montgomery	537
Ned Doig	418
Len Ashurst	409
Stan Anderson	402
Charlie Buchan	379
Gary Bennett	369

‑‑‑› *Kevin Phillips averaged 22 goals per year in all competitions in his six seasons with Sunderland. His eight England caps came while he was on Wearside.*

GOLDEN BOY PHILLIPS

Kevin Phillips won the Premier League Golden Boot in 1999/00. The Black Cats enjoyed an impressive seventh-place finish that term, with Phillips and strike partner Niall Quinn scoring 44 of the club's 57 goals. Phillips finished the campaign with 30 in the league, seven more than nearest rival Alan Shearer. He scored a hat-trick in a 5–0 win at Derby and two in a stunning 4–1 victory against Chelsea.

ENTER THE LIGHT

Sunderland moved to the Stadium of Light in 1997. The club were relegated from the Premier League in their final season at Roker Park, meaning the first campaign at their new home was in the second tier. The Black Cats missed out on promotion that term after losing the Play-Off Final to Charlton, but they went up in style the following year. The capacity of the stadium was expanded to around 49,000 in 2002, making it the fifth largest of any English football ground.

SUNDERLAND

ROY KEEN TO IMPRESS

Roy Keane led Sunderland to the Championship title in 2006/07 after the club had got off to the worst possible start. The Black Cats lost their first four matches, with Keane in the stands to watch them secure a first win against West Brom on August 28 2006. He started work the next day and a run of 17 games unbeaten – 14 of them wins – put the club firmly in the promotion hunt. A 5–0 victory at Luton on May 6 2007 clinched the title and with it a place in the top flight.

↑ Roy Keane turned around Sunderland's fortunes in 2006/07, working for former international team-mate Niall Quinn, who had recently taken over as club chairman.

SUNDERLAND'S RED CARD RECORD

Kieran Richardson	v Manchester United	2–2
Kenwyne Jones	v West Ham	2–2
Lorik Cana	v Aston Villa	0–2
Michael Turner	v Manchester City	3–4
Lee Cattermole	v Portsmouth	1–1
David Meyler	v Portsmouth	1–1
Alan Hutton	v Hull	1–0
Jack Colback	v Wolves	1–2
Michael Turner	v Wolves	1–2

┄→ Michael Turner (4) is shown a straight red card at Eastlands at the end of Sunderland's 4–3 defeat to Manchester City.

BENT WAVES BYE-BYE

Fans were left stunned when goal-machine Darren Bent was sold to Aston Villa in January 2011. The England striker, who had been the Black Cats' record signing before the arrival of Asamoah Gyan for £13million in August 2010, left having scored eight Barclays Premier League goals before the turn of the year. A club-record £18million fee, which could eventually rise to £24million, was agreed with the Villans and Bent waved goodbye to the Stadium of Light. He ended the season with 17 top-flight goals.

↑ Darren Bent had netted 91 top-flight career goals by the end of the 2010/11 campaign.

BLACK CATS SEE RED

Sunderland set a new record in 2009/10 when they became the first side to have nine players sent off in a single Premier League season. Michael Turner saw red on two occasions, with the first coming in the dying seconds of a 4–3 defeat at Manchester City in December and the second in the latter stages of a 2–1 loss at Wolves on the final day. A double dismissal proved costly at Portsmouth in February, with Aruna Dindane snatching a last-gasp equaliser three minutes after substitute David Meyler had joined Lee Cattermole in being sent off.

⟵ Striker Ryan Noble is one of an exciting clutch of young players who have come through the ranks at Sunderland.

GOAL-MAD GURNEY

Bobby Gurney is the club's all-time record goalscorer, having netted 228 times in 390 games in all competitions. The prolific striker was the club's top scorer for six successive seasons during the 1930s and grabbed the Black Cats' first-ever goal at Wembley in the FA Cup final victory of 1937. Gurney earned one England cap against Scotland in 1935. Charlie Buchan holds the record for the most league goals for the Wearsiders, with 209 between 1911 and 1925.

GOALLESS STALEMATE

Sunderland made an uninspiring start to life in the Premier League in August 1996, as their first game in the competition ended goalless. The Black Cats took on Leicester, who had also been promoted the season before, at Roker Park, but neither of the top-flight new-boys could find a breakthrough.

EUROPEAN TOUR

The Black Cats made it into the second round of the European Cup Winners' Cup in 1973/74, having qualified via their FA Cup success. They played Vasas SC of Hungary in the first round, winning 2–0 at home and 1–0 in the away leg, to land a tricky test against Sporting Lisbon. The Portuguese side proved too strong and they claimed a 3–2 aggregate win, despite Sunderland securing a 2–1 success at Roker Park. It remains the Wearsiders' only taste of European competition.

SUNDERLAND'S TOP LEAGUE GOALSCORERS SINCE 2000/01

2000/01	Kevin Phillips	14
2001/02	Kevin Phillips	11
2002/03	Kevin Phillips	6
2003/04	Marcus Stewart	14
2004/05	Marcus Stewart	16
2005/06	Liam Lawrence	3
	Anthony Le Tallec	
	Tommy Miller	
2006/07	David Connolly	13
2007/08	Kenwyne Jones	7
2008/09	Djibril Cisse	10
	Kenwyne Jones	
2009/10	Darren Bent	24
2010/11	Asamoah Gyan	10

BLACK KITTENS

The 18 players named on the teamsheet for Sunderland's home clash with Wolves in May 2011 included nine Academy graduates. Jordan Henderson and Jack Colback started the game, while Louis Laing, Craig Lynch and Ryan Noble all came on as substitutes. Such were the Black Cats' injury problems at the time, the bench was made up of Billy Knott, Blair Adams, Trevor Carson and Jordan Cook. The seven subs that day had an average age of just 19. Steve Bruce's side lost the game 3–1.

⟵ Republic of Ireland international defender Charlie Hurley holds a number of Sunderland records and was named as Player of the Century by fans during the club's centenary celebrations in 1979.

HURLEY IS THE KING

Charlie Hurley is widely regarded as the best player ever to turn out for the club. The classy defender recovered from a 7–0 defeat to Blackpool on his debut to spend 12 seasons on Wearside, making 401 appearances in all competitions and scoring 26 goals. Hurley missed out on the Footballer of the Year award to Bobby Moore in 1964. He is Sunderland's most capped player, with 38 of his 40 caps for the Republic of Ireland having come during his time at Roker Park.

SWANSEA CITY

Swansea became the first Welsh club to reach the Barclays Premier League in May 2011. The Swans have a proud history that has taken in plenty of highs, as well as some lows. They have endured mixed fortunes since their best-ever finish to a season in 1981/82, when they were sixth in the top flight, but they are now back in the big time.

SWANS' ANFIELD MISERY

Liverpool inflicted Swansea's heaviest cup defeat in January 1990. The 8–0 reverse came in a replay in the third round of the FA Cup after the Swans had held their top-flight opponents to a goalless draw at the Vetch Field. Welsh goalscoring legend Ian Rush netted a hat-trick and John Barnes grabbed two as the Reds went goal crazy. Swansea suffered the same fate against Monaco in the European Cup Winners' Cup in October of the following year. Arsenal manager Arsene Wenger was in charge of the French side at the time.

The Liberty Stadium in Swansea is a multi-purpose arena – the home of Swansea City AFC, Ospreys RUFC and a rock concert venue too. Elton John attracted a 25,000 crowd in 2008.

HOME COMFORTS

The club moved into the Liberty Stadium in time for the 2005/06 season. They had played their home matches at the Vetch Field since 1912, but the all-seater stadium, which can hold just over 20,500 spectators, became their new home in July 2005. The first match to take place there was a pre-season clash against Fulham which ended 1–1. The first league game was a 1–0 success against Tranmere, with Adebayo Akinfenwa scoring the only goal. A record crowd of 19,816 watched the npower Championship Play-Off Semi-Final against Nottingham Forest in May 2011.

STATUE OF LIBERTY

Ivor Allchurch is Swansea's record goalscorer, having netted 164 times in almost 450 appearances for his home-town club in two separate spells between 1949 and 1968. He jointly held the record as Wales' all-time leading scorer with Trevor Ford until 1986, when the duo were overtaken by Ian Rush. A statue of Allchurch stands outside the Liberty Stadium to commemorate his achievements.

Jason Scotland's 45 league goals from 2007 to 2009 earned him a transfer to top-flight Wigan, the £2million fee being a Swansea club record.

SWANSEA'S LEAGUE GOALS 2010/11

Scott Sinclair	19
Stephen Dobbie	9
Darren Pratley	9
Fabio Borini	6
Craig Beattie	4
Luke Moore	3
Ashley Williams	3
Joe Allen	2
Nathan Dyer	2
Angel Rangel	2

SWANNING AROUND

The Swans finished in their highest-ever league position in 1981/82. It was their first season in the top tier and John Toshack's side proved to be a surprise package, beating established teams such as Liverpool, Manchester United, Arsenal and Tottenham as they finished in sixth place. Only a succession of injuries later in the season prevented them from finishing even higher.

SCOTLAND THE BRAVE

Jason Scotland finished as League 1's top goalscorer in 2007/08 as Swansea claimed the title with a club-record points total. Scotland's 24 goals helped the Swans to a 92-point haul, 10 more than runners-up Nottingham Forest. Scotland scored 21 goals in the Championship the following term before moving to Wigan for £2million in July 2009 – a record fee received by the Welsh outfit.

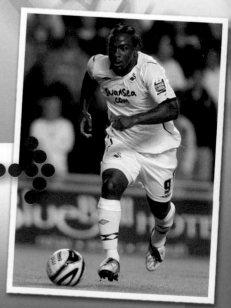

SINCLAIR IS SPOT ON

Scott Sinclair converted seven penalties during the regular 2010/11 season – more than any other player in the npower Championship. Sinclair, who joined the club from Chelsea in the summer of 2010 following a successful season-long loan spell at Wigan, added two more spot-kicks as he netted a hat-trick in the 4–2 Play-Off Final victory over Reading. That treble made it 27 goals in all competitions – not a bad return for a winger!

→ A chart-topping haul of seven spot-kicks meant that Scott Sinclair played a key part in Swansea's promotion to the Barclays Premier League.

CUP OF DREAMS

Swansea have reached the semi-finals of the FA Cup on two occasions, with the 1964 campaign particularly memorable. The Swans were struggling in the second tier when they came up against Liverpool, who were leading the top flight, in the sixth round at Anfield. Amazingly, the underdogs found themselves 2–0 up at half-time thanks to goals from Jimmy McLaughlin and Eddie Thomas. The Reds pulled a goal back and were then awarded a penalty nine minutes from time. But more drama followed as Noel Dwyer saved Ronnie Moran's spot-kick to secure a last-four clash with Preston. They lost that game 2–1 despite taking the lead.

DE VRIES KEEPS IT OUT

Swansea, aided by goalkeeper Dorus De Vries, broke a 10-year club record during the 2009/10 campaign as they surpassed a clean-sheet mark set by Roger Freestone and the title-winning side of 1999/2000. The new milestone was set on April 5 when De Vries made it 23 games without conceding in the 3–0 victory at home to Scunthorpe. 'To keep a clean sheet and break the record of a Swansea legend is absolutely amazing,' De Vries said. The Dutchman kept 21 in the npower Championship in 2010/11.

↓ Wolves are now benefiting from Dorus De Vries' shot-stopping abilities after the Dutchman left Swansea to sign for them in June 2011.

A FIRST FOR WALES

Swansea became the first club from Wales to reach the Premier League following their promotion in 2010/11. The Swans were last in the top flight in 1983, dropping out after finishing second from bottom, while Cardiff were relegated after two seasons in the highest division in 1961/62 and have not made it back since. Newport County and Wrexham are the only other Welsh sides to have featured in the Football League post-war.

DERBY DEADLOCK

South Wales derby clashes with Cardiff are competitive affairs, but interestingly neither side has ever done the double – winning both home and away league games in the same season. The current head-to-head stands at 20 wins for Swansea, 18 for the Bluebirds, with 16 ending all square. In 2010/11, the Swans claimed a 1–0 win at the Cardiff City Stadium with on-loan striker Marvin Emnes grabbing the only goal. But a single strike from Craig Bellamy was enough to earn Cardiff the points at the Liberty Stadium in February 2011.

TOTTENHAM HOTSPUR

Spurs have an illustrious history. They were the first club in the 20th Century to achieve a league and cup double and were also the first English club to taste success in Europe when they lifted the Cup Winners' Cup in 1963. They have won the UEFA Cup twice, the League Cup four times and the FA Cup on eight occasions.

ROUGH DIAMONDS

Tottenham legends Glenn Hoddle and Chris Waddle released a single called 'Diamond Lights' in April 1987. The song reached number 12 in the charts, with the pair performing the track on *Top of the Pops*. Hoddle left White Hart Lane for Monaco at the end of the 1986/87 season, although it's not thought that the embarrassment of his short music career had anything to do with him leaving the country!

⬅ Glenn Hoddle was probably ranked higher than 12 in the England football charts when 'Diamond Lights' peaked.

EURO FIRST FOR SPURS

Spurs became the first English side to lift a European trophy when they crushed Atletico Madrid 5–1 in the European Cup Winners' Cup final of 1963. Jimmy Greaves and Terry Dyson both scored twice against the Spaniards, with John White completing the victory. The win went some way to erasing the memory of the previous season's European Cup campaign, which had ended in semi-final disappointment.

DOUBLE DELIGHT

The Londoners were the first double winners of the 20th Century in 1961. Tottenham scored 115 goals on their way to the top-flight title, finishing eight points ahead of Sheffield Wednesday. They then claimed a 2–0 win against Leicester in the FA Cup final at Wembley to complete a memorable campaign. Captain Danny Blanchflower landed the Player of the Year award for the second time. Spurs then repeated their FA Cup win by triumphing again in 1962.

SPURS' MAJOR HONOURS

Top flight
Champions   1950/51, 1960/61
Runners-up   1921/22, 1951/52, 1956/57, 1962/63

Second tier
Champions   1919/20, 1949/50
Runners-up   1908/09, 1932/33

FA Cup
Winners   1900/01, 1920/21, 1960/61, 1961/62, 1966/67, 1980/81, 1981/82, 1990/91

League Cup
Winners   1970/71, 1972/73, 1998/99, 2007/08

European Cup Winners' Cup
Winners   1962/63

UEFA Cup
Winners   1971/72, 1983/84

⬅ Bobby Smith (left) and Maurice Norman chair captain Danny Blanchflower after Tottenham had beaten Burnley in the 1962 FA Cup final.

GREAVES IS THE GREATEST

Jimmy Greaves is widely regarded as one of the greatest goalscorers of all time, with an incredible 220 league goals in 321 appearances from a nine-year stay at Tottenham between 1961 and 1970. He also holds the distinction of having scored the most league goals in a single season for Spurs – 37 as the club lifted the title in 1962/63. His record in cup competitions was also amazing, with the striker netting 32 goals in 36 FA Cup games, five in eight League Cup matches and nine goals in 14 games on the European stage.

SPURS' LEADING GOALSCORERS

Jimmy Greaves	266
Bobby Smith	208
Martin Chivers	174
Cliff Jones	159
George Hunt	138

ARGIE BARGY

Tottenham pulled off a transfer coup in 1978 when they signed two of Argentina's World Cup-winning squad. Ossie Ardiles and Ricky Villa arrived at White Hart Lane fresh from starring at the finals in their home country. Villa scored 25 goals in 179 appearances but is best remembered for a stunning solo effort against Manchester City in the replay of the 1981 FA Cup final. He left in 1983, but Ardiles stayed on to add a UEFA Cup winners' medal to his collection a year later. He also netted 25 goals but played 311 games.

UP FOUR THE CUP

Spurs won the League Cup for the fourth time in 2008, beating London rivals Chelsea 2–1 after extra time. Didier Drogba had put the Blues ahead in the first half, but a Dimitar Berbatov penalty made it 1–1 and a 94th-minute header from Jonathan Woodgate snatched victory. Tottenham were also winners of the competition in 1971, 1973 and 1999, while they finished runners-up in 1982, 2002 and most recently 2009, when they lost on penalties to Manchester United.

KLINSMANN DIVES IN

Jurgen Klinsmann made a huge impact in his one full season at White Hart Lane in 1994/95. The German striker scored 20 Premier League goals and 29 overall as Spurs finished seventh and reached the semi-finals of the FA Cup. Klinsmann returned to the club in December 1997 to aid their successful battle against relegation and scored nine times before the end of the campaign, including four goals in a 6–2 win at Wimbledon.

⤑ Jurgen Klinsmann's first goal for Spurs, at Sheffield Wednesday in 1994, was followed by a dive on the Hillsborough turf. It has become one of the most copied goal celebrations.

↓ Manager Keith Burkinshaw is flanked by Ricky Villa (left) and Ossie Ardiles, who had just starred in Argentina's 1978 World Cup win.

TOP OF THE BILL

Bill Nicholson both played for and managed Tottenham during their golden era. Having made over 300 appearances for the club, winning two titles, he became manager in October 1958 and enjoyed a hugely successful 16-year spell in charge. Nicholson led Spurs to the double in 1961 and won the FA Cup again in 1962. The Londoners claimed the European Cup Winners' Cup in 1963, the FA Cup again in 1967, the League Cup in 1971 and 1973 and the UEFA Cup in 1972. Nicholson scored after just 19 seconds of his only England appearance.

↓ Bill Nicholson (second left) with (left–right) Frank Saul, Joe Kinnear, Terry Venables and Pat Jennings before the 1967 FA Cup final.

TOTTENHAM HOTSPUR

GUNNERS SHOT DOWN

Mark Falco and Chris Hughton both scored twice when Tottenham equalled their biggest victory against arch-rivals Arsenal in April 1983. Spurs first claimed a 5–0 win on Christmas Day 1911, and 72 years later they matched that success. More recently, there were five different goalscorers when a young Gunners side were beaten 5–1 in the Carling Cup at White Hart Lane in January 2008.

A UEFA FIRST

The north London club were the first winners of the UEFA Cup in 1972. That year saw an all-English final, with Spurs claiming a 3–2 aggregate victory over Wolves. The first leg at Molineux finished 2–1 to the visitors, with Martin Chivers scoring a stunning late winner. A 1–1 draw in the second leg at White Hart Lane was enough to secure the trophy. Tottenham won the same competition for the second time in 1984, beating Anderlecht of Belgium 4–3 on penalties after both legs had finished 1–1.

DEFOE REACHES LANDMARK

Jermain Defoe scored his 100th Premier League goal during season 2010/11, becoming the 20th player to reach the total. The Spurs striker was spotted by TV cameras wearing a '100 goals' vest underneath his playing shirt during a clash with West Ham in March as he prepared to celebrate the occasion. Unfortunately, it proved premature, as he failed to reach his target for another six matches – a 2–2 draw at home to West Brom. Defoe scored with a superb 20-yard shot to put his side 2–1 ahead, only for the Baggies to snatch a point.

⋯➔ A typically-clinical finish saw Jermain Defoe join the '100 club' of Premier League goals against West Brom in April 2011.

☦ Happy captain Alan Mullery waves to Tottenham fans after the team had beaten Wolves 3–2 on aggregate to win the UEFA Cup in 1972.

BILL'S FLYING START

October 11 1958 was an unforgettable afternoon for Spurs as it marked both the start of legendary manager Bill Nicholson's reign and Tottenham's highest-scoring league match. Nicholson's spell as manager could not have begun better – his new side claiming an incredible 10–4 win against Everton at White Hart Lane. The Londoners were leading 6–1 at the break, with Bobby Smith going on to score four goals and Alfie Stokes helping himself to a brace. Nicholson led the club from 1958 to 1974 and is widely regarded as Spurs' greatest boss.

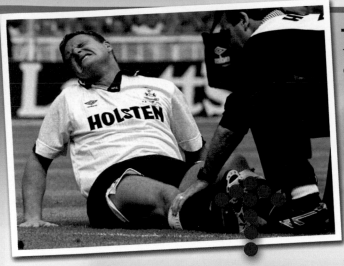

↑ Paul Gascoigne's 1991 FA Cup final – the last game of his Tottenham career – was over after less than 20 minutes. Spurs went on to beat Nottingham Forest 2–1.

THE GREAT EIGHT

The club have won the FA Cup on eight occasions, with their most recent success coming back in 1991. That final is best remembered for Paul Gascoigne's reckless challenge on Gary Charles that saw the Tottenham playmaker come off worst. Gascoigne left the field with a serious knee injury. In his absence, Gary Lineker had a penalty saved by Mark Crossley with Forest 1–0 up, but Paul Stewart equalised to force extra time. An own goal from Des Walker eventually handed Tottenham the cup. The Londoners were a non-League club when they won the trophy for the first time in 1901, while their other wins came in 1921, 1961, 1962, 1967, 1981 and 1982.

SPURS MAKE IT 1,000

Spurs became the sixth team to reach 1,000 Premier League points when they claimed a 2–1 win against Sunderland in February 2011. Goals from Michael Dawson and Niko Kranjcar secured the points at the Stadium of Light. Of the seven ever-present teams since the competition began in 1992, Everton are now the only club to have failed to break the barrier, sitting on 978 points at the end of the 2010/11 campaign. Harry Redknapp's side ended the season on 1,017 points.

ON CLOUD NINE

Tottenham's biggest margin of victory came in a second-tier clash with Bristol Rovers in 1977 when they claimed a 9–0 win at White Hart Lane. Colin Lee scored four goals on his debut, having signed from Torquay for £60,000, with Ian Moores netting a hat-trick. Glenn Hoddle and Peter Taylor completed the rout. Spurs went close to matching that feat when they beat Wigan 9–1 in 2009/10.

A RECORD RUN

Steve Perryman is Spurs' record appearance holder, having featured in 854 games for the club between 1969 and 1986. Defender Perryman also holds the distinction of having won more medals than any other Tottenham player. He lifted two League Cups, two FA Cups and two UEFA Cups in his 17-year stay at White Hart Lane and also scooped the Football Writers' Player of the Year award in 1982.

MILAN DUO BEATEN

Tottenham got the better of both Milan clubs as they enjoyed a memorable first Champions League campaign in 2010/11. Spurs topped a group containing Inter, Dutch side FC Twente and Werder Bremen of Germany. Gareth Bale announced his arrival on the world stage with a sublime hat-trick at the San Siro, although the Italian side held on for a thrilling 4–3 win. Harry Redknapp's side gained revenge with a 3–1 win at White Hart Lane, before beating AC Milan over two legs in the last 16. Unfortunately, the Londoners drew Real Madrid in the quarter-finals and were beaten 5–0 on aggregate.

SPURS APPEARANCES

Steve Perryman	854
Gary Mabbutt	611
Pat Jennings	590
Cyril Knowles	506
Glenn Hoddle	490
Ted Ditchburn	452
Alan Gilzean	439
Jimmy Dimmock	438
Phil Beal	420
Maurice Norman	411

↑ Steve Perryman made his Spurs debut at the age of 17 and, as a 20-year-old, became the youngest player in modern times to be appointed club captain.

← Sensational performances against both Milan clubs saw Gareth Bale catch the eye of his peers, as he was voted the PFA Player of the Year in 2011.

WEST BROMWICH ALBION

Formed in 1878, West Brom were crowned champions of the top flight in 1919/20 and have also lifted the FA Cup on five occasions. More recently, they have yo-yoed between the second tier and the top division, which has made for some exciting — if at times nervous — watching for the club's loyal supporters.

ASTLE THE CUP KING

West Brom have won the FA Cup five times. The Baggies were victorious in 1888 – the year The Football League was formed – and followed that up with further success in 1892, 1931, 1954 and 1968. Alan Ashman led the club to glory against Everton in the 1968 final, with Jeff Astle scoring the only goal of the game in extra time. Striker Astle scored in every round of the competition that year.

⤑ As well as his cup exploits for West Brom, Jeff Astle was a prolific marksman in The Football League, scoring 137 goals in 292 games for the Baggies from 1964 to 1974.

BOMBER BROWN WINGS IN

Tony Brown holds plenty of records for West Brom. The forward is the club's all-time leading goalscorer, having scored 279 from an 18-year spell between 1963 and 1981, with 218 of those coming in the league – also a Baggies record. 'Bomber', as he was known by fans, was involved in 720 games for West Brom in total – an overall club appearance landmark – and featured 574 times in league matches.

ALBION STROLL ON

West Bromwich Albion is one of the most famous names in English football, but the club has not always been called as such. They were originally known as West Bromwich Strollers after their founders had to walk to Wednesbury to buy a match ball! They took on the name Albion in 1880.

WEST BROM'S 10-YEAR LEAGUE RECORD

2001/02 (second tier)	2nd
2002/03 (Premier League)	19th
2003/04 (second tier)	2nd
2004/05 (Premier League)	17th
2005/06 (Premier League)	19th
2006/07 (second tier)	4th
2007/08 (second tier)	1st
2008/09 (Premier League)	20th
2009/10 (second tier)	2nd
2010/11 (Premier League)	11th

BOING, BOING BAGGIES

West Brom have developed an amazing ability to bounce back following relegation from the Premier League. The Baggies were promoted to the top flight in season 2001/02, and since then they have experienced the joy of promotion or the agony of relegation in seven of the last 10 seasons. They were 11th in the Barclays Premier League last term after finishing as runners-up in the Championship in 2009/10. It's never dull at The Hawthorns!

CAPTAIN MARVEL

Bryan Robson's switch from West Brom to Manchester United in October 1981 was a British transfer record at the time. Robson followed manager Ron Atkinson and team-mate Remi Moses to Old Trafford in a £1.5million deal. That figure for a transfer between two British clubs was not beaten until Liverpool paid Newcastle £1.9million to sign striker Peter Beardsley in the summer of 1987. Robson returned to West Brom as manager from 2004–2006, keeping the club in the top flight in his first season in charge.

⤑ Midfielder Bryan Robson had made almost 200 league appearances for West Brom, and made his full England debut, when Manchester United broke the British transfer record to sign him in 1981.

PRICELESS PETER

Peter Odemwingie set a new record for the most goals in a Premier League season by a West Brom player in 2010/11. The Nigerian forward scored 15 to beat the previous best of 11 set by Robert Earnshaw during the 2004/05 campaign. Odemwingie also managed to find the net in five consecutive top-flight matches between April 9 and May 8 2011, becoming the first Albion player since Tony Brown over 40 years ago to achieve the feat.

⤺ Before joining Albion, Nigerian ace Peter Odemwingie was prolific for Lille in France and Lokomotiv Moscow in the Russian Premier League.

HOLES IN THE BAGGIES

West Brom set an unwanted Premier League record of 34 successive games without keeping a clean sheet during the 2010/11 season. The Baggies kept out Sunderland in a 1–0 win in August – a week after Chelsea had hit them for six – but had to wait until the home victory over Everton on May 8 for their second shut-out of the campaign! The club's porous defence was at it again on the final day of the season, though, as Roy Hodgson's men came from three goals down to draw 3–3 at Newcastle.

PAUL TAKES IT TO EXTREMES

Adrenaline junkie Paul Scharner loves extreme sports. Scharner's thrill-seeking led to his former club Wigan banning him from parachuting and bungee-jumping! The fun-loving midfielder, who can speak five languages, revealed it was written into his contract at the DW Stadium to 'be careful'. The Austrian is not afraid to stand out either, having sported a number of unusual haircuts during his time in the Barclays Premier League.

⤏ With this hairstyle there was no mistaking Paul Scharner on the pitch.

WE'RE GUNNER BEAT YOU!

West Brom's stunning 3–2 win at Arsenal in September 2010 was the first time they have beaten one of the perceived 'Big Four' away from The Hawthorns in the Premier League era. Two goals in as many minutes at the start of the second half from Peter Odemwingie and Gonzalo Jara put the visitors firmly in command at the Emirates Stadium, with Jerome Thomas adding a third. Samir Nasri pulled a goal back shortly afterwards and added his second at the death, but Albion held on. West Brom were also the only team to take a point off Manchester United at Old Trafford last term, drawing 2–2 having been two goals down.

⤏ Midfielder Jerome Thomas celebrates scoring the all-important third goal as West Brom cling on to claim a memorable win against Arsenal in September 2010.

WEST BROMWICH ALBION

JOY FOR ROY

Roy Hodgson had an instant impact at the club after taking charge in February 2011. The experienced boss took the Baggies on a six-game unbeaten run which included an impressive 3–1 derby win at Birmingham, a 2–1 success against Liverpool and a 2–2 draw at home to Arsenal – although Albion had been leading that game 2–0. Hodgson replaced Roberto Di Matteo as West Brom manager having been sacked by Liverpool a month earlier.

↑ *After his time at Liverpool, Roy Hodgson's managerial career quickly got back on track following his arrival at West Brom in February 2011.*

MID-SEASON MISERY

Albion suffered a club-record 11 straight defeats during the 1995/96 campaign but still managed to finish 11th in the second tier. The Baggies went into their October 28 clash with Millwall on the back of three successive victories, but a 2–1 loss in London sparked a miserable run. Alan Buckley's side were beaten heavily by Norwich (4–1) and Huddersfield (4–1), with a goalless draw at home to Wolves in January 1996 finally ending the sequence.

RUN SENDS ALBION UP

Season 2001/02 saw West Brom clinch a place in the Premier League by overhauling an 11-point gap over the last 42 days of the campaign to snatch the runners-up spot from Wolves. The Baggies were unbeaten during the last 10 matches, winning eight and drawing the other two. Albion, under manager Gary Megson, ended the season on 89 points, with champions Manchester City finishing 10 ahead. At the time, it was Albion's highest total since three points for a win were introduced. They managed 91 points in 2009/10.

HAWTHORNS HIGH

The Hawthorns has the distinction of being the highest stadium above sea level in the top four tiers of English football. It is at an altitude of 551 feet (168 metres). Hull and Southampton are playing at grounds almost on the same level as the sea – they are six feet or lower than that mark.

↓ *Opposition fans and players need to have a head for heights when they visit The Hawthorns. The famous old ground has been Albion's home since 1900.*

TAYLOR MADE FOR BAGGIES

Bob Taylor became the first Albion player since Jeff Astle to score 35 goals in a season in 1992/93. 'Super Bob' bagged on his home debut in 1992 against Brentford and grabbed two more at St Andrew's as Birmingham were beaten 3–0. The following term was when Taylor came into his own, though, finishing as the third tier's top scorer with 30 goals. He netted 37 in all competitions as the Baggies secured promotion. Taylor left for Bolton in 1998 but returned to The Hawthorns for a second three-year stay in 2000.

----> More than 100 goals over two spells made 'Super' Bob Taylor a real fans' favourite during his time with Albion.

TRIPLE DEBUT FOR HURST

Teenage defender James Hurst may have only made three first-team appearances for West Brom in 2010/11, but each time he was making his debut. Hurst, who turned 19 in January, featured in three different competitions, starting with a 90-minute run-out in Albion's 1–0 defeat at Ipswich in the Carling Cup in December 2010. He played in a 3–0 defeat at Fulham in the Barclays Premier League in January and kept his place for the FA Cup clash at Reading.

↓ James Hurst (left) battles for the ball on one of his three debuts in 2010/11 – this time against Fulham in the Barclays Premier League.

APPLETON AGONY

Injury forced Michael Appleton to retire at the age of 27 in 2003, but he is now carving out a career as a coach at West Brom. Appleton was a Baggies player when he tore posterior cruciate ligaments in his right knee in an accidental training-ground collision with team-mate Des Lyttle in 2001. He returned in a reserve-team match against Manchester United in February 2003 but was forced to quit in November of that year. Having been in charge of Albion's youth and reserve teams, he is now Roy Hodgson's assistant.

LAURIE IS THE REAL DEAL

Laurie Cunningham became the first English player to turn out for Real Madrid when he left West Brom for the Bernabeu in 1979. Flying winger Cunningham moved in a £995,000 deal and went on to make almost 50 appearances for the Spanish giants, scoring 13 goals. His finest display saw him receive a standing ovation from the home fans after helping Madrid to a 2–0 win against Barcelona at the Nou Camp. Cunningham was the first black player to represent England at any level when he played for the Under-21s against Scotland in 1977 and the first to represent the full England side in a competitive match two years later.

DOUBLE HOODOO BROKEN

Most clubs have a 'bogey' team – an opponent they have struggled to beat. West Brom finally got the better of theirs when they edged out Liverpool in 2010/11 – the first time since 1981! They hadn't even taken a point against the Reds since 1984, but that all changed when two penalties from Chris Brunt secured a 2–1 win in April 2011. The Baggies also took three points off derby rivals Aston Villa for the first time since 1985 in the same month as goals from Peter Odemwingie and Youssuf Mulumbu snatched another 2–1 success.

SICK OF THE SIGHT

West Brom played fierce rivals Wolves five times during the 2006/07 season. The Baggies claimed a comfortable 3–0 victory in the first league meeting in October 2006, with an FA Cup game following at Molineux which Albion won by the same scoreline. Wolves gained revenge with a 1–0 win in the second-tier clash of March 2007, before the two teams met in the play-offs. Kevin Phillips was the West Brom hero, scoring three times over the two legs in a 4–2 aggregate success.

<--- The Baggies were thankful for the goals of Kevin Phillips in 2006/07, particularly against arch-rivals Wolves.

WIGAN ATHLETIC

Wigan reached the top flight for the first time in 2005 and have now established themselves in the Barclays Premier League. They have won the Football League Trophy twice, but the nearest they have come to claiming a major domestic trophy was in 2006 when they were beaten finalists in the Carling Cup.

WIGAN'S HONOURS

Second tier
Runners-up   2004/05

Third tier
Champions   2002/03

Fourth tier
Champions   1996/97
Promoted (third) 1981/82

Football League Trophy
Winners   1984/85, 1998/99

League Cup
Runners-up   2005/06

A TOP FINISH

Wigan achieved their best top-flight finish in their debut season back in 2005/06. The Lancashire club's first Barclays Premier League game ended in a last-gasp 1–0 defeat at home to Chelsea but, after losing by the same scoreline at Charlton, the Latics embarked on an impressive run of nine games without defeat – eight of those victories – to climb to second in the table. Paul Jewell's side were unable to sustain that impressive form, but they still finished 10th.

LEAGUE CUP LATICS

Wigan made it to their first major domestic final in 2006 when they played Manchester United in the Carling Cup at the Millennium Stadium. Jason Roberts had scored with only a few seconds remaining in extra time of the semi-final second-leg clash against Arsenal at Highbury to secure a win on away goals. That earned the Latics their Cardiff date but, unfortunately for Paul Jewell's side, they were beaten 4–0 by a Wayne Rooney-inspired United.

⇢ Jason Roberts (right) scored in the opening minute of his Wigan debut, in a Lancashire derby against Preston, and quickly formed a dangerous partnership with Nathan Ellington (left).

DEADLY DUO

Nathan Ellington and Jason Roberts formed a superb strike partnership in the club's promotion-winning team of 2004/05. The Latics scored 79 league goals that term, with the pair contributing 45 of them. Ellington netted 24 times, with Roberts scoring 21 as the duo finished first and second in the scoring charts.

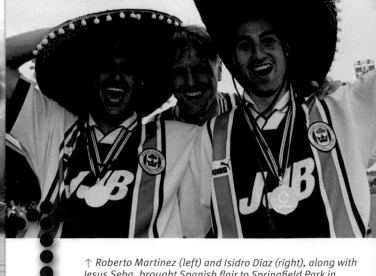

† Roberto Martinez (left) and Isidro Diaz (right), along with Jesus Seba, brought Spanish flair to Springfield Park in 1995. Two seasons later, they were celebrating promotion.

THE THREE AMIGOS

The 'Three Amigos' arrived at Wigan amid a wave of publicity in the summer of 1995. Spanish trio Roberto Martinez, Isidro Diaz and Jesus Seba were signed from Balaguer and Zaragoza by chairman Dave Whelan when the club were playing in the fourth tier. Playmaker Martinez made the biggest impact, completing 187 league appearances and scoring 17 goals for the Latics. He is now the manager of the club.

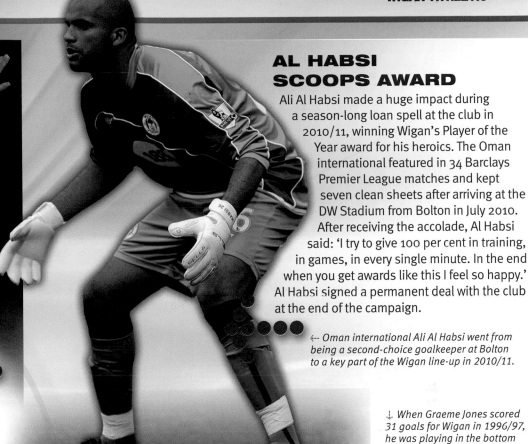

AL HABSI SCOOPS AWARD

Ali Al Habsi made a huge impact during a season-long loan spell at the club in 2010/11, winning Wigan's Player of the Year award for his heroics. The Oman international featured in 34 Barclays Premier League matches and kept seven clean sheets after arriving at the DW Stadium from Bolton in July 2010. After receiving the accolade, Al Habsi said: 'I try to give 100 per cent in training, in games, in every single minute. In the end when you get awards like this I feel so happy.' Al Habsi signed a permanent deal with the club at the end of the campaign.

←·· Oman international Ali Al Habsi went from being a second-choice goalkeeper at Bolton to a key part of the Wigan line-up in 2010/11.

↓ When Graeme Jones scored 31 goals for Wigan in 1996/97, he was playing in the bottom tier. Eight seasons later, the Latics were promoted to the Barclays Premier League.

JEWELL IN THE CROWN

Paul Jewell masterminded a meteoric rise that saw Wigan move from the third tier to the Barclays Premier League within four seasons. They reached the second tier for the first time in emphatic fashion by winning the title with 100 points – their biggest-ever haul. The Latics narrowly missed out on the play-offs the following term, before they finished second to Sunderland in 2004/05 to secure automatic promotion and a place in the top flight for the first time in their history.

↑ Paul Jewell makes a point during Wigan's December 2006 match against West Ham at Upton Park. The Latics just avoided relegation at the end of the season, after which Jewell resigned.

KEEPING UP WITH THE JONESES

Assistant manager Graeme Jones was a goalscoring legend for the club between 1996 and 1999. Jones established the Latics record for the most goals in a single season when he netted 31 times in the promotion-winning campaign of 1996/97. He scored four hat-tricks during that term, including two in consecutive games against Leyton Orient and Darlington.

DOUBLE TROPHY SUCCESS

The Latics have won the Football League Trophy on two occasions. Their first success came in 1985 when goals from Mike Newell, Tony Kelly and David Lowe secured a 3–1 win against Brentford, and they won it again in 1999 in dramatic fashion. Midfielder Paul Rogers scored the only goal of the final against Millwall in the dying seconds.

A LEAGUE OF THEIR OWN

The Lancashire outfit are the youngest club in the top division, having formed in 1932. The Latics were elected to the fourth tier of The Football League in 1978 thanks to a slice of good fortune. They had finished second to Boston United in the Northern Premier League, but the champions' ground did not meet the required criteria for a Football League club and so Wigan went up instead.

WIGAN ATHLETIC

THE DW STADIUM

The Lancashire club moved to the DW Stadium – or the JJB Stadium as it was first known – in time for the start of the 1999/2000 campaign. The Latics share the 25,133-capacity ground with the town's rugby league team, Wigan Warriors. Simon Haworth scored the first league goal at the stadium, going on to grab a brace in a 3–0 win against Scunthorpe. Prior to their move, Wigan had played their home games at Springfield Park for 67 years.

←-- Record goalscorer Andy Liddell (centre) is congratulated by Nicky Eaden (left) and Jimmy Bullard after scoring Wigan's second equaliser in a 2–2 home draw with Nottingham Forest.

↓ Kevin Langley scored 12 goals in his 317 appearances for Wigan in their early years in The Football League. He returned to the club as a coach in the Centre of Excellence.

LONG-SERVING LIDDELL

Andy Liddell scored a club-record 70 league goals for Wigan between 1998 and 2004. Liddell joined the Latics from Barnsley in a £350,000 switch in October 1998 and went on to score 10 goals in his first season. He was Wigan's top scorer in the 2001/02 campaign, netting two hat-tricks against Brighton and Cambridge on his way to an 18-goal haul. He was the club's longest-serving player when he left for Sheffield United in 2004.

WIGAN'S TOP SCORERS SINCE 2001/02

Season	Player	Goals
2001/02	Andy Liddell	18
2002/03	Andy Liddell	16
2003/04	Nathan Ellington	18
2004/05	Nathan Ellington	24
2005/06	Henri Camara	12
2006/07	Emile Heskey	8
2007/08	Marcus Bent	7
2008/09	Amr Zaki	10
2009/10	Hugo Rodallega	10
2010/11	Hugo Rodallega	9
	Charles N'Zogbia	

A LANG TIME COMING

Kevin Langley made 317 league appearances in two spells with Wigan – a club record. Midfielder Langley was 17 when he made his debut in September 1981, and he went on to feature 160 times before moving to Everton five years later. He returned to Springfield Park from Birmingham in 1990 for another four-year stay, adding another 157 appearances.

CAP FITS FOR HESKEY

Emile Heskey became the first full-time Wigan player to represent England when he started the European Championship qualifier against Israel on September 8 2007. The striker failed to get on the scoresheet, but England were 3–0 winners at Wembley. Goalkeeper Chris Kirkland had earned his first cap in a friendly against Greece while with the Latics in August 2006, but he was only on loan from Liverpool at the time.

LAST EIGHT FOR LATICS

Wigan's best run in the FA Cup saw them reach the sixth round in 1986/87. The Latics, who were playing in the third tier at the time, claimed a 3–1 win against Lincoln in the first round and then scored five without reply at Darlington. A 2–1 victory against Gillingham got them into the fourth round, where they knocked out Norwich, who finished fifth in the top flight that season. Second-tier Hull were brushed aside 3–0 to secure a quarter-final clash with Leeds, before the Latics were eventually beaten 2–0 at Springfield Park.

VALENCIA WINGS IT

Antonio Valencia cost Manchester United in the region of £16million when he left the DW Stadium in June 2009 – a record transfer fee received by the Latics. The Ecuador winger had been snapped up by Paul Jewell from Spanish side Villarreal in 2006, initially on loan, before penning a full-time deal in January 2008 when Steve Bruce was in charge. Valencia scored seven goals in 84 league games for Wigan before moving to Old Trafford.

→ Antonio Valencia spent 18 months on loan at Wigan before a permanent deal was done. A year and a half later, he was sold for £16million.

LOSING STREAK

A 1–0 home loss to Arsenal in 2006/07 led to the club's worst league run of eight straight defeats in a row. Having been beaten by the Gunners, the Latics also went down to Chelsea, twice (3–2 and 4–0), and they were also second best against Manchester United (3–1), Everton (0–2), Sheffield United (1–0), Blackburn (3–0) and Reading (3–2). They finally secured a long-overdue win on February 3 2007 when Lee McCulloch scored the only goal of the game against Portsmouth.

HEADS YOU WIN

Wigan only scored three headed goals during the whole of the 2010/11 season, but one of them kept the club in the Barclays Premier League! Hugo Rodallega's 78th-minute header at Stoke on the final day ensured the Latics' survival and also moved the Colombian striker two goals ahead of Henri Camara as Wigan's top scorer since they joined the top flight in 2005/06. Rodallega has now scored 22 times.

SPOT THE DIFFERENCE

Wigan are the only side in Premier League history to have conceded more than 74 goals in a season and still avoided relegation. The Latics' goal was breached a total of 79 times in 2009/10, with 24 of those coming at the DW Stadium, compared to 55 on their travels. Roberto Martinez's side ended the campaign with a goal difference of -42, which was the worst in the top flight. There wasn't much in it, though, with relegated duo Hull and Burnley ending the season on -41 and -40 respectively.

↓ Hugo Rodallega used his head to keep Wigan in the Barclays Premier League, nodding home a decisive goal against Stoke on the final day of last season.

↑ Roberto Martinez's reputation is for producing teams playing open football. Wigan set a new record in 2009/10 when they conceded the most goals by a team avoiding relegation.

WOLVERHAMPTON WANDERERS

Wolves were one of the leading names in English football during the 1950s and early 1960s, making back-page headlines both domestically and in Europe. They have been top-flight champions three times, have won the FA Cup on four occasions and were League Cup winners in 1974 and 1980.

BADGE OF HONOUR

Wanderers have used their current club badge since 1979. The first crest worn on the famous gold and black shirts was Wolverhampton's coat of arms, which was then changed in the late 1960s to a single leaping wolf. The badge was redesigned again in the 1970s, this time to show three leaping wolves, until the current crest was introduced. The city's coat of arms made a brief return between 1993 and 1996.

A RUN TO REMEMBER

Wolves set a club record when they went 21 league matches unbeaten in 2005. The run started on January 15 with a 4–2 win at home to West Ham. Kenny Miller scored twice in that game, with Paul Ince and Carl Cort also on target. Wanderers didn't lose any of their remaining 18 games that term, and their streak continued into the 2005/06 campaign. They managed three more league matches before they were finally beaten 2–0 by Leeds at Elland Road on August 20.

WOLVES' MAJOR HONOURS

Top flight
Champions 1953/54, 1957/58, 1958/59

Second tier
Champions 1931/32, 1976/77, 2008/09

Third tier
Champions 1923/24 (North), 1988/89

Fourth tier
Champions 1987/88

FA Cup
Winners   1892/93, 1907/08, 1948/49, 1959/60

League Cup
Winners   1973/74, 1979/80

Football League Trophy
Winners   1987/88

SYLVAN HAS GOLDEN TOUCH

Sylvan Ebanks-Blake enjoyed a season to remember in 2008/09, claiming the second tier's Golden Boot for the second year running to help the club into the Barclays Premier League. The striker finished the campaign with 25 league goals – two better than the previous term – and he was named the Championship Player of the Year. He also scored his first professional hat-trick in a 3–3 draw against Norwich at Molineux.

↑ Sylvan Ebanks-Blake was released by Manchester United without playing a Premier League game for them, but he has found great success with Wolves.

STEVE IS UNBEATA-BULL

There was no shortage of goals at Wolves when Steve Bull was around. The prolific striker holds the record as the club's all-time top goalscorer, having netted 306 times in all competitions and scored 250 in the league between 1986 and 1999. Bull scored an incredible 52 times in season 1987/88 – a club record for the most goals in a single campaign – and he also grabbed 18 hat-tricks for Wanderers.

← Steve Bull, the last third-tier player to earn a full England cap, acknowledges the Wolves fans after his testimonial against Brazil's Santos in August 1997.

JODY'S ART ATTACK

Defender Jody Craddock may be best known as a vital part of Wolves' rearguard, but off the pitch he has also made quite a name for himself as an artist. The centre-back, who has made over 200 appearances for the club, has sold paintings at art shows across the country and shown his work in several top galleries. His recent work has included paintings of England stars Wayne Rooney and David Beckham, as well as Wolves club legend Steve Bull and several of his team-mates.

↑ As well as painting pictures in his spare time, Jody Craddock has made an art of stopping goals as a key part of the Wolves defensive line.

PLAY-OFF JOY

Wolves reached the Premier League for the first time by beating Sheffield United 3–0 at Cardiff's Millennium Stadium in the 2003 Play-Off Final. Wanderers had finished fifth in the second tier that season and played Reading in a two-legged semi-final. Goals from Mark Kennedy, Nathan Blake and Kenny Miller cut down the Blades in the final to seal promotion.

⇢ (Left to right) Wolves goalscorers Kenny Miller, Nathan Blake and Mark Kennedy celebrate with the second-tier play-off trophy after the 3–0 defeat of Sheffield United won them promotion in 2003.

EUROPE'S

Wolves' back-to-back t
the added bonus of Eu
competition for two su
round of the 1958/59 o
by German side Schalk
get through the prelimi
round, with Bobby Mas
on aggregate. Stan Cull
the last eight.

ALL HAIL THE DOUG

Derek Dougan netted 12 European goals during his
career with Wolves to mak
him the club's leading sc
continental competition. N
those came in the memor
run to the UEFA Cup final i
1971/72, as Dougan finish
that season as the compet
top scorer. The popular str
grabbed four goals agains
Portuguese side Academic
de Coimbra, two against D
outfit Den Haag and a brac
the home leg against Carl Z
Jena. Dougan scored again
when Wolves faced Italian
Juventus in the last eight, b
failed to find the net in the
final success against Feren
or the aggregate defeat to
Tottenham in the final.

↑ Billy Wright receives the FA Cup from Princess Elizabeth after Wolves defeated Leicester City 3–1 in the 1949 final.

JARVIS LOSES OUT

Matt Jarvis took part in more Barclays Premier League defeats than any other player in the 2010/11 campaign. Wolves lost more matches than any other side in the top flight last term, 20, and Jarvis, who was the club's top appearance-maker, was involved in all of them, missing just one league game all season. The England winger, though, scored to help Wanderers to a 4–0 win against Blackpool and also grabbed the only goal of the game at Aston Villa in March 2011.

← Winger Matt Jarvis was Wolves' unluckiest player in the Barclays Premier League last season.

CAPTAIN BILLY

Billy Wright captained Wolves and England with distinction. The defender, who was never booked or sent off, won three top-flight titles with Wanderers in 1954, 1958 and 1959 and the FA Cup in 1949. He also skippered England in three World Cup finals on the way to making a total of 105 appearances for his country. He was the first player in the world to win a century of international caps. Wright captained England a record 90 times and played in 70 consecutive internationals. There is a bronze statue of him outside Wolves' Molineux ground and also a stand named in his honour.

HONVED HEROES

Newspaper headlines hailed Wolves as the best team in the world when they restored some national pride with a 3–2 win over Budapest Honved on December 13 1954. England had been thumped 6–3 by Hungary at Wembley in 1953 and 7–1 in Budapest a year later, and seven of those Hungarian players, including striker Ferenc Puskas, were in the Honved line-up. Wanderers found themselves 2–0 down in the early stages, with Sandor Kocsis and Ferenc Machos scoring for the visitors. But Wolves hit back in the second half, with Johnny Hancocks pulling a goal back from the penalty spot and Roy Swinbourne scoring twice in as many minutes to snatch a famous victory.

WOLVES ARE SAVAGED

The club made the worst possible start to life in the Barclays Premier League when they were beaten 5–1 by Blackburn on the opening day of the 2003/04 campaign. Wanderers were already losing 3–0 when Steffen Iversen pulled a goal back, but two late strikes from Andrew Cole ensured that Rovers got their campaign off to a flying start. Dave Jones' side went on to suffer relegation that season.

← Steffen Iversen was signed by Wolves in 2003 to get goals, but he played in only 16 Barclays Premier League matches and scored just four times.

WANDERERS COMPLETE THE SET

When Wolves were crowned fourth-tier champions in 1987/88 they became the first club to have won all four professional leagues in English football. Their first success came in the third tier in 1923/24, while they scooped the second-tier title for the first time in 1931/32. The top-flight championship followed in 1953/54, and they completed the set 34 years later by claiming the fourth-tier title. The feat has since been matched by Burnley in 1992 and Preston in 1996.

WOLVERHAM
WANDERERS

LATE DRAMA FOR WOLVES

There was plenty of late drama in Wolves' matches during the 2010/11 campaign, with Mick McCarthy's men conceding 10 goals in the last five minutes of games or the injury time that followed. This cost Wanderers seven points in total, with Carlos Vela's equaliser for West Brom in a 1–1 draw at The Hawthorns hurting the most as they dropped two valuable points – and lost the derby bragging rights. However, Wolves did manage to score seven goals themselves between 85 and 90 minutes, gaining four points in the process.

CUP OF PL

Wolves have been FA
lifted the trophy back
game against Everton
high-flying Newcastle
success against Leices
Midlands club to a 3–

TONS OF GO

Wolves became the first te
in three consecutive leagu
They hit the net 103 times i
1957/58 and managed 110
again celebrated the cham
ahead of Manchester Unite
confirmed in 1959/60 whe
than Burnley – but they ha

PARKIN FINE FOR WO

Derek Parkin holds the club record for the most a
having featured 609 times in all competitions – 5
league games – between 1968 and 1982. Full-bac
who joined the club from Huddersfield, claimed tw
Cup winners' medals and a second-tier champions
with the club before signing for Stoke in 1982.

← Derek Parkin was almost an ever-present for Wolves throughout the 1970s. He was called into the full England squad once, in Malta in 1971, but didn't play.

NPOWER CHAMPIONSHIP CLUB RECORDS

The npower Championship is the second tier of English football and, according to recent statistics, is the fourth most popular division in Europe, beating Italy's Serie A and Ligue 1 in France in terms of total attendance. Three clubs – Leeds, Derby and Leicester – played in front of home crowds of over 30,000 fans during the 2010/11 season, while the addition of West Ham, Birmingham and Southampton will mean a total of 10 teams at this level who have the capacity to house that number of supporters.

Norwich's David Fox (left) and David Nugent of Portsmouth battle for the ball during their npower Championship clash at Fratton Park in May 2011.

Nottingham Forest fans in full voice at the City Ground during the 2010/11 campaign.

BARNSLEY

Barnsley joined The Football League in 1898 and play their home games at Oakwell. The South Yorkshire club spent one season in the top flight in the mid-1990s but have since flitted between the second and third tiers. The Tykes finished the 2010/11 season 14 points and five places clear of the npower Championship relegation zone.

BIG GUNS BEATEN

Barnsley stole the headlines in 2008 when they stunned two of the Barclays Premier League's big guns on the way to the semi-finals of the FA Cup. Brian Howard scored the winner as they knocked Liverpool out in the fifth round with a stunning 2–1 victory at Anfield. A home tie against Chelsea followed in the quarter-finals, with a header from Kayode Odejayi enough to dump the Londoners out of the competition. Barnsley's dream died in the last four when Cardiff claimed a 1–0 win at Wembley.

BARNSLEY BOSSES SINCE DANNY WILSON

John Hendrie	1998–1999
Dave Bassett	1999–2000
Nigel Spackman	2001
Steve Parkin	2001–2002
Glyn Hodges	2002–2003
Gudjon Thordarson	2003–2004
Paul Hart	2004–2005
Andy Ritchie	2005–2006
Simon Davey	2006–2009
Mark Robins	2009–2011
Keith Hill	2011–Present

‥⤳ Danny Wilson failed to keep Barnsley in the Premier League in 1997/98, but his was a hard act to follow.

ROVERS AND OUT FOR WARD

The £4.5million deal that saw Ashley Ward leave for Blackburn in December 1998 remains the record transfer fee received by Barnsley. Striker Ward had moved to Oakwell from Derby for £1.3million ahead of the club's Premier League campaign, and he ended that season with 10 goals. He scored 15 times for the Tykes in 1998/99 before making his big-money move to Ewood Park.

‥⤳ Ashley Ward scored 10 goals for Barnsley in their 1997/98 Premier League season and had netted 15 in half a season before the Tykes received a record transfer fee for him.

TOP-FLIGHT TYKES

The Tykes made it to the Premier League for the only time in their history when they were promoted at the end of 1996/97. Danny Wilson was in charge as they finished runners-up to Bolton in the second tier. Sadly, all three teams promoted that season went down the following term, with the Yorkshire club finishing 19th, ahead of Crystal Palace.

HINE HOLDS SCORING MARK

Ernie Hine is the club's record league goalscorer, having netted 123 times overall in two separate spells. Hine spent five years at Oakwell between 1921 and 1926 before leaving for Leicester, where he also became a crowd favourite. Hine rejoined the Tykes in 1934 having also played for Huddersfield and Manchester United. During his time at Leicester, he played six games for England and scored four goals.

BIRMINGHAM CITY

Birmingham may have spent the majority of their history in the top flight of English football but they find themselves in the npower Championship for the 2011/12 campaign. Their most successful period came in the 1950s and early 1960s, and they won the League Cup in 1963. Blues repeated that feat in 2011, despite going on to suffer relegation.

GLOBAL APPEAL

Birmingham's globe crest was adopted by the club in 1972. It was the winning entry in a newspaper competition to design a new badge. It consists of a globe resting on top of a football, with a ribbon draped around it which carries the name of the club and the year of their formation – 1875. The crest was not worn on City's shirts until the 1976/77 campaign.

A FINE FINISH

The 1955/56 season saw Birmingham finish in their highest league position and reach the final of the FA Cup for the second time in their history. They ended the campaign in sixth place in the top flight, just four points behind runners-up Blackpool. Arthur Turner's side were beaten 3–1 by Manchester City in the FA Cup, with Noel Kinsey scoring Birmingham's goal. Blues' only other final appearance came in 1931 when they lost 2–1 to West Brom.

CARLING CUP BLUES

Blues celebrated winning their first major trophy in 48 years at Wembley in 2011, lifting the Carling Cup following a surprise 2–1 victory over Arsenal, although they did go on to suffer the heartache of relegation from the Barclays Premier League at the end of the season. Birmingham were two points above the drop zone and had two games in hand on most of the teams around them on the day of the Carling Cup final, February 27, but two wins from their last 13 league games – including five defeats in their last six matches – saw them consigned to the drop.

↑ Birmingham were the first team in Premier League history to win the League Cup and be relegated in the same season.

TRICKY TREV

Trevor Francis was 16 years and 139 days old when he set the record as the youngest player ever to pull on a Birmingham shirt. Francis, who went on to become Britain's first £1million footballer, was sent on as a substitute in a second-tier clash against Cardiff on September 5 1970. He played 328 games for Blues and scored 134 goals before moving to Nottingham Forest in 1979. Francis later returned to St Andrew's as manager, leading the club to the League Cup final in 2001.

⇢ Birmingham's most precocious teenager, Trevor Francis, burst onto the football scene in spectacular fashion.

A TRUE BLUE

One of the most famous names in Birmingham's history passed away in 2010. Goalkeeper Gil Merrick was a one-club man, spending 22 years at St Andrew's between 1938 and 1960. That spell makes him the longest-serving Blues player ever, while he also holds the record for the most appearances in a City shirt. Merrick featured in 551 post-war matches, although if you include wartime games that tally is boosted to 713. Merrick went on to manage the club, leading them to the Fairs Cup final in 1961 and League Cup glory in 1963.

⇠ Gil Merrick, saving at the feet of Sunderland's Charlie Fleming (stripes) in 1956, was honoured by Birmingham in 2009 when the Railway Stand at St Andrew's was renamed the Gil Merrick Stand.

BLACKPOOL

The Seasiders have enjoyed an illustrious history, with some of English football's finest players having graced Bloomfield Road over the years. Season 2010/11 saw the club playing in the top flight once again, but although they played an entertaining brand of football, Ian Holloway's side failed to stave off relegation.

↑ Blackpool's longest-serving player, Jimmy Armfield, is approaching 'National Treasure' status.

ARMFIELD A BLACKPOOL LEGEND

Jimmy Armfield spent the whole of his 17-year career with Blackpool and holds the club record for the most appearances, making a total of 568 in the league. Armfield, who played 43 times for England, was part of the Blackpool team that finished the 1955/56 campaign as runners-up in the top flight. Now working in the media as a radio pundit, Armfield is widely regarded as one of the finest players English football has ever produced. He is held in such high esteem at Blackpool that he has a stand at Bloomfield Road named after him, with a statue outside the ground.

THE MATTHEWS FINAL

The 1953 FA Cup final is fondly remembered as 'The Matthews Final' thanks to wing-wizard Stanley Matthews' amazing display in helping Blackpool come from 3–1 down to lift the trophy. Another club legend, Stan Mortensen, scored a hat-trick as the Seasiders hit back to snatch a 4–3 win against Bolton at Wembley, but it was Matthews who really shone. Bill Perry scored the winning goal from a Matthews cross in injury time.

⌐ Charlie Adam's spot-kick prowess helped earn him a move to Liverpool for the 2011/12 campaign.

TROPHY JOY FOR SEASIDERS

The club have won the Football League Trophy on two occasions. They eased to a 4–1 victory against Cambridge in March 2002, with John Murphy, Chris Clarke, John Hills and Scott Taylor on the scoresheet. Two years later, they made it back to Cardiff's Millennium Stadium, with striker Murphy on target again in a 2–0 win over Southend.

↑ Blackpool had to wait for 49 years after 'The Matthews Final' before they won another major trophy, beating Cambridge United 4–1 in the 2002 Football League Trophy final in Cardiff.

BIG-TIME CHARLIE

Record signing Charlie Adam took more penalties individually than 16 of the other 19 Barclays Premier League clubs did in total in 2010/11. The talented midfielder, who joined the Seasiders for £500,000 on a permanent deal from Rangers at the start of the 2009/10 campaign, had eight attempts from the spot. He took two in quick succession against Tottenham at the start of May 2011, missing the first one but keeping his nerve to notch the second a minute later. Adam scored 12 league goals in total, including a stunning 25-yard free-kick at Old Trafford.

GOING DOWN IN STYLE

No side in Premier League history has scored as many goals as Blackpool did in 2010/11 and still been relegated. Ian Holloway's entertainers netted 55 times in their 38 games, putting four past Wigan at the DW Stadium on the opening day to announce their return to the top flight in emphatic style. They also scored four against Bolton in a seven-goal thriller at Bloomfield Road in May 2011 and only failed to score in eight top-flight matches.

BRIGHTON & HOVE ALBION

Promotion to the npower Championship at the end of the 2010/11 campaign ensured a real feelgood factor for Brighton, with the club also having recently moved into their brand new 22,500-seater stadium. The Seagulls last played in the top flight in 1983 – the same season that they made their one and only appearance so far in an FA Cup final.

SEAGULLS SOARING HIGH

Brighton claimed back-to-back promotions as champions in 2000/01 and 2001/02. Micky Adams was in charge as the Seagulls soared to the fourth-tier title. They finished the campaign with 92 points which, until last season's title success, had been their best total since three points for a win was introduced. Adams left for Leicester in October the following year but Peter Taylor successfully completed the job.

←··· Danny Cullip celebrates after scoring for Brighton against Cheltenham during the Seagulls' run to the fourth-tier championship in 2000/01.

BOBBY DAZZLER

England striker Bobby Zamora shot to prominence while playing for Brighton. He moved to the club from Bristol Rovers in August 2000 following a successful loan spell and left for Tottenham in a club-record £1.5million switch three years later having netted 77 goals in 130 league and cup appearances.

↑ Bobby Zamora was an instant hit for Brighton after leaving Bristol Rovers in 2000 and he earned the Seagulls a club-record £1.5million transfer fee when Spurs signed him in 2003.

WARDY WONDERLAND

Peter Ward holds the record for the most goals scored in a single season by a Brighton player. Seagulls legend Ward netted 32 times in the league during the 1976/77 campaign as Albion finished runners-up to Mansfield in the third tier.

GROUNDS FOR OPTIMISM

The club's 13-year wait for a new home finally came to an end in 2011 when the 22,500-seater Falmer Stadium opened. The site was first identified in 1998, with the Seagulls originally expecting the ground to be finished by the mid-2000s. However, delays in gaining planning permission meant that Brighton had to be patient. Their first npower Championship match at the stadium took place on August 6 2011 against Doncaster.

BRIGHTON ROCKING

The Seagulls suffered just two home defeats on their way to the npower League 1 title in 2010/11. Gus Poyet's men took 55 points from a possible 69 at the Withdean Stadium, only losing their last two games of the season to Southampton and Huddersfield. They managed some thrilling home victories, winning 4–3 against both Carlisle and Dagenham and scoring four or more against Hartlepool, Leyton Orient and Plymouth.

····≽ Overjoyed Brighton players celebrate their promotion after clinching the npower League 1 title in some style.

BRISTOL CITY

Bristol City have played their home games at Ashton Gate since 1904, although the club are hoping to move to a new stadium by the summer of 2013. They reached the top flight in 1976 and stayed there for four seasons before suffering relegation in 1980. They have never returned, but came mightily close in 2008 when they were beaten in the Championship Play-Off Final by Hull.

TIGERS TAME ROBINS

The Robins were on the verge of reaching the Barclays Premier League when they made it to the Championship Play-Off Final in 2007/08, but they suffered heartbreak in the Wembley showpiece. They had only been promoted to the second tier that season but defied the pundits to move within sight of making it into the top flight at the first attempt. However, they lost out to a solitary strike from veteran Dean Windass, as he volleyed home to give Hull a 1–0 victory.

⟵ Dejected Bristol City players (left to right) Dele Adebola, Liam Fontaine, Louis Carey and Marvin Elliott after losing to Hull City at Wembley in 2008.

ATYEO IS GOAL KING

John Atyeo is both Bristol City's record appearance holder and their all-time leading goalscorer. He played 645 times for the Robins in a 15-year spell with the club between 1951 and 1966, helping himself to 351 goals – better than a goal every other game! Goal-machine Atyeo, who was only ever a semi-professional footballer, won six England caps, scoring five times.

WALSH WALLOPS GILLS

Tommy 'Tot' Walsh was one of the most prolific marksmen to pull on a City shirt, and he enhanced that reputation when he scored six times in a single match. The striker achieved the amazing feat against Gillingham in a 9–4 win on January 15 1927. The Robins went goal crazy during the course of that season, scoring a club-record haul of 104.

ROBINS NICK STRIKER

City broke their transfer record to sign Nicky Maynard from Crewe for £2.25million in August 2008. Maynard had scored prolifically during two full seasons at Gresty Road, prompting then Robins boss Gary Johnson to pounce. The striker repaid his new manager's faith with 11 goals in 2008/09 and he netted 21 times the following term. Maynard scooped The Football League's Goal of the Year award for 2009 after an acrobatic effort at QPR on Boxing Day.

⟵ Nicky Maynard became Bristol City's most expensive signing when he joined the Robins from Crewe in the summer of 2008.

CITY'S LEADING GOALSCORERS

John Atyeo	351
Tom Ritchie	132
Arnold Rodgers	111
Jimmy Rogers	108
Alan Walsh	99

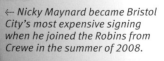

BURNLEY

The Clarets have one of the brightest young managers in The Football League in Eddie Howe and will be targeting the Play-Offs in 2011/12. The Lancashire club have won the top-flight title twice in their history and the FA Cup once, while in 2009 just missed out on another Wembley appearance in the Carling Cup Final.

SO CLOSE FOR CLARETS

The Clarets were two minutes away from reaching the Carling Cup final in 2009. It was the fourth time that Burnley had made it to the last four of the competition, and they had done it the hard way, knocking out London trio Fulham, Chelsea and Arsenal before losing 4–1 in the first leg of their semi-final at Tottenham. The Lancashire club, who were playing in the second tier at the time, managed to force extra time with a stunning 3–0 win at Turf Moor, but goals in the 118th and 120th minutes from Roman Pavlyuchenko and Jermain Defoe snatched victory for Spurs.

⇢When Burnley defender Clarke Carlisle appeared on the TV words and numbers game show Countdown, he managed to avoid asking for a 'foul'!

DAWSON'S DECISION

Jerry Dawson, Burnley's record appearance maker, missed the 1914 FA Cup final at his own request. Goalkeeper Dawson told manager John Haworth the day before the game that he did not think he would be able to play the full 90 minutes due to a rib injury he had sustained the week before. There were no substitutes in those days, meaning that the Clarets could have been left without a keeper. Dawson, who played 522 league games for the club between 1907 and 1928, was given a special winners' medal in recognition of his selfless decision.

ELLIOTT WADES IN

Wade Elliott scored the goal that earned Burnley a place in the top tier in 2008/09. The Clarets finished fifth in the second tier to secure a play-off spot. A 3–0 aggregate win over Reading in the semi-finals set up a clash with Sheffield United at Wembley. Winger Elliott sent the Burnley fans wild with a stunning strike, finding the top corner with a superb first-time curling effort after he had created the chance with a jinking run from inside his own half.

† Wade Elliott (11) turns away after scoring the only goal of the Championship Play-Off Final against Sheffield United at Wembley.

CARLISLE'S COUNTDOWN

Clarke Carlisle proved himself to be something of a brainbox when the Burnley centre-back beat 12 other players to scoop the title of Britain's Brainiest Footballer in 2002 and then featured on popular daytime TV game show Countdown in February 2010. Carlisle was a winner on two occasions before losing on his third Countdown appearance. Following his first victory, the defender admitted: 'I can't say it's better than winning a big football game – but it's up there!'

GOLDEN GRAHAM

Graham Alexander became only the second player to reach 1,000 competitive outfield appearances in English football history during the 2010/11 season. He achieved the amazing landmark during the Clarets' 2–1 win against Swansea on April 16, coming on for the last three minutes. Easter Monday was designated 'Graham Alexander Day' by the club, with the veteran defender receiving an award on the pitch in recognition of his feat and a guard of honour from his team-mates and opponents Portsmouth. The Scot holds the record as the oldest Premier League debutant and turned 40 in 2011.

† Graham Alexander reached his landmark almost 20 years to the day after making his debut for Scunthorpe.

CARDIFF CITY

Cardiff were formed as Riverside FC in 1899 and play their home games at the Cardiff City Stadium. The Bluebirds have not played top-flight football since 1962 but went close in both of the last two seasons. They made it to the Championship Play-Off Final in 2010 before losing out to Blackpool, and they were beaten by Reading in the semi-finals last term.

↑ Alan Cork's reign as Cardiff manager saw the Bluebirds score goals at a record pace.

BLUEBIRDS ARE FLYING

Cardiff established a new club mark for the most league goals scored in a single season in 2000/01. Under boss Alan Cork, they rattled in 95 on their way to a second-place finish and automatic promotion from the fourth tier. They finished 10 points behind champions Brighton but had scored 22 more goals. Notable victories included a 6–1 win at home to Exeter and 5–2 success at Macclesfield. Cardiff scored four or more goals on nine occasions in the league that season. More success came as they managed to go through the entire term unbeaten at home in the league, completing that run with a 3–1 victory over Shrewsbury on the penultimate weekend of the campaign.

WELSH WONDERS

The Bluebirds have the honour of being the only club from outside of England to have won the FA Cup. Their solitary success came in 1927 when they beat pre-match favourites Arsenal 1–0 at Wembley. Forward Hughie Ferguson scored the only goal of the game to give the Welshmen a memorable victory. Captain Fred Keenor received the trophy from King George V just seven years after Cardiff had entered The Football League.

CARDIFF'S MAJOR HONOURS

FA Cup	Winners	1926/27
FA Cup	Runners-up	1924/25, 2007/08
FA Charity Shield	Winners	1927/28
Top flight	Runners-up	1923/24
Second tier	Runners-up	1920/21, 1951/52, 1959/60
Third tier (South)	Champions	1946/47
Third tier	Champions	1992/93
Third tier	Runners-up	1975/76, 1982/83
Fourth tier	Runners-up	1987/88, 2000/01

⇢ Cardiff's winning goal in the 1927 FA Cup final came courtesy of an error by Arsenal's Welsh international goalkeeper Dan Lewis.

↙ The Bluebirds became the ninth club of striker Craig Bellamy's career.

HOME-TOWN HERO RETURNS

The Welsh club pulled off an amazing transfer coup when Craig Bellamy arrived at Cardiff City Stadium on a season-long loan deal from Manchester City in August 2010. He had played regularly in the top flight in 2009/10 but was deemed surplus to requirements by Roberto Mancini. Bellamy was desperate to help his home-town club achieve their Premier League dream, and although he scored 11 goals as Cardiff finished fourth, they were beaten by Reading in the play-offs.

↓ Goalscorer Rob Earnshaw celebrates another strike at Ninian Park in February 2003, one of his 31 for the Bluebirds that season.

ROB NETS A HATFUL

Robert Earnshaw has scored the most league goals in a single season for Cardiff. The Wales international netted 31 times in 2002/03 as the Bluebirds gained promotion from the third tier via the play-offs. Earnshaw, who came through the Cardiff ranks and has also scored regularly for his country, netted two hat-tricks in the league that season and another treble in the League Cup. He left the club when he signed for West Brom in August 2004.

COVENTRY CITY

Coventry were in the top flight for 34 years between 1967 and 2001 but have since occupied the second tier. They have played their home games at the Ricoh Arena since 2005, with some notable players having pulled on the famous Sky Blue shirt both there and at their former Highfield Road ground.

HAPPY AS CLARRIE

A superb career at Coventry helped make Clarrie Bourton one of the most prolific strikers ever to have graced English football. He is the Sky Blues' all-time top marksman, with 171 league goals between 1931 and 1937. He also holds the club record for scoring the most league goals in a single season – 49 in 1931/32.

DUBLIN'S NET RETURN

Dion Dublin scored a record-equalling 23 goals in a top-flight season for the club in 1997/98. Dublin, who joined the Sky Blues for £2million from Manchester United in September 1994 and scored 61 goals in 145 league matches, could not surpass the record set by Ian Wallace in the 1977/78 campaign. Dublin left City for Aston Villa in 1998.

⇢ *Dion Dublin celebrates yet another goal for Coventry during the 1997/98 season. His haul of 23 goals is a joint club record in the top flight.*

OGGY, OGGY, OGGY!

Steve Ogrizovic holds a special place in Coventry folklore as the club's record appearance holder. He featured in 601 matches in all competitions during a 16-year spell with the Sky Blues between 1984 and 2000. Goalkeeper Ogrizovic is also the third oldest player to have appeared in a Premier League game, aged 42 years and 237 days.

↑ *Robbie Keane's year at Coventry saw his transfer value double, with the Sky Blues paying and receiving club-record fees for his services in 1999 and 2000.*

ROBBIE THE BANK

Robbie Keane holds two transfer records for Coventry. His arrival for a reported £6.5million from Wolves in August 1999 is the most the Sky Blues have ever paid for a player, although that record is held jointly with Craig Bellamy, who cost the same amount from Norwich in August 2000. Keane was sold for £13million to Italian giants Inter Milan in July 2000 – the biggest transfer fee that City have received.

SKY BLUES' CUP OF CHEER

Coventry won the FA Cup for the only time in their history in 1987. John Sillett and George Curtis were in charge as the Sky Blues beat Tottenham 3–2, with Keith Houchen scoring one of the great FA Cup final goals. The striker arrived in the box to power home a stunning diving header which sent the game into extra time. City went on to secure the trophy thanks to an own goal from luckless Tottenham defender Gary Mabbutt, with the Spurs centre-back inadvertently turning the ball into his own net when he failed to deal with a cross from Lloyd McGrath.

↑ *Keith Houchen's flying header is probably the most famous goal in Coventry's history. It was the second equaliser in their 3–2 FA Cup final defeat of Tottenham at Wembley in 1987.*

CRYSTAL PALACE

Crystal Palace are an established npower Championship side based in south-east London. The Eagles have spent 12 of the last 13 seasons in the second tier, surviving in 2009/10 despite a 10-point deduction for financial difficulties. They avoided relegation again in 2010/11 under the guidance of club legend Dougie Freedman, who has taken well to a move into management.

UNSTOPPABLE SIMPSON

Peter Simpson scored 19 hat-tricks for the Eagles between September 1929 and November 1933 on his way to becoming the club's all-time leading goalscorer. Simpson, who scored six times in one game against Exeter in October 1930, also holds the club landmark for the most goals in a single campaign – 46 in 1930/31. He grabbed 165 goals for the club in total.

↓ Ian Wright is third on Crystal Palace's all-time scoring charts, but is the leader in post-war goals.

TOFFEES STUCK ON JOHNSON

Palace received a club-record £8.6million from Everton for Andrew Johnson in May 2006. The hot-shot striker had netted 17 goals for the Eagles in the 2005/06 season, prompting interest from the Toffees. The Barclays Premier League outfit were impressed enough to beat their previous biggest spend in order to sign the prolific frontman. Johnson, who made 160 appearances in total for Palace, got off the mark after 15 minutes of his Everton debut – a 2–1 win against Watford. He later left the Toffees to sign for Fulham in 2008.

←··· Andrew Johnson's 84 goals for Crystal Palace came at a rate of better than one every other match for the Eagles.

PALACE'S LEADING GOALSCORERS

Peter Simpson	165
Ted Smith	124
Ian Wright	117
Clinton Morrison	113
Mark Bright	113
Dougie Freedman	108
George Clarke	106
Johnny Byrne	101
Albert Dawes	92
Andrew Johnson	84

BOSTOCK SOARS FOR EAGLES

John Bostock is the youngest player to have pulled on a Palace shirt. He was 15 years and 287 days old when he came on as a substitute with 20 minutes remaining in a 2–0 home defeat against Watford in October 2007. Bostock left Selhurst Park for the Barclays Premier League at the age of 16, joining Tottenham. He spent part of the 2009/10 season on loan at Brentford and was sent out to Hull for five months last term.

↓ Alan Pardew (11) heads home the Crystal Palace winner in the 1990 FA Cup semi-final.

SEMI-FINAL STUNNER

The Eagles were involved in one of the greatest FA Cup semi-finals of all time when they enjoyed their best-ever run in the competition in 1990. They lost the final to Manchester United following a replay, but their 4–3 extra-time success against Liverpool to reach Wembley is fondly remembered. Andy Gray's header in the last minute of normal time made it 3–3, with Alan Pardew grabbing the winner.

DERBY COUNTY

Derby were among the 12 founder members of The Football League in 1888. They were one of the dominant forces in the top flight during the 1970s and impressed in Europe during that time. Current boss Nigel Clough is the son of legendary Rams manager Brian, who was in charge during the club's glory years.

EURO DREAM DIES

The Rams were 180 minutes away from a place in the European Cup final in 1973. Under the late, great Brian Clough, they had already knocked Eusebio's Benfica out of the competition in an earlier round when they came up against Juventus in a two-legged semi-final. The Italian giants won the first tie 3–1, and that proved too much for Derby to overcome, as they had Roger Davies sent off and Alan Hinton missed a penalty in a goalless return.

TITLE TRIUMPH FOR RAMS

Derby were top-flight champions twice during the 1970s. Brian Clough guided the Rams to the first title in their history in 1971/72 as they beat Leeds, Liverpool and Manchester City by a point. Dave Mackay then took over the helm and ensured further glory in 1974/75 in his first full season as manager, edging out Liverpool and Ipswich by two points.

← *Brian Clough (left, with assistant Peter Taylor) made Derby a top club in the 1970s, winning their first league title in 1972.*

GOAL WOE FOR WARD

Ashley Ward scored Derby's last league goal at the Baseball Ground and the first at their Pride Park Stadium – although the second has since been wiped from the history books. Arsenal ran out 3–1 winners in May 1997 after Ward had opened the scoring in the final game at the Rams' old ground. The striker was then the first name on the scoresheet in the clash with Wimbledon in August of that year as they began life at their new stadium, only for the floodlights to fail and the match to be abandoned shortly after half-time with Derby leading 2–1.

← *Ashley Ward's first competitive goal at Pride Park was negated when Derby's match with Wimbledon was abandoned.*

HECTOR SETS APPEARANCE MARK

Kevin Hector holds the record for the most appearances in a Derby shirt. Hector, who played in the successful Rams team of the 1970s, featured in 486 league games and 589 in total in two spells at the club, with a stint at Canadian side Vancouver Whitecaps sandwiched in between.

↑ *Kevin Hector (taking the ball past Everton's Henry Newton) scored 201 goals in all competitions for Derby in two spells, having netted 113 for Bradford Park Avenue before first joining the Rams. He earned two England caps in 1973, both as a substitute.*

BLOOMING MARVELLOUS

Steve Bloomer holds a special place in the club's history following his extraordinary goalscoring exploits. He netted 292 league goals and 332 in total for the Rams in two spells from 1892–1905 and 1910–1913. He is Derby's record all-time goalscorer – a feat that is celebrated by a bust of Bloomer next to the home dugout at Pride Park.

DONCASTER ROVERS

Doncaster Rovers only returned to The Football League in 2003 but have gone on to make it to the npower Championship in impressive fashion, gaining promotion from the third tier in 2007/08. They have also won the Johnstone's Paint Trophy since making their return. Rovers enjoyed their best season for 59 years with a 12th-place finish in 2009/10 but had to settle for 21st in 2010/11.

DONCASTER'S ASCENT TO THE CHAMPIONSHIP

2002/03	Conference National	3rd (Promotion)
2003/04	Fourth tier	1st (Promotion)
2004/05	Third tier	10th
2005/06	Third tier	8th
2006/07	Third tier	11th
2007/08	Third tier	3rd (Promotion)

TROPHY GLORY FOR ROVERS

Doncaster won their first cup final in April 2007 when they took the Johnstone's Paint Trophy, beating Bristol Rovers 3–2. Two goals in the opening five minutes from Jonathan Forte and Paul Heffernan put Doncaster in command, but the Pirates fought back to take the game into extra time. Graeme Lee's header won it for Doncaster. A year later, Doncaster beat Leeds 1–0 in the League 1 Play-Off Final.

↑ *Thirteen months after winning their first major cup final, Doncaster Rovers were back at Wembley and they were celebrating again following a 1–0 defeat of Leeds United to win the League 1 Play-Off Final.*

GOODBYE TO BELLE VUE

Rovers played their first competitive game at the Keepmoat Stadium on New Year's Day 2007, having spent 84 years at their Belle Vue ground. Huddersfield were the first visitors, beaten 3–0. Mark McCammon had the distinction of scoring the first goal at the new stadium, while Town's Adnan Ahmed was shown the first red card, with Pawel Abbott and Doncaster's Gareth Roberts also dismissed that day.

LUCKY BREAK FOR ALICK

Alick Jeffrey is the youngest player to have appeared for Doncaster in The Football League, aged 15 years and 229 days. Jeffrey made 262 appearances in two spells between 1954 and 1969, scoring 129 goals. Amazingly, Jeffrey actually retired from professional football in 1957 after failing to fully recover from a broken leg. But, after moving to Australia and taking up playing again, he returned to the club in 1963, going on to make another 191 appearances.

ROVERS MAKING PROGRESS

Doncaster made a remarkable leap from playing Conference football to becoming an established npower Championship club in just a few years. They made it back into The Football League in 2003 with a 3–2 play-off victory against Dagenham & Redbridge, before going on to claim the fourth-tier title the following season. A period of consolidation followed before a third-place finish in 2007/08 saw them book another play-off date, this time against Leeds. James Hayter scored the only goal of the game to send Rovers up.

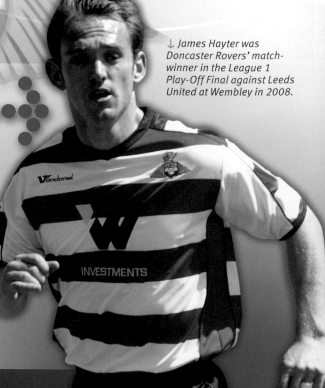

↓ *James Hayter was Doncaster Rovers' match-winner in the League 1 Play-Off Final against Leeds United at Wembley in 2008.*

HULL CITY

'THE TIGERS'

Prior to 2008, Hull was the biggest city in Europe never to have had a top-flight football team, but that all changed when they were promoted via the play-offs for their first Barclays Premier League campaign. The Tigers avoided relegation in 2008/09, but they could not repeat the feat a year on and they are now back in the second tier.

DUANE AT THE DOUBLE

Duane Darby scored a double hat-trick for Hull in an extraordinary FA Cup tie against Whitby Town in November 1996. The non-League side had forced a replay at Boothferry Park after holding City to a goalless draw. However, the two teams more than made up for a lack of goals in the first match, with the Tigers going on to claim an amazing 8–4 victory! Striker Darby scored four goals in normal time – the fourth coming in the 89th minute to send the game into extra time – and he went on to net two more as Hull finally secured their progress.

THE GREAT ESCAPE

Hull were bottom of The Football League in November 1998 and they looked likely to slip into the Conference when Warren Joyce replaced Mark Hateley in the managerial hot-seat. It was not until the turn of the year that results finally began to pick up, but City lost just four times in their last 22 games to pull clear of danger, confirming their fourth-tier status with just a few games to spare.

⤏ As player-manager, Warren Joyce oversaw Hull's escape from relegation to the Conference in 1998/99.

† Martin Carruthers models one of the most memorable kits in English football history. These Tigers didn't scare too many teams as they tried vainly to climb out of the third tier.

MUTRIE'S THE MAN

Les Mutrie set a club record when he scored 14 goals in nine consecutive games in season 1981/82. The sequence started on February 13 1982 with a brace in a 2–2 draw at Tranmere, and the prolific striker followed that up with four goals in a 5–2 success against Hartlepool. The last game of his remarkable scoring run came on March 20, with Mutrie netting in a 3–1 win at home to Port Vale. Keith Edwards came close to equalling the record in 1989 when he managed 13 goals in eight consecutive matches.

EYE-SORE OF THE TIGERS

Several clubs have sported some 'questionable' kits over the years, but Hull fans have had to endure a few of their own. From 1992 until the end of the 1994/95 season the Tigers made the most of their nickname, taking their famous amber and black stripes one step further by wearing tiger-print shirts!

VOLLEY GOOD SHOW

Dean Windass cemented his popularity with Hull fans by scoring the goal that earned the club a place in the top flight. Windass, who scored 77 goals in 236 league appearances for City over two spells, volleyed home the only goal of the game in the 2008 Championship Play-Off Final against Bristol City to complete a remarkable campaign.

⤏ Dean Windass celebrates the final whistle after his goal had given Hull City their first-ever place in England's top tier. His goals had already made him a legend on Humberside.

IPSWICH TOWN

Ipswich have a proud history which has seen them win the top-flight title and the UEFA Cup, among other trophies. Two of English football's greatest managers – Sir Alf Ramsay and Sir Bobby Robson – enjoyed success with the Suffolk club, while Paul Jewell is the man who has more recently been tasked with continuing the traditions of Portman Road.

TOP BOSSES GET TOWN HONOUR

Ipswich have paid a special tribute to two of their greatest managers with statues which stand outside their Portman Road ground. Sir Alf Ramsey, who led the club to the top-flight title in 1961/62 before taking charge of England and guiding them to the 1966 World Cup, was first to be immortalised with a bronze sculpture in 2000, with a life-size statue of the late Sir Bobby Robson following two years later. Robson guided Town to FA Cup glory in 1978 and won the UEFA Cup with the club in 1981.

⟵ A scarf adorns the statue of Sir Bobby Robson outside Portman Road in July 2009, placed there by a fan following the former manager's death.

JOHN WALKS OFF WITH AWARD

John Wark is the only Ipswich player to have won the PFA Player of the Year trophy. The Scot scooped the accolade following a string of impressive performances during the 1980/81 season which saw the Tractor Boys win the UEFA Cup. Wark scored 14 goals on the way to the final, netting 36 times in total over the course of the campaign. Another Town player has, however, won the PFA's Young Player of the Year award – Kevin Beattie claiming the inaugural prize in 1973/74.

WICKHAM HITS THE BIG TIME

Connor Wickham's stunning form for Ipswich in 2010/11 helped to secure a big-money move to the Barclays Premier League. Dozens of scouts had descended on Portman Road throughout the campaign as Wickham continued to improve, but in the end he opted for a move to Sunderland ahead of the new season for a fee that could rise to £12million. In his last 19 league games in a Town shirt he scored an impressive nine goals. That included a hat-trick at Doncaster in a 6–0 win. Wickham made his debut aged 16 years and 11 days, becoming the youngest player ever to pull on an Ipswich shirt.

BADGE IS NO COMPETITION

Town's club badge actually came about as the result of a competition, run back in 1972. The winning entry, designed by John Gammage – a former treasurer of the Town supporters club – features the famous Suffolk Punch horse with a football at its feet. The current badge was given a facelift again in 2005, with a red border replacing the original yellow one.

↓ Connor Wickham beat the record held by Jason Dozzell when he became Town's youngest player in April 2009.

IPSWICH HONOURS LIST

Top flight

Champions	1961/62
Runners-up	1980/81, 1981/82
Second tier	
Champions	1960/61, 1967/68, 1991/92
Play-off winners	1999/00
Third tier (South)	
Champions	1953/54, 1956/57
FA Cup	
Winners	1977/78
UEFA Cup	
Winners	1980/81

↑ John Wark's performances in 1980/81 earned him the PFA Player of the Year award. He also set a UEFA Cup record with 14 goals from midfield as Ipswich won their only European trophy.

LEEDS UNITED

Leeds are a club steeped in history, having won the top-flight title three times. They were FA Cup winners in 1972 and have also competed in the Champions League, making it to the semi-finals in 2001. The Whites are one of the best supported npower Championship teams, with the Elland Road faithful as strong and passionate as ever.

FOND MEMORIES FOR LEEDS

Leeds may have been playing in the third tier recently, but it was not so long ago that they competed in a UEFA Champions League semi-final. In season 1999/00, the Yorkshire club finished third in the Premier League to qualify for Europe's top competition. They went on to reach the last four in May 2001, where they were beaten 3–0 over two legs by Spanish club Valencia.

⋯▸ John Charles was a Leeds legend. The 'Gentle Giant' made a brief return to the club in 1962, between spells at Juventus and Roma.

HIS NAME IS RIO

Rio Ferdinand's move to Manchester United in July 2002 netted Leeds a cool £12million profit. The Whites had broken their club record by splashing out £18million to sign the classy defender from West Ham in November 2000 but the England international just got better and better and left Elland Road two years later for a then British transfer record of £30million!

GOALSCORING GIANT

John Charles is second in the list of Leeds' all-time Football League goalscorers, but he does hold the club record for the most goals in a single season. The 'Gentle Giant', as he was affectionately known, netted 42 times in the league in Leeds' 1953/54 campaign. He left Elland Road for Italian giants Juventus in 1957 for a then British record transfer fee of £65,000.

TITLE-WINNING WHITES

Leeds were top-flight champions in 1991/92 – the year before the Premier League began. Howard Wilkinson was in charge of a side featuring the talents of Gary Speed, Gordon Strachan and Gary McAllister. Striker Lee Chapman ended the campaign with 16 goals in 38 games as the Whites claimed the title by four points from Manchester United. Bizarrely, Leeds finished the following season just two points above the relegation zone having failed to win a game away from Elland Road!

LEEDS' LONGEST-SERVING MANAGERS

Don Revie	1961–1974
Billy Hampson	1935–1947
Howard Wilkinson	1988–1996
Dick Ray	1927–1935
Arthur Fairclough	1920–1927

⟵ Howard Wilkinson's success with Leeds in 1991/92 makes him the last English manager to win the top-flight title.

⟵ It proved to be a transfer masterstroke when Leeds signed Rio Ferdinand during the 2000/01 season.

LEICESTER CITY

The Foxes have established themselves as a force in the npower Championship. With former England coach Sven-Goran Eriksson attracting a host of exciting signings, Leicester are one of the most talked-about teams in the division. Arguably the Foxes' most impressive achievements have come in The League Cup (now called the Carling Cup), which they have lifted three times.

TITLE CRUISE

The Foxes' haul of 96 points on the way to winning the League 1 title in 2008/09 is the most they have managed in a single season. Their relegation from the Championship the previous term was quickly banished from memory as manager Nigel Pearson led them to three wins from their first four games. They kept their good form going for the rest of the campaign and promotion was finally confirmed with a 2–0 win at Southend on April 18 2009.

MATT FINISHES FASTEST

Matt Fryatt broke the record for the fastest goal in Leicester's history when he scored after just nine seconds against Preston in 2006. Gareth Williams' chip over the defence released Fryatt, and he coolly slotted past Preston goalkeeper Carlo Nash. Unfortunately for Leicester, they went on to lose the game 2–1. Three other players – Tom Dryburgh, Derek Hines and Ian McNeil – had scored after 10 seconds for the Foxes in the 1950s. Fryatt also rewrote the record books in 2008/09 when he became the first Leicester player since Derek Dougan 42 years earlier to net 20 goals before Christmas.

Matt Fryatt didn't only score early for Leicester, he also scored often, especially in the 2008/09 season, when he netted 32 times.

Graham Cross (white) is denied by Manchester United's David Gaskell and Maurice Setters in the 1963 FA Cup final.

A move to join the Foxes helped to reignite Nigerian striker Ayegbeni Yakubu's career.

LEICESTER'S LEADING APPEARANCES

Graham Cross	599
Adam Black	557
Hugh Adcock	460
Mark Wallington	460
Steve Walsh	449
Arthur Chandler	419
John Sjoberg	413
Mal Griffiths	409
Steve Whitworth	400
Sep Smith	373

FOXES' SECOND HOME

City were regular visitors to Wembley between 1990 and 2000, featuring in seven finals. They reached the League Cup final three times during that period, drawing 1–1 with Middlesbrough then winning the replay 1–0 at Hillsborough in 1997, losing 1–0 to Tottenham in 1999 and beating Tranmere 2–1 in 2000. They also played in four play-off finals, losing against Blackburn (1992) and Swindon (1993) and beating Derby (1994) and then Crystal Palace (1996).

FEED THE YAK!

Ayegbeni Yakubu proved a big hit for the Foxes when he arrived on loan from Barclays Premier League side Everton in January 2011. The burly Nigerian striker bagged 11 goals in 19 starts, opening the scoring on his debut at Preston and netting a superb hat-trick in a 3–3 draw against his former club Middlesbrough in April. After scoring four goals in his final three matches, Yakubu returned to Goodison Park.

MIDDLESBROUGH

Boro have become a big name again with the help of chairman Steve Gibson, winning their first major trophy, the Carling Cup, in 2004. The Riverside Stadium club ended the 2010/11 campaign as one of the division's form sides and secured a 12th-place finish, with the challenge now to build on that for 2011/12.

REACH FOR THE STARS

Teenage winger Adam Reach scored on his senior debut as a substitute in Middlesbrough's 3–0 win against Doncaster on the last day of the 2010/11 season. The 18-year-old was one of eight players aged 21 or under to be handed first-team experience by Boro boss Tony Mowbray that term. Goalkeeper Connor Ripley, the son of club legend Stuart, endured a tough start to his senior career, conceding three times in a 5–2 defeat at Reading after replacing the injured Jason Steele.

⋯ Probably England's most successful Brazilian import, midfielder Juninho had three spells with Middlesbrough, lastly from 2002 to 2004.

BY GEORGE, THAT'S A RECORD!

George Camsell scored 59 league goals in a single season in the second tier in 1926/27 and netted 325 league goals in total for Middlesbrough between 1925 and 1939 – both club records. Camsell, who cost Middlesbrough just £600 from Durham City, scored 24 hat-tricks during his 14-year career on Teesside. He also made nine appearances for England, scoring 18 times.

⬆ George Camsell's 59 goals in a season, in 1926/27, was a Football League record for only 12 months, but it remains the best ever in England's second tier.

MIDDLESBROUGH'S BIGGEST LEAGUE VICTORIES

9–0	v Brighton	(1958)
8–0	v Huddersfield	(1950)
8–0	v Sheffield Wednesday	(1974)
10–3	v Sheffield United	(1933)
9–2	v Blackpool	(1938)

ARMSTRONG THE EVER-PRESENT

David Armstrong has made the most consecutive appearances for Boro. 'Spike', as he was affectionately known, played a remarkable 305 league games in a row for the club – 356 in all competitions – between March 1973 and August 1980. He was voted Middlesbrough's Player of the Year in 1980 and made his England debut in the same year against Australia. Ray Yeoman is second in the list of unbroken league appearances for Boro with 190.

SAMBA DUO DANCE IN... AND OUT

The club's record transfer cost them £12million, with the same figure also representing the biggest fee they have ever received for a player – and both deals involved Brazilians. Samba star Juninho moved to Teesside from Sao Paulo in October 1995, wowing the crowds for two years to make himself a fans' favourite before leaving for Atletico Madrid in a £12million move. He returned for two more spells with the club from 1999–2000 and 2002–2004. Afonso Alves is Boro's record signing, costing £12million from Dutch side Heerenveen in January 2008. He made just 42 Barclays Premier League appearances and scored 10 goals before he left for Qatar in September 2009.

MILLWALL

MILLWALL

Millwall originally played their home matches on the Isle of Dogs, moving to the London Borough of Lewisham in 1910. They were a top-flight club for two seasons between 1988 and 1990, securing their highest-ever finish of 10th in that time. The Lions were a second-tier side when they reached the FA Cup final under Dennis Wise in 2004.

LIONS HUNGARY FOR EUROPE

Millwall made it all the way to the FA Cup final in 2004 and as a result qualified for the UEFA Cup the following year. The Lions avoided Premier League opposition until the FA Cup final, where they lost 3–0 to Manchester United. Their European adventure ended at the first hurdle, as they were beaten 4–2 over two legs by Hungarian champions Ferencvaros.

HARRIS ROARS INTO HISTORY BOOKS

Neil Harris is Millwall's all-time leading goalscorer. Harris, who turned 34 in 2011, overtook Teddy Sheringham's record with his 112th goal for the Lions in an FA Cup tie against Crewe in January 2009. He improved the mark to 117 by the end of that campaign and went on to make it 138 in all competitions by the time he left the club for npower League 2 Southend on a free transfer in June 2011.

GRAHAM HAS MILLWALL MOVING UP

George Graham began his managerial career at Millwall. The Lions were bottom of the third tier when he took over during 1982/83 and, after saving the club from relegation, he guided them to promotion two years later. Graham left the club for Arsenal in 1986, where he went on to spend nine successful years.

↑ *Neil Harris overcame illness and injury to become Millwall's all-time leading scorer. This goal celebration was in the FA Cup against AFC Wimbledon in 2009.*

←··· *Steve Morison actually played eight times for England C before switching allegiance to make his full international debut for Wales.*

LIONS' TOP LEAGUE SCORERS SINCE 2002/03

2002/03	Neil Harris	12
2003/04	Tim Cahill/Neil Harris	9
2004/05	Barry Hayles	12
2005/06	Ben May	10
2006/07	Darren Byfield	16
2007/08	Gary Alexander	7
2008/09	Gary Alexander	11
2009/10	Steve Morison	20
2010/11	Steve Morison	15

MORISON HARD TO REPLACE

Millwall will miss Steve Morison's goals in 2011/12. The Wales international was the Lions' leading scorer in both 2009/10 and last term, netting 35 goals during his time at the club. Morison, who cost just £130,000 from Stevenage in the summer of 2009, joined Barclays Premier League new-boys Norwich for a fee that is thought to be higher than the record £2.3million received for Mark Kennedy in March 1995.

NOTTINGHAM FOREST

Nottingham Forest are one of the oldest football clubs in the world and one of the most successful in England. Among other things, they have won the top-flight title, the FA Cup, the League Cup and back-to-back European Cups, with their greatest spell of success coming in the late 1970s and early 1980s.

FOREST MANAGERS SINCE BRIAN CLOUGH

Frank Clark	1993–1996
Stuart Pearce	1996–1997
Dave Bassett	1997–1998
Ron Atkinson	1999
David Platt	1999–2001
Paul Hart	2001–2004
Joe Kinnear	2004
Gary Megson	2005–2006
Colin Calderwood	2006–2008
Billy Davies	2009–2011
Steve McClaren	2011–Present

FOREST SOW THE SEED

Nottingham Forest were the second English club to win back-to-back European Cups when they triumphed in 1979 and 1980. Forest enjoyed outstanding success under then manager Brian Clough, beating Swedish side Malmo 1–0 in Munich's Olympic Stadium in 1979 before retaining the trophy a year later with a 1–0 victory against Hamburg in Madrid. Martin O'Neill was in the Forest side that day, while Kevin Keegan was playing for the Germans. Liverpool were the first English back-to-back winners, having achieved the feat in 1977 and 1978.

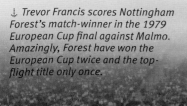

↓ Trevor Francis scores Nottingham Forest's match-winner in the 1979 European Cup final against Malmo. Amazingly, Forest have won the European Cup twice and the top-flight title only once.

CLOUGH REIGNS SUPREME

Brian Clough is the most successful manager in Nottingham Forest's history and is widely regarded as one of the greatest English football has ever seen. Clough also had spells in charge of Hartlepool, Derby, Brighton and Leeds during his long career, but his finest achievements came at the City Ground. Arguably his greatest feat was leading Forest to back-to-back European Cup triumphs in 1979 and 1980. Those successes came after the club had won the old Division One title in 1977/78 and claimed the runners-up spot the following season. Clough also took Forest to six League Cup finals during his 18 years in charge of the club from 1975–1993 – winning four and losing two. He also reached the FA Cup final in 1991.

↑ The charismatic Brian Clough (left) won two European Cups and one top-flight title at Forest.

FOREST RECORD CHOPPED DOWN

After going through the entire 2003/04 Premier League season unbeaten, Arsenal broke a record that had been held by Nottingham Forest for 26 years. Prior to the Gunners' 49-game streak, the previous benchmark was 42, which the Reds had achieved under Brian Clough between November 26 1977 and November 25 1978. Forest's run spanned across two seasons, starting with a goalless draw at home to West Brom and ending almost a year later at Liverpool, where they lost 2–0.

FRANCIS IS ONE IN A MILLION

Nottingham Forest were the first British club to pay £1million for a player when they signed Trevor Francis from Birmingham in February 1979. Francis scored the winning goal in the European Cup final against Malmo in May of that year but missed out against Hamburg the following season due to injury.

← Trevor Francis repaid Brian Clough's faith in him by scoring the winner in the 1979 European Cup final.

PETERBOROUGH UNITED

Peterborough are relative newcomers to The Football League, having been admitted in 1960. The London Road club took little time to make their mark among English football's elite, and they have since gone from strength to strength. After suffering relegation from the second tier in 2009/10, they now find themselves back there following an npower League 1 Play-Off Final win against Huddersfield.

POSH SPICE UP THE LEAGUE

Peterborough scored a remarkable 134 league goals on the way to the fourth-tier title in 1960/1961. Incredibly, striker Terry Bly scored 52 of those as Posh also recorded a club-record 28 wins. Peterborough had only been elected to The Football League that season on the back of five successive title wins in the Midland League.

← Terry Bly (back row, one from right) provided the firepower for Peterborough in their 1960/61 fourth-tier title run.

ETHERINGTON WINGS IN

Matthew Etherington is the youngest player to have represented Peterborough, appearing for 87 minutes of a 1–0 win at Brentford in May 1997 aged 15 years and 262 days. Etherington made almost 60 appearances for Posh before being sold to Tottenham in December 1999. Spurs snapped up Simon Davies at the same time, with Peterborough receiving a then club-record £700,000 for the Welsh winger.

BENNETT BREAKS RECORD

The club broke their transfer record to sign highly-rated defender Ryan Bennett from Grimsby in 2009/10. He penned a long-term deal after a successful loan spell. Although the exact fee was undisclosed, it did supersede the £400,000 paid to Norwich for goalkeeper Joe Lewis in January 2008.

LIKE FATHER, LIKE SON

Posh enjoyed back-to-back promotions in 2008 and 2009. Darren Ferguson secured runners-up spot in the fourth tier in his first full season as manager and then guided the club to another second-place finish the following year, taking them into the second tier. Ferguson, the son of Manchester United manager Sir Alex, left Peterborough by mutual consent in November 2009 but returned in January 2011 to oversee yet another promotion!

PARTY TIME FOR POSH

Craig Mackail-Smith scored 27 of Peterborough's league-high 106 goals during the 2010/11 promotion-winning season. Winger George Boyd added a further 15, while midfielder Grant McCann notched nine. Posh edged a nine-goal thriller against Swindon and hit five or more goals against Carlisle, Dagenham & Redbridge, Oldham and Sheffield Wednesday – and that was just at London Road! The club finished fourth in npower League 1, seeing off MK Dons in the semi-finals of the play-offs and beating Huddersfield 3–0 in the final. All three goals came in a crazy eight-minute spell late in the second half.

→ Peterborough's players celebrate their promotion back to the second tier after beating Huddersfield in the 2011 npower Championship Play-Off Final.

PORTSMOUTH

Portsmouth's recent spell in the top flight came to an end in 2010 after a difficult season both on and off the field ended in relegation, but the club still managed to reach the FA Cup final for the second time in three years. Following a campaign of consolidation under Steve Cotterill in the npower Championship in 2010/11, they are now looking to rebuild for another crack at the big time.

HAPPY AS HARRY

Harry Redknapp became the first English manager to lift the FA Cup since 1995 when Portsmouth beat Cardiff 1–0 at Wembley in 2008. A single goal from Nigerian striker Nwankwo Kanu was enough for victory as the south-coast club won the trophy for the second time in their history. Cliff Parker was the hero in the 1939 final, scoring twice to help Pompey to a 4–1 win against Wolves.

← In 2008, Harry Redknapp became the first English manager to win the FA Cup since 1995.

GENTLEMAN JIM

Jimmy Dickinson holds the record for the most appearances in a Portsmouth shirt and is also the club's most capped player. Dickinson, who earned the nickname 'Gentleman Jim' due to the fact that he was never booked or sent off, featured 845 times in all competitions for Pompey between 1946 and 1965. His 764 league appearances for one club is bettered only by John Trollope, who played 770 games for Swindon. Dickinson was capped 48 times by England and went to both the 1950 and 1954 World Cups.

BACK-TO-BACK TITLES

Only five teams have won back-to-back top-flight titles since World War II – and Portsmouth are one of them. Bob Jackson led the club to glory in 1948/49 and again in 1949/50, with a team featuring club legends such as Jimmy Dickinson, Jack Froggatt, Duggie Reid and Peter Harris. Harris finished the first championship-winning season as top scorer with 22 goals, while Ike Clarke led the way with 20 the following term.

↓ Benjani (25) is congratulated by Niko Kranjcar after scoring Portsmouth's first goal in the 11-goal thriller against Reading in 2007.

WHAT A GUY!

Guy Whittingham scored a club-record 42 league goals in season 1992/93, but Pompey missed out on promotion to the top flight on goal difference. They finished third in the second tier, with Newcastle and West Ham going up automatically before Portsmouth were beaten by Leicester at the semi-final stage of the play-offs. Prolific striker Whittingham scored over half of the club's total goals that term and left for Aston Villa in the summer of 1993 having scored 88 times in 160 league matches.

← It was ironic that despite 42 goals in the league from striker Guy Whittingham, Portsmouth missed out on promotion into the Premier League on goal difference.

↑ Jimmy Dickinson retired soon after his 40th birthday, having helped to save Portsmouth from relegation to the third tier.

A COMMON SCORELINE

The amazing 7–4 win against Reading in September 2007 was nothing new – it was actually the fourth time the club have been involved in games with that scoreline. The first came against Newcastle in November 1930, with the club winning on Tyneside. It was raining goals again on Christmas Day 1957, but there was no festive cheer for Portsmouth, who lost out to Chelsea. Charlton were 7–4 victors in October 1960, before the most recent battle against the Royals. Striker Benjani Mwaruwari scored a hat-trick for Pompey in that game.

READING

Reading are one of the oldest clubs in England but they did not join The Football League until 1920. They created their own piece of history in 2005/06 when they were promoted to the top flight for the first time and although they were relegated at the end of their second term, the Royals remain a club with big ambitions. They were beaten by Swansea in the 2010/11 npower Championship Play-Off Final.

⇠ Reading's domination of the Championship in 2005/06 broke many long-standing Football League records, and their Barclays Premier League debut season was pretty good too.

RECORD-BREAKING READING

Reading enjoyed their best-ever season in 2005/06 when they won the Championship title with a massive haul of 106 points – a Football League record. The Royals also broke a host of other records during that 46-game campaign as they lost just two league matches – one of those away from home – conceded the fewest goals (32) and secured the most wins (31). With Steve Coppell in charge, Reading also became the team to have clinched promotion the earliest, beating Plymouth by one day and Notts County by three.

ROYALS KEEP IT CLEAN

The Royals created more Football League history when they went 1,103 minutes without conceding a goal in 1979. The run began on March 24 when they kept a clean sheet for 84 minutes of their clash with Rochdale. They didn't concede for 11 more games that season before goalkeeper Steve Death was finally beaten 29 minutes into the start of the 1979/80 campaign against Brentford. Edwin van der Sar has since broken that record for Manchester United, although that is classed as a Premier League statistic.

A RECORD RUN

Reading started the 1985/86 season with 13 consecutive league wins – a Football League record. Here's how they did it:

v Blackpool	1–0
v Plymouth	1–0
v Bristol Rovers	3–2
v Cardiff	3–1
v Walsall	2–1
v Rotherham	2–1
v Brentford	2–1
v Swansea	2–0
v Doncaster	1–0
v Chesterfield	4–2
v Bolton	1–0
v Newport	2–0
v Lincoln	1–0

KITSON MAKES HIS MARK

Striker Dave Kitson scored Reading's first Barclays Premier League goal in a 3–2 win against Middlesbrough on the opening day of the 2006/07 season. The Royals were 2–0 down when Kitson struck, and that sparked an impressive comeback as goals from Steve Sidwell and Leroy Lita earned the newcomers victory.

LONG FALLS SHORT

Shane Long proved himself to be one of the npower Championship's hottest prospects in 2010/11, scoring 21 league goals for the Royals. Only Watford's Danny Graham hit the net more times than the young Republic of Ireland international. Long's brace at Cardiff secured Reading their npower Championship Play-Off Final date with Swansea in May 2011.

⇢ The 2010/11 campaign marked the best goalscoring season so far of Shane Long's career, as he ended with 28 goals for club and country.

SOUTHAMPTON

Saints marched into the npower Championship at the end of 2010/11 after two seasons in the third tier, with manager Nigel Adkins helping to revive the south-coast club's fortunes. Southampton, who celebrated their 125th anniversary in 2010/11, have won the FA Cup once in their history in 1976, while their highest-ever finish was second in the top flight in 1984.

DELL BOYS

The Saints moved from The Dell to their current St Mary's Stadium in 2001. Matt Le Tissier scored the last goal at their old ground as they beat Arsenal 3–2. Marian Pahars was the first home player to score a league goal at St Mary's, but Southampton lost 3–1 to Aston Villa.

LE TISS IS SPOT ON

Matt Le Tissier is a Southampton legend. The attacking midfielder joined the club as a youngster in 1986 and played for the Saints until his retirement in 2002. Le Tissier is second only to Mick Channon in the list of all-time Southampton goalscorers, while he was also incredibly reliable from the penalty spot. He took nearly 50 spot-kicks for the club and missed just once!

◄— When they moved into St Mary's, Southampton may have had a beautiful new ground, but the tight confines of The Dell, their old home, had been a big advantage.

SAINTS MARCH TO GLORY

Southampton won the FA Cup for the only time in their history in 1976, stunning Manchester United 1–0 at Wembley. United had finished third in the top flight that year but a late Bobby Stokes goal snatched victory for the unfancied Saints.

◄— Matt Le Tissier's record from the penalty spot was almost perfect. Only Nottingham Forest goalkeeper Mark Crossley saved one of his attempts.

◄— Rickie Lambert has scored goals wherever he has played, netting over 150 times in the league in total for five different clubs.

SOUTHAMPTON'S 10-YEAR RECORD

2001/02 (Top flight)	11th
2002/03 (Top flight)	8th
2003/04 (Top flight)	12th
2004/05 (Top flight)	20th
2005/06 (Second tier)	12th
2006/07 (Second tier)	6th
2007/08 (Second tier)	20th
2008/09 (Second tier)	23rd
2009/10 (Third tier)	7th
2010/11 (Third tier)	2nd

LAMBERT TOPS THE CHARTS

Rickie Lambert finished as League 1's top scorer for two consecutive seasons between 2008 and 2010 and wasn't far away last term. The prolific striker netted 29 times for Bristol Rovers during the 2008/09 campaign, sharing the Golden Boot with Simon Cox of Swindon. That impressive haul earned him a £1million move to Southampton, where he went one better in 2009/10, hitting 30 league goals. Lambert was joint third on the list in 2010/11, although his 21-goal haul was six less than Peterborough's Craig Mackail-Smith.

WATFORD

Watford's glory years came in the early 1980s when Elton John was chairman and they were competing for the top-flight title, and there are signs that they have begun to move back to being competitive and successful. The Hornets finished the 2010/11 campaign comfortably in mid-table, with former defensive lynchpin Sean Dyche the man now at the helm.

YOUNG IS OLD FAVOURITE

Ashley Young's move to Aston Villa in January 2007 is the record transfer fee the club have received. England international winger Young left for Villa Park for £9.65million, having scored 22 goals for the Hornets in all competitions. Young scored on his debut for Villa in a 3–1 defeat at Newcastle and went on to make his international bow in November 2007 in a friendly against Austria.

↑ It took almost £10million for Aston Villa to sign Ashley Young from Watford, the biggest transfer fee the Hornets have received.

OH DANNY BOY!

Danny Graham equalled a near 80-year-old club record by scoring in seven consecutive games during the 2010/11 season. He netted nine goals during the impressive run, which started against Leicester on December 4 and continued until mid-January. He finished as the npower Championship's top scorer with 24 and moved to Barclays Premier League new-boys Swansea for £3.5million in June 2011.

⇢ Luther Blissett's first spell at Vicarage Road coincided with the Hornets' meteoric rise up the English football ladder.

LEGEND LUTHER

Luther Blissett holds the Watford club records for both the most Football League appearances and the most Football League goals. Blissett appeared in 415 league games for the Hornets across three separate spells, scoring 148 goals in that time. He finished as the top scorer in the top flight in 1982/83 and as a result secured a £1million move to Italian giants AC Milan. He failed to make an impact at the San Siro, though, and promptly returned to Vicarage Road.

↗ Under Graham Taylor, Watford went from the fourth tier of English football in 1977/78 to top-division runners-up in 1982/83.

ELTON CALLS THE TUNE

Superstar singer-songwriter Elton John has been chairman of Watford on two separate occasions. Taking over in 1976, the multi-million selling artist was then bought out by Jack Petchey in 1987. Sir Elton resumed the role in the late 1990s but stepped down again in 2002, although he is still an avid follower of the Hornets. He has also held the position of club president.

TAYLOR-MADE FOR TOP FLIGHT

Watford finished as runners-up in their first-ever season in the top flight in 1982/83. Graham Taylor was in charge as the Hornets finished the campaign a point ahead of Manchester United but 11 behind champions Liverpool. It completed a meteoric rise by the club under Taylor's management, as Watford had been playing in the fourth tier just five years previously. Taylor enjoyed a second spell as manager of the club between 1996 and 2001, leading them to the Premier League.

WEST HAM UNITED

Sam Allardyce is the new man in charge at West Ham, who will be hoping to take the npower Championship by storm. A club steeped in tradition, the Hammers may not have won the top-flight title, but they have lifted the FA Cup on three occasions. The east London club also claimed the now defunct European Cup Winners' Cup back in 1965.

TEVEZ TIMES HIS RUN

Carlos Tevez wrote his name into West Ham folklore in season 2006/07 when his goals helped the club to survive relegation. The Argentina international opened his Hammers account in a 4–3 defeat at home to Tottenham on March 4 2007, starting a spree of seven goals in 10 games. Tevez was on target against Manchester United at Old Trafford on the final day of the campaign to secure a shock 1–0 win that guaranteed the club's top-flight status.

---→ Trevor Brooking acknowledges the crowd after his goal decided the 1980 FA Cup final. Two of West Ham's three FA Cup final wins have been in London derbies.

TRIPLE WHAMMY FOR HAMMERS

The club have won the FA Cup on three occasions, with their last success coming in 1980. The Hammers' first triumph in the competition came in 1964, when a last-gasp goal from Ron Boyce snatched a 3–2 win against Preston. Alan Taylor scored twice as Fulham were beaten 2–0 in the 1975 final, while Trevor Brooking was practically on the floor when he headed the only goal of the game against Arsenal in 1980.

THE TWO FRANKIES

Two generations of the Lampard family have played for the London club, with Frank Snr turning out between 1967 and 1985 and his son, Frank Jnr, making his name at Upton Park from 1995 until 2001. Frank Snr won two FA Cups with the club, in 1975 and 1980, and was also part of the promotion-winning team of 1981. He is second only to Billy Bonds in the list of record appearance makers. Frank Jnr, who now plays for Chelsea, helped West Ham to their highest Premier League finish in 1998/99.

ON THE UP

The club achieved their highest Premier League finish of fifth in 1998/99, but their best overall top-flight position came in the 1985/86 campaign. West Ham – under the management of John Lyall and with Frank McAvennie and Tony Cottee forging a superb strike partnership – finished third, but they were in with a chance of the title going into the last week of the season. Liverpool were the eventual winners, with Everton two points behind and the Londoners a further two adrift on 84.

WORLD CUP WONDERS

West Ham had three players in England's World Cup-winning squad of 1966 – and the trio played a major part in claiming the trophy. Defensive rock Bobby Moore captained the side and midfielder Martin Peters was on target in the final, but it was striker Geoff Hurst who stole the headlines. Having scored the only goal against Argentina in the quarter-final, Hurst netted a hat-trick in the final as England beat West Germany 4–2 after extra time.

↖ Between them, the two Frank Lampards made more than 850 appearances for West Ham. Frank Senior (left) is second on the all-time list with nearly 700, while Frank Junior played more than 170 times before joining Chelsea in 2001.

↓ West Ham fans like to say that their team won the World Cup in 1966. (Left to right) Bobby Moore captained England to glory in the final, Martin Peters scored the second goal and Geoff Hurst got the other three.

NPOWER LEAGUE 1 CLUB RECORDS

Some big names have graced League 1 in recent times, with the likes of Southampton, Leicester, Norwich, Charlton and Leeds having all played in the third tier. Saints played in front of over 30,000 spectators last term – attracting a crowd of 31,653 against Walsall in May 2011 – while Sheffield Wednesday and the Addicks were close to 25,000 on occasion, proving just how well supported some of the teams in the lower reaches of English football are.

Peterborough's Craig Mackail-Smith in action during the 2010/11 campaign. The Posh striker ended the season as npower League 1's top scorer.

Paul Benson of Charlton (right) holds off the challenge of Gary MacKenzie during MK Dons' 2–0 victory in March 2011.

AFC BOURNEMOUTH

CHERRIES PICK OFF BIG GUNS

Bournemouth enjoyed their greatest FA Cup run in 1956/57, reaching the sixth round, where they were narrowly beaten by Manchester United. Having knocked out Burton, Swindon and Accrington, the Cherries landed a trip to Wolves, who were third in the top flight at the time. They went on to claim a stunning 1–0 win at Molineux and earn a home game against Tottenham. Another superb performance brought a 3–1 victory and a meeting with United. However, the dream ended there, although Bournemouth did gain revenge in 1984 when, under manager Harry Redknapp, they stunned the reigning FA Cup holders 2–0 to record one of their most famous results.

↑ Darren Anderton's Bournemouth career began with a 40-yard goal on his debut in 2006 and ended with a match-winning volley in 2008, after which he retired.

ANDERTON GOES OUT ON A HIGH

Former England international midfielder Darren Anderton enjoyed a fairytale end to his career at Bournemouth in December 2008. Having come on as a substitute just before the hour mark, Anderton scored the only goal of the game against Chester with two minutes remaining – a stunning volley. Anderton made almost 500 league appearances for five different clubs.

BRETT THE HITMAN

Striker Brett Pitman's move to Bristol City ahead of the 2010/11 campaign earned the Cherries their biggest-ever transfer fee. The Jersey-born goal ace left the club after six years, during which time he scored 62 goals in 197 appearances, and although the final figure was undisclosed, it is believed that it bettered the £800,000 fee that Bournemouth recouped on the sale of midfielder Matt Holland to Ipswich in 1997.

BRENTFORD

ALL RHODES LEAD TO GOALS

Jordan Rhodes joined an elite group of players to have scored a 'perfect' hat-trick when he netted a treble for Brentford at Shrewsbury in January 2009. The young striker, who is now banging in the goals for Huddersfield, scored three in a row – the first with his right foot, the second with his left foot and the final one a header – as the Bees claimed a 3–1 victory.

←⋯ Jordan Rhodes was on loan from Ipswich when he netted a 'perfect' hat-trick for Brentford at Shrewsbury in a League 2 match in January 2009. Rhodes become the Bees' youngest-ever hat-trick scorer.

HOME COMFORTS FOR BEES

Griffin Park was a fortress during the 1929/30 season as the Bees won all 21 of their home matches. That was still not enough for them to win the title, though, as they finished runners-up to Plymouth, who they had beaten 3–0 at home earlier in the campaign.

THE ICE MAN

Brentford paid a club-record £750,000 to sign defender Hermann Hreidarsson from Crystal Palace in September 1998, but he only stayed for 13 months before creating more Bees history. The Iceland international's performances in helping the club to the fourth-tier title in 1998/99 saw him make a £2.5million move to the Premier League with Wimbledon – the biggest fee received by Brentford.

BURY

A NEW HIGH FOR LOWE

Ryan Lowe went close to equalling a post-war English football record for the number of goals scored in consecutive matches during season 2010/11. The Bury forward netted 10 times in nine straight games between January and March 2011, bagging a brace in a 4–2 win at Macclesfield. The current record stands at 10 successive games, with Ruud van Nistelrooy (Manchester United), Jermain Defoe (Bournemouth) and John Aldridge (Liverpool) all having achieved the feat. Lowe ended the campaign with 27 league goals.

⋯⋯> *Ryan Lowe's goals were a crucial factor in securing Bury their promotion to npower League 1 in 2010/11.*

CRAIG'S GOAL MAD

Craig Madden netted the most league goals for Bury in a single season on his way to becoming the Shakers' all-time leading scorer. Madden scored 35 times in the 1981/82 season as the club finished ninth in the fourth tier. In eight years at the club, Madden netted 129 league goals.

LANDMARK SEASON FOR SHAKERS

Bury celebrated their 125th anniversary in 2010. The club was formed in 1885, with the first match at Gigg Lane taking place in September of that year – a 4–3 friendly win against Wigan. To mark the anniversary, the Shakers wore a brown and sky blue shirt with white shorts for the 2009/10 campaign – the same colours they wore in their very first season.

⋯⋯> *Scorer Daniel Nardiello (right) and Danny Racchi celebrate in Bury's 125th anniversary shirts against Notts County at Gigg Lane in November 2009.*

CARLISLE UNITED

⋯⋯> *On-loan goalkeeper Jimmy Glass (red shirt) runs away in celebration after his last-minute goal against Plymouth at Brunton Park preserved Carlisle's Football League status in 1999.*

THE TOP AND BOTTOM OF IT

Carlisle were in dreamland at the start of the 1974/75 season as they led the top flight after the opening three games. They claimed 2–0 victories at Chelsea and Middlesbrough in their first two matches and followed that with a 1–0 success at home to Tottenham. Unfortunately for the Cumbrians, they ended their one and only top-flight campaign at the bottom of the table.

CARLISLE MANAGERS SINCE 2000

Ian Atkins	2000–2001
Roddy Collins	2001–2002, 2002–2003
Paul Simpson	2003–2006
Neil McDonald	2006–2007
John Ward	2007–2008
Greg Abbott	2008–Present

TOUCH OF GLASS

Goalkeeper Jimmy Glass earned a place in Carlisle folklore when he scored an injury-time winner against Plymouth on the last day of the 1998/99 season to secure the club's Football League status in dramatic fashion. There were just 10 seconds of the Brunton Park clash remaining when shot-stopper Glass, who had come up for a corner, volleyed home after Scott Dobie's header had been parried. That was enough to earn the Cumbrians the win they needed to avoid the drop as Scarborough were relegated to the Conference instead.

CHARLTON ATHLETIC

CHARLTON'S CENTENARY AWARDS

Greatest Manager	Alan Curbishley
Greatest Goalkeeper	Sam Bartram
Greatest Defender	Richard Rufus
Greatest Midfielder	Mark Kinsella
Greatest Striker	Derek Hales
Greatest Overseas Player	Eddie Firmani

MENDONCA'S THE MAN

Charlton were involved in one of the most memorable play-off wins ever in May 1998. The Addicks beat Sunderland 7–6 on penalties after a ding-dong battle had finished 4–4 at the end of extra time. Clive Mendonca scored a hat-trick for the Londoners – his third coming in the 103rd minute to send the game to penalties. Michael Gray missed the crucial kick for Sunderland to send Charlton into the Premier League.

BARTRAM STANDS TALL

There is a nine-foot statue of Charlton goalkeeping legend Sam Bartram outside The Valley. Bartram is the club's record appearance holder, having featured 623 times in all competitions from 1934–1956. He was immortalised as part of the Addicks' centenary celebrations in 2005, when he was also voted as Charlton's greatest goalkeeper.

⟵ Clive Mendonca slides in to score his third and Charlton's fourth goal in their memorable 1998 play-off win against Sunderland at Wembley.

CHESTERFIELD

CUP OF CHEER

Chesterfield enjoyed their best FA Cup run in 1997, eventually losing in the semi-finals to Middlesbrough. The Spireites knocked out Bolton and Nottingham Forest on their way to the last four, where they took a 2–0 lead against Middlesbrough at Old Trafford. Jonathan Howard had a goal disallowed and their top-flight opponents hit back to take the game into extra time. Chesterfield forced an equaliser through Jamie Hewitt late on but lost the replay 3–0.

⟵ A disallowed goal from Jonathan Howard denied Chesterfield the chance to lead Middlesbrough 3–0 in their 1997 FA Cup semi-final. Boro hit back and eventually won the tie after a replay.

DAVIES STARTS AS A SPIREITE

Barclays Premier League striker Kevin Davies began his career at Chesterfield and ranks as one of their most famous former players. Davies scored 22 goals in 129 league games for the Spireites before making a club-record £750,000 move to Southampton in May 1997. Blackburn then paid £7.5million to take him to Ewood Park just over a year later. He is now captain of Bolton.

⟶ Craig Davies' 23 league goals last season earned him a move to npower Championship Barnsley in time for the 2011/12 campaign.

GOAL CRAZY

The Spireites scored 85 goals on their way to the npower League 2 title in 2010/11 – the highest total in the division. Craig Davies was the club's top scorer with 23 goals, while veteran striker Jack Lester weighed in with 17. John Sheridan's side finished five points ahead of Bury at the top of the table.

COLCHESTER UNITED

LEEDS LEFT REELING

Colchester reached the quarter-finals of the FA Cup in 1970/71 – their best-ever run in the competition. In the fourth tier at the time, they were drawn against Leeds in the fifth round, who were flying high in the top flight under manager Don Revie. Colchester pulled off one of the greatest shocks in the competition's history with a 3–2 victory. Everton proved too strong for them in the last eight, however, running out 5–0 winners.

COMMUNITY SPIRIT

The Us left their home of 71 years to move into a new £14million all-seater stadium in July 2008. Richard Cresswell was the last player to score at Layer Road as they were beaten 1–0 by Stoke. Athletic Bilbao striker Aritz Aduriz netted the first goal at the new Colchester Community Stadium in a pre-season friendly in August 2008.

Us RIDING HIGH

Colchester enjoyed their highest league finish in 2006/07 when they ended the season in 10th place in the Championship. The Us had been tipped to make an instant return to the third tier having gained automatic promotion in 2005/06. But they defied the pundits, with Jamie Cureton ending the campaign as the league's top scorer with 23 goals.

Jamie Cureton acknowledges the Colchester fans. His 23 goals helped the Us to a best-ever league finish in 2006/07.

EXETER CITY

GRECIANS HOLD FIRM

Exeter recorded one of the most famous results in their history in 2004/05 when they held mighty Manchester United to a goalless draw in the FA Cup third round at Old Trafford. The Grecians were in the Conference at the time, but they held their own against a United side featuring the likes of Cristiano Ronaldo, Paul Scholes and Ryan Giggs before losing out in a replay.

Kwame Ampadu (left) and Gary Sawyer (3) combine to frustrate Manchester United's Ryan Giggs during Exeter's 0–0 FA Cup draw at Old Trafford in 2005.

MOVING ON UP

The Grecians returned to The Football League after a five-year absence in 2008, and they made it back-to-back promotions the following term. A stunning comeback in the semi-final of the Conference play-offs against Torquay – they scored four second-half goals to win 5–3 on aggregate – set up a Wembley date with Cambridge. A single goal from Rob Edwards was enough to secure victory, and in 2008/09 they finished second in the fourth tier to move up again.

THE BOY DONE GOOD

Goalscoring great Cliff Bastin was handed his Football League debut by Exeter at the age of 16 years and 31 days – making him the youngest player to feature for the club. Winger Bastin was sold to Arsenal for £2,000 when he was 17 and went on to become the Gunners' all-time leading goalscorer in the league until he was surpassed by Thierry Henry in 2006.

Rob Edwards' goal in the Conference Play-Off Final against Cambridge restored Exeter's Football League status in May 2008.

HARTLEPOOL UNITED

FINAL WOE FOR POOLS

Hartlepool's highest Football League finish is sixth in the third tier. They achieved that in both 2003/04 and again the following campaign. The 2004/05 season was the most successful in the club's history so far as they reached the League 1 Play-Off Final, where they were beaten 4–2 by Sheffield Wednesday after extra time at the Millennium Stadium in Cardiff. Pools were relegated from the third tier the following year.

···▷ *No one could question former England Under-21 international Ritchie Humphreys' loyalty to the Hartlepool cause.*

RITCHIE'S RECORD RUN

Ritchie Humphreys holds the record for the most consecutive league appearances in a Hartlepool shirt – a feat that earned him recognition from Buckingham Palace! He didn't miss a game in his first five years at the club and was honoured by the Queen for a remarkable run of 234 unbroken matches. Humphreys, who has played at left-back, in midfield and attack for Pools, was also named Hartlepool's Player of the Century in May 2008.

THAT WINNING FEELING

Season 2006/07 was one of the most memorable in Hartlepool's history. It started poorly, with the club taking six games to secure their first league win, but just when it looked like their promotion dream was struggling, a 2–1 victory at Accrington on November 18 2006 sparked a club-record run of nine consecutive league wins, the following eight without conceding, which carried Pools to a second-place finish.

HUDDERSFIELD TOWN

RECORD RUN NOT ENOUGH

Lee Clark's Huddersfield went an incredible 27 games unbeaten in the league and play-offs in 2010/11, only to miss out on promotion at the final hurdle. The Terriers were unlucky not to go up automatically, with Brighton and Southampton equally impressive. Town posted a best-ever total of 13 away wins, and the six straight victories they managed on the road between March and May was also a club record. They were beaten 3–0 by Peterborough in the npower League 1 Play-Off Final at Old Trafford.

◁··· *After an impressive playing career for the likes of Newcastle United and Fulham, Lee Clark has made management look easy.*

TRIPLE WHAMMY FOR TOWN

In 1926, Huddersfield became the first team in history to win three successive top-flight titles, a feat that only three other clubs – Arsenal, Liverpool and Manchester United – have been able to match.

UNLUCKY SEVEN FOR TERRIERS

Huddersfield were the losing side in one of the most amazing comebacks in Football League history in December 1957. The Terriers were leading 5–1 at Charlton with half an hour to go against 10 men, but they ended up losing 7–6! Bill Shankly was manager of Huddersfield as they allowed Johnny Summers to score five goals – including a quick-fire hat-trick – and set up two more to snatch Charlton a stunning victory.

◁··· *Bill Shankly would not have been a happy man when his Huddersfield team lost 7–6 at Charlton in 1957.*

LEYTON ORIENT

LAST FOUR FOR ORIENT

Leyton Orient reached the semi-finals of the FA Cup while playing in the second tier in 1977/78. They finished 14th in the league that season, but an impressive cup run saw them beat then top-flight teams in Norwich, Chelsea and Middlesbrough along the way before they lost 3–0 to Arsenal at Stamford Bridge in the last four. The Os played the Gunners again in 2011, holding them to a 1–1 draw at Brisbane Road in the fifth round before losing the replay 5–0.

⇢ *Jonathan Tehoue's last-gasp goal against Arsenal was one of the stories of the FA Cup in season 2010/11.*

GIFT OF THE GAB

The biggest transfer fee ever received by Leyton Orient is £1million from Fulham for Gabriel Zakuani in July 2006. Defender Zakuani made more than 90 appearances for the club between 2002 and 2006, scoring three goals.

Os ON THE RUN

Between October 1993 and September 1995, Leyton Orient failed to win a single game away from home in The Football League. Following Colin West's goal at Hull in a 1–0 triumph on October 30 1993, Orient embarked on a 42-game winless run on the road which resulted in them being relegated from the third tier. They failed to win any of their first three games of the 1995/96 season in the fourth tier, before goals from Ian Hendon and Alex Inglethorpe finally secured a 2–1 victory at Northampton.

MILTON KEYNES DONS

McLEOD HAS SILVER LINING

Izale McLeod is MK Dons' all-time leading scorer, having netted 60 goals in a three-year spell at the club between 2004 and 2007. McLeod scored on his Dons debut against Barnsley and went on to score 17 more times in his first season. A haul of 24 goals in 2006/07 helped the Dons to a play-off place, but they were beaten at the semi-final stage by Shrewsbury.

⇠ *No one has scored more goals for the MK Dons since the club was formed than Izale McLeod. His form earned him an England Under-21 cap in 2006.*

FIVE-STAR DONS

The Dons equalled their record margin of victory when they beat Hartlepool 5–0 at Victoria Park in 2009/10. Jermaine Easter opened the scoring against one of his former clubs, with a Gary Liddle own goal and further strikes from Peter Leven, Sam Baldock and Jason Puncheon securing a memorable win. They had won by the same scoreline in December 2007 when Accrington were the opponents.

ROVERS AND OUT

Keith Andrews created a new transfer record for the MK Dons when he left for Blackburn in 2008. Paul Ince, then in charge at Rovers having previously been with the Dons, took his former captain to Ewood Park with him in a £1.2million deal.

NOTTS COUNTY

WARNOCK WORKS HIS MAGIC

Neil Warnock led Notts County to back-to-back promotions in 1989/90 and 1990/91. They secured a play-off spot with a third-place finish in 1989/90, beating Tranmere 2–0 in the final with goals from Tommy Johnson and Craig Short. Seven consecutive wins towards the end of the following campaign earned County another play-off appearance, and Johnson was the goal hero again, scoring twice in a 3–1 win against Brighton to send them up. The Magpies were relegated in season 1991/92, however.

⋯⋙ Neil Warnock's first league job was as Scarborough manager, but he became well-known as Notts County boss.

COUNTY'S RECORD GOALSCORERS

Les Bradd	137
Tony Hateley	114
Jackie Sewell	104
Tommy Lawton	103
Tom Keetley	98
Don Masson	97
Tom Johnston	92
Ian McParland	90
Harry Daft	81
Gary Lund, Trevor Christie, Mark Stallard	79

⬆ Mark Stallard is equal 10th on the list of Notts County goalscorers. His 79 came between 1999 and 2005.

OLD TIMERS

Notts County hold the honour of being the oldest league club in the world. They were first formed in 1862 – although their official formation came two years later – and they were one of the founding members of The Football League in 1888.

OLDHAM ATHLETIC

OLDHAM MANAGERS SINCE 1982

Joe Royle	1982–1994
Graeme Sharp	1994–1997
Neil Warnock	1997–1998
Andy Ritchie	1998–2001
Mick Wadsworth	2001–2002
Iain Dowie	2002–2003
Brian Talbot	2004–2005
Ronnie Moore	2005–2006
John Sheridan	2006–2009
Joe Royle	2009
Dave Penney	2009–2010
Paul Dickov	2010–Present

PLASTIC LATICS

Oldham were one of four English clubs to install a plastic pitch during the 1980s. Artificial surfaces were also introduced at QPR, Luton and Preston in an effort to reduce maintenance costs and limit the number of postponements. However, they proved unpopular, and Oldham got rid of their plastic pitch in 1991.

BY ROYLE APPOINTMENT

Joe Royle established his managerial reputation with Oldham, leading the club to the top flight in 1991 and also taking them to the final of the League Cup, where they lost to Nottingham Forest. Oldham also reached the last four of the FA Cup on two occasions during Royle's 12-year spell in charge, losing both times to Manchester United.

⬅ Joe Royle ended Oldham's 68-year absence from England's top division when he took the Latics up in 1991, and his cup record was also quite impressive. He returned to Boundary Park briefly in 2009.

PRESTON NORTH END

AFFINITY WITH FINNEY

The name of Sir Tom Finney is synonymous with Preston. The legendary forward was a one-club man, spending 14 years at Deepdale between 1946 and 1960, during which time he emerged as one of the finest players of his generation. He is North End's all-time leading goalscorer, having netted 210 goals for the club in 473 games. Finney also won 76 caps for England during that time, scoring 30 goals for his country. He is ranked fifth in the list of England's top goalscorers, level with Nat Lofthouse and Alan Shearer. Finney received a knighthood in 1998, while there is also a stand named after him at Deepdale and a sculpture in his honour outside the ground.

There is no argument about who is the greatest player in Preston North End history – Sir Tom Finney stands head and shoulders above all others.

PRESTON FIRST PAST THE POST

Preston hold the distinction of being English football's first champions. North End were founder members of The Football League in 1888, and they beat 11 other teams to win the title in its inaugural season. Preston also became the first team to achieve a league and FA Cup double in the 1888/89 campaign. They won the championship again the following year and finished as runners-up in 1890/91, 1891/92 and 1892/93.

MAGIC MOYES

Everton boss David Moyes started his managerial career at Preston, enjoying a successful spell at Deepdale between 1998 and 2002. He led North End to the play-offs in 1998/99 and the third-tier title in 1999/00, with the club racking up their best-ever points total in the process – 95. The play-offs were achieved again in 2000/01 before Moyes left for Goodison Park in March 2002.

ROCHDALE

JONES KEEPING UP APPEARANCES

Gary Jones became Rochdale's record appearance holder in 2007/08 and is increasing his tally with every game he plays for the club. Jones, who has already written himself into the history books at Spotland, surpassed Graham Smith's previous landmark of 345 appearances in all competitions in March 2008. He was a regular in the promotion-winning side of 2009/10 and managed 17 goals last term – easily his best-ever total.

At the heart of Rochdale's first promotion for 41 years in 2010 was Gary Jones, who holds the club record for appearances. In all competitions, he has more than 400 to his name.

DALE MOVE ON UP

Rochdale fans will not forget 2009/10 in a hurry after the club were promoted for only the second time in their history. Dale spent a total of five seasons in the third tier on their first visit to that level before they were relegated at the end of the 1973/74 campaign. However, they finally had cause to celebrate for a second time on April 17 2010 as Chris O'Grady's close-range strike against Northampton secured their first promotion since 1969. They had been the longest-serving club in the bottom division of The Football League.

WHITEHURST GOAL BURST

Albert Whitehurst scored a club-record 44 league goals during the 1926/27 season. He netted 117 times in the league in total for Dale – two less than all-time top scorer Reg Jenkins – and also bagged 10 hat-tricks for the club.

SCUNTHORPE UNITED

DUO SHINE IN GREAT EIGHT

Barrie Thomas and Andy McFarlane both put in outstanding individual displays on the two occasions that Scunthorpe recorded 8–1 wins – their biggest-ever victories. Luton were the opponents on April 24 1965 as Thomas, who is second on the list of the Iron's top scorers (his 93 goals in 143 matches in two spells is bettered only by Steve Cammack) netted five times – a club record for the most goals in a single game. McFarlane grabbed four goals as Torquay were beaten by the same scoreline at Plainmoor 30 years later.

← When Scunthorpe sold Barrie Thomas to Newcastle in 1962, the club was top of the second tier, but they fell away and missed promotion.

RAZOR-SHARP BILLY

The Iron received a club-record £2million fee when hot-shot striker Billy Sharp left for Sheffield United in July 2007. Sharp had joined from the Blades for just £100,000 in August 2005 and quickly established himself as a first-team regular for the club. However, after scoring 53 goals in just 82 league games over two seasons at Glanford Park, he returned to his roots and headed back to Bramall Lane in a deal that also saw winger Jonathan Forte move in the opposite direction.

IRON ON SMOKING RUN

Scunthorpe's promotion from The Football League's bottom division in 2004/05 sparked a real purple patch for the club that saw them playing in the second tier just two years later. They followed up their initial success with yet more glory the following season and went a club-record 19 games unbeaten on their way to winning the League 1 title in 2006/07 to complete their remarkable ascent.

↓ Scunthorpe's players celebrate with the 2006/07 League 1 championship trophy. It was the first time the Iron had finished top of the table for 49 years, when they won the final Division 3 North crown.

SHEFFIELD UNITED

↑ Michael Tonge fires home the winner in the Carling Cup semi-final first leg against Liverpool at Bramall Lane.

BLADES CHOPPED DOWN

United have won the FA Cup four times – in 1899, 1902, 1915 and 1925 – but their best-ever run in the League Cup came more recently in 2003. The Blades reached the semi-finals, where they were beaten over two legs by Liverpool. Two goals from Michael Tonge had given them a slender 2–1 lead at Bramall Lane going into the return, but the Reds claimed a 2–0 victory to progress 3–2 on aggregate. Neil Warnock also led the club to the last four of the FA Cup that year.

NO GO FOR 'HAND OF GOD'

Legend has it that Diego Maradona was close to signing for Sheffield United in the late 1970s. Maradona was 17 when then Blades boss Harry Haslam spotted him playing for Argentinos Juniors. There are conflicting reports as to why a deal fell through, but ultimately Maradona never pulled on a red-and-white-striped shirt. Fellow Argentinian playmaker Alex Sabella arrived at the club instead for a then record fee of £160,000, but he managed just eight league goals in 76 appearances.

→ Micky Adams could not help his local team avoid the drop in 2010/11.

AGONY FOR ADAMS

Micky Adams was handed the task of helping his home-town club avoid relegation from the npower Championship in 2010/11. Unfortunately for Adams and the Blades, he failed. His first victory came at the 14th attempt against Nottingham Forest on March 8 2011. When Adams took over, the South Yorkshire side were two places and two points above the relegation zone. But by the end of the campaign they were second from bottom, having taken just 17 points from a possible 69. Adams was sacked at the end of the season and returned to npower League 2 side Port Vale.

SHEFFIELD WEDNESDAY

DEJA VU FOR OWLS

The Owls completed a remarkable achievement in 1993 when they reached both the FA Cup and League Cup finals in the same season, although their joy was shortlived, as they suffered defeat to Arsenal on both occasions. It is the only time in the history of the professional game that both of England's major domestic cup finals have been contested by the same two teams in the same season. Wednesday lost out in both matches to the same scoreline, 2–1.

WHY WEDNESDAY?

Wednesday rank as one of the more unusually named teams in The Football League. They actually started life as a cricket club, initially being formed as The Wednesday Cricket Club after the day of the week on which they held their matches. The local craftsmen who founded the club used to take half a day off on the same afternoon each week to play. It wasn't until June 1929 that the club's name was officially changed to Sheffield Wednesday.

SHERI THE TOAST OF SHEFFIELD

Sheffield Wednesday were in the second tier when they beat Manchester United to win the League Cup for the first and only time in their history in 1991. They knocked top-flight trio Derby, Coventry and Chelsea out of the competition on their way to reaching the Wembley showpiece. The Owls were promoted in the same season, while United finished sixth in Division One. A single goal from midfielder John Sheridan won the cup for the South Yorkshire side.

⤑ John Sheridan scored the only goal for Sheffield Wednesday when they won the 1991 League Cup. It was the Owls' first cup final victory since they beat West Brom to win the FA Cup in 1935.

STEVENAGE

MOUSINHO MAGIC

John Mousinho scored the only goal of the game as Stevenage earned a place in the third tier for the first time in their history by beating Torquay in the 2010/11 npower League 2 Play-Off Final at Old Trafford. It capped a remarkable two seasons for the club, who had only reached The Football League for the first time in 2009/10. Boro finished sixth in npower League 2 to secure a two-legged semi-final against Accrington and, after claiming a 3–0 aggregate victory, they went on to beat the Gulls and secure promotion.

⤑ Stevenage's John Mousinho celebrates with the npower League 2 Play-Off trophy following his side's promotion in May 2011.

GOING UP – AT LAST!

Stevenage won the Conference title in 1995/96 but were denied entry into The Football League as their Broadhall Way ground did not meet the necessary standards. Boro improved the stadium to meet the criteria but had to wait until 2010 before they finally achieved promotion.

BORO DENIED BY BLUES EXIT

Boro were on course to set a new Conference points record in 2009/10 until Chester City were removed from the competition. Graham Westley's side had already beaten the Blues 1–0 away and 2–0 at Broadhall Way, but the six points were later taken off them when the north-west club were expelled due to financial problems. That meant Stevenage finished as champions with 99 points from 44 games when they could have had 105 from 46. Crawley managed that total in 2010/11.

TRANMERE ROVERS

ALDRIDGE ON FORM

John Aldridge holds the post-war record for scoring the most goals in a season for Tranmere. The former Republic of Ireland striker, who also holds the club record for the most international caps, with 30, netted 40 times during the 1991/92 campaign.

⋯▶ John Aldridge scored 138 goals in 221 league games for Tranmere and later managed the club.

ROVERS OUT-FOXED

Tranmere recorded one of the most memorable achievements in their history when they reached the final of the League Cup in 2000. Having edged past Blackpool in the first round, Rovers beat Premier League Coventry 6–4 on aggregate. Wins against Oxford and Barnsley followed before a quarter-final against Middlesbrough and a semi-final with Bolton, which they won 4–0 over two legs. However, their dream run ended when they were beaten by Leicester at Wembley.

IN SAFE HANDS

Goalkeeper Eric Nixon kept a club-record 25 clean sheets as Rovers finished runners-up in the fourth tier and gained promotion in 1989. Nixon spent nine years at Prenton Park between 1988 and 1997 and, when he returned to the club for a second spell in 1999, he became the oldest player to appear for the club aged 39 years and 352 days.

⋯ Eric Nixon played his final competitive match for Tranmere in September 2002, just two weeks before his 40th birthday.

WALSALL

SMITH IN THE SADDLE

Dean Smith helped Walsall to pull off a miraculous escape from relegation in 2010/11. Smith was initially handed the manager's job on a temporary basis following the departure of Chris Hutchings in January. At the time, the Saddlers were rock-bottom of npower League 1 and eight points adrift of safety. But, after a brief settling-in period, results started to improve under Smith, and a run of 13 points from their last 10 games saw them survive by a point from Dagenham.

⋯ Dean Smith was Walsall's Head of Youth before taking over the reins as manager.

UNBEATABLE INCE

Goalkeeper Clayton Ince set a new club record of 22 clean sheets in all competitions when he helped Walsall to the League 2 title in 2006/07. The Saddlers lost just seven league games that season.

⋯▶ Walsall's Trinidad & Tobago international goalkeeper Clayton Ince kept 22 clean sheets during the Saddlers' League 2 championship campaign of 2006/07.

HARRISON HITS 500

Colin Harrison is Walsall's record all-time appearance holder in The Football League, having turned out for the club 467 times between 1964 and 1981. He is one of three players to have made over 500 appearances for the Saddlers in all competitions, with Nick Atthey and Colin Taylor also achieving the feat.

WYCOMBE WANDERERS

WYCOMBE'S FOOTBALL LEAGUE MANAGERS

Martin O'Neill	1993–1995
Alan Smith	1995–1996
John Gregory	1996–1998
Neil Smillie	1998–1999
Lawrie Sanchez	1999–2003
Tony Adams	2003–2004
John Gorman	2004–2006
Paul Lambert	2006–2008
Peter Taylor	2008–2009
Gary Waddock	2009–Present

--→ Martin O'Neill took his first real steps in football management at Wycombe in 1990. It took him just three seasons to guide the Chairboys into The Football League and win two FA Trophies.

O'NEILL EARNS HERO STATUS

Martin O'Neill was responsible for taking Wycombe into The Football League in 1993, and he cemented his hero status by guiding the club to a second successive promotion via the play-offs the following season. The Chairboys finished sixth in the third tier the season after that before O'Neill left to take charge at Norwich.

EXTRAORDINARY ESSANDOH

Wycombe famously reached the semi-finals of the FA Cup in 2001, thanks in no small part to a striker signed via a television text service! Lawrie Sanchez, who was Wanderers' manager at the time, placed an advert appealing for a new forward and Roy Essandoh's agent got in touch. Essandoh came off the bench to score a 90th-minute winner against Leicester and set up a semi-final clash with Liverpool at Villa Park, although the dream ended there as they were beaten 2–1.

YEOVIL TOWN

PHIL YOUR BOOTS

Phil Jevons holds the distinction of scoring the most league goals in a single season for Yeovil. The former Everton trainee netted 27 times in 2004/05 to help the Glovers claim the League 2 title. Jevons, who left the club to link up with his former Yeovil boss Gary Johnson at Bristol City in the summer of 2006, scored a total of 42 times for the club in The Football League.

SKIVERTON BOSSES RECORDS

Yeovil manager Terry Skiverton holds the club record for the most Football League appearances. A talismanic captain during his playing days at Huish Park, Skiverton made 195 appearances before he stopped playing to focus on his managerial duties. He replaced Russell Slade in the Yeovil dugout in February 2009.

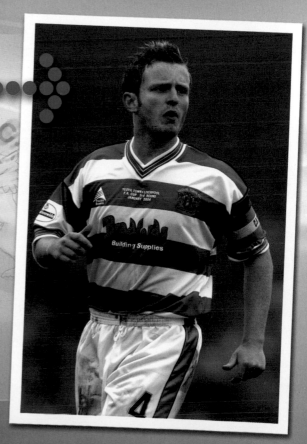

--→ Terry Skiverton, here playing in an FA Cup tie against Liverpool in 2004, is a Yeovil legend. As a player, he is the club's record Football League appearance holder and in 2009, he took over as boss at Huish Park.

PLAY-OFF WOE FOR GLOVERS

Yeovil's highest-ever league finish came in 2006/07 when they reached the play-offs after ending the season in fifth place in League 1. The Glovers made it to the final by overcoming Nottingham Forest 5–4 over two legs, but they were beaten 2–0 by Blackpool at Wembley.

NPOWER LEAGUE 2 CLUB RECORDS

There is always a lot to play for in npower League 2, with automatic promotion extending to the top three places in the table while relegation sends the bottom two teams out of The Football League. New faces such asBurton Albion, Dagenham & Redbridge, Crawley and AFC Wimbledon have arrived in the fourth tier over recent seasons, while Bradford were playing in the Premier League a decade ago.

Clark Keltie of Lincoln (left) and Chesterfield's Craig Davies in action during their npower League 2 clash in September 2010.

Accrington's Phil Edwards (right) slides to make a challenge against Byron Harrison of Stevenage during the 2011 npower League 2 Play-Off Semi-Final.

ACCRINGTON STANLEY

ACCRINGTON STANLEY, WHO ARE THEY?

Accrington resigned from The Football League in 1962 after suffering financial difficulties, but they returned after a 44-year gap in 2006. Their first game back in the fourth tier was away at Chester, where they lost 2–0. They finished their comeback season in 20th place.

⇢ *Paul Mullin's goals helped the reformed Accrington Stanley return to The Football League in 2006.*

STANLEY GO OUT FIGHTING

Stanley enjoyed their best FA Cup run since their reformation in season 2003/04. Having knocked Huddersfield out of the competition, they then got the better of Bournemouth in the second round. Paul Mullin was on the scoresheet in a 1–1 draw at Dean Court and following a goalless draw in the replay, Accrington went through on penalties. They were beaten 2–1 by Colchester in the next round.

MULLIN'S THE MAN

Paul Mullin was the first player since Accrington's reformation to top 400 appearances for the club. The veteran striker is a Stanley hero, having scored almost 200 goals in an eight-year spell. After a loan spell at Bradford, Mullin finally left Accrington to join Morecambe in August 2009.

ALDERSHOT TOWN

DONNELLY EARNS DISTINCTION

Scott Donnelly scored Aldershot Town's first-ever Football League goal at Accrington on August 9 2008. The Shots won the game 1–0 and followed that with a 1–1 draw against Bournemouth – Louie Soares scoring the club's first home Football League goal.

←– *Goalkeeper Nikki Bull was first choice for Aldershot in the Ryman League, Conference and League 2, and he played in 173 consecutive games between 2005 and 2009.*

TOWN'S LEADING GOALSCORERS

Mark Butler	155
Gary Abbott	120
Steve Stairs	75
Roy Young	75
John Grant	57

BULL GRABS THE RECORD

Nikki Bull holds the record for the most consecutive appearances in an Aldershot shirt since the club's formation in 1992. Goalkeeper Bull played 173 matches in a row for the Shots from August 13 2005 to April 15 2009. Bull, who moved to Brentford on a free transfer in August 2009, is second on Aldershot's list of all-time appearance holders with 313 – 176 less than Jason Chewins, who played 489 games for the club.

BARNET

BEES BUZZING

Barnet's first campaign in The Football League in 1991 got off to an amazing start when they were beaten 7–4 at home by Crewe. Barry Fry's side then drew 5–5 at home to Brentford in the first leg of their debut League Cup game!

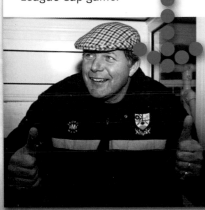

FREEDMAN ON FIRE

Dougie Freedman holds Barnet's record for scoring the most league goals in a season. The 1994/95 campaign saw the prolific striker score 24 times in the fourth tier as the Bees finished 11th. Freedman also shares the club record for the most goals in a single game, scoring four in a 6–2 victory over Rochdale in September 1994. Lee Hodges also netted four against Dale two years later. Freedman moved to Crystal Palace for a club-record fee of £800,000 in September 1995.

⤙ Barry Fry's first match as a Football League boss, with Barnet in 1991, saw 11 goals; his first game in the League Cup brought another 10.

LAST-DAY LUCK

Martin Allen, Giuliano Grazioli and Lawrie Sanchez all played their part in keeping Barnet in The Football League in 2010/11. The Bees were three points adrift of third-from-bottom Burton when Allen replaced Mark Stimson as manager in March 2011. However, a morale-boosting 2–2 draw with table-topping Chesterfield in his first game was followed by back-to-back wins against the Brewers and Crewe. Allen left for Notts County after those three games, with Sanchez coming in to help Grazioli in the dugout for the last four matches. A last-day 1–0 win against Port Vale kept them up.

⤑ Helping to keep Barnet up marked another notable achievement in Lawrie Sanchez's coaching career.

BRADFORD CITY

⤙ The first English club for Aussie goalkeeper Mark Schwarzer was Bradford City, and he helped them to avoid relegation to the third tier in 1996/97.

SOUTHALL TURNS BACK THE CLOCK

Neville Southall is the oldest player to have turned out for Bradford. The former Everton goalkeeper was 41 years and 178 days old when he made his only appearance for the Bantams in a 2–1 defeat to Leeds at Valley Parade on March 12 2000. That one-off display made Southall the fourth oldest player ever to appear in the Premier League.

SELECTION POSER

The Bantams used a total of 42 players in the 1996/97 campaign – a club record that still stands. Their squad that year was made up of players from 11 different nations, including two Australians (Mark Schwarzer and George Kulcsar) a Finn, two Swedes, a Norwegian, a Brazilian (Edinho) and players from Portugal and Holland, as well as the home nations.

BANTAMS ON THE RUN

Bradford's record number of consecutive victories is 10, achieved during the 1983/84 season. Their impressive run started on November 26 1983 against Brentford, with the last win coming on February 3 the following year. They finished that season in seventh place in the third tier.

BRISTOL ROVERS

BRADFORD BONANZA

Geoff Bradford holds a number of goalscoring records for Bristol Rovers. He is the club's all-time top scorer, having netted 242 times in the league during a 15-year stay between 1949 and 1964. Bradford also scored the most league goals in a single season for Rovers in 1952/53, grabbing 33 as the club claimed the third-tier title. He scored four goals in one game against Rotherham in March 1959 – a feat he shares with 10 other players.

⇢ It's all too much to bear for Rovers' Will Hoskins as his side slip further towards relegation to the fourth tier.

ROVERS ARE OUT

Rovers dropped down into npower League 2 after four seasons in the third tier at the end of the 2010/11 campaign. Paul Trollope, who had been in charge at the Memorial Stadium since 2005, left in December after the club slipped into the relegation zone. Darren Patterson was placed in temporary charge, before Dave Penney was appointed in January 2011. He lasted just 13 games, overseeing two wins, two draws and nine defeats before he was axed. Stuart Campbell took over for the last 12 matches but could not keep Rovers up.

PIRATES STEAL VICTORY

Bristol Rovers equalled their best run in the FA Cup in 2008 when they reached the quarter-finals. The highlight was a penalty shootout victory in the third round against top-flight Fulham after the Pirates had forced a replay. Rovers slipped to a 5–1 home defeat against West Brom in the last eight – the first time they had reached that stage since 1958.

BURTON ALBION

BREWERS MAKE THE BIG TIME

Burton Albion were promoted to The Football League for the first time in their history in 2008/09. Nigel Clough was in charge at the start of the campaign, helping them to open up a 13-point lead at the top of the Conference. When he left to take over at Derby, Roy McFarland was placed in charge until the end of the season, and he extended their advantage to 19 points. However, Burton's season stuttered and they eventually won the title by just two points from Cambridge following a tense finish.

⇠ Nigel Clough spent 10 years as Burton Albion manager, but left them a few months before they won promotion to League 2.

UNITED HELD

Albion held Manchester United to a goalless draw in the third round of the FA Cup in 2005/06 – one of their most famous results. They were up against a team containing the likes of Ole Gunnar Solskjaer, Louis Saha and Giuseppe Rossi, while Cristiano Ronaldo and Wayne Rooney came on for United with an hour gone. Battling Burton held their own to secure a memorable draw and a replay at Old Trafford, where they were eventually beaten 5–0.

ROBINS LEAVE ALBION RED-FACED

Burton were involved in one of the most bizarre games in Football League history in 2009/10 when they were beaten 6–5 at home by Cheltenham. The hosts were leading 5–3 with just five minutes remaining but incredibly lost the game when Justin Richards completed an astonishing comeback in injury time. Substitute Michael Pook was the Cheltenham hero, scoring a hat-trick in six minutes.

CHELTENHAM TOWN

CHELTENHAM TOWN FC

HAPPY RETURNS

Julian Alsop's return to Cheltenham paved the way for him to become the club's record goalscorer in The Football League. Following a successful three-year spell with the Robins between 2000 and 2003, during which he scored 35 goals in 117 games, the big striker was brought back to the club by Martin Allen at the age of 36 in July 2009. He went on to beat Martin Devaney's 38-goal record in the 2009/10 campaign.

VICTORY FOR JAMIE

Jamie Victory has made the most Football League appearances for Cheltenham, playing 258 games in 11 years. Club legend Victory, who made the left-back spot his own between 1996 and 2007, retired from football in 2008 due to injury. Roger Thorndale is the Robins' all-time record appearance holder with 702 to his name.

····⇥ Jamie Victory gave Cheltenham Town 11 years' great service, from their days in the Conference in 1996, through to League 1 in 2007.

MIDDLE MAN ARRIVES IN STYLE

Cheltenham paid a club-record fee of £50,000 to sign midfielder Grant McCann from West Ham in January 2003. He played almost 200 games for the Robins, scoring more than 30 goals between 2003 and 2007. McCann is also Cheltenham's most capped player, having made seven starts and 22 substitute appearances for Northern Ireland while at the club. Cheltenham equalled their transfer record by paying Stoke £50,000 for Brian Wilson in March 2004.

CRAWLEY TOWN

TERRIFIC TUBBS

Matt Tubbs almost single-handedly fired Crawley into The Football League in 2010/11, netting 37 Conference goals and 40 in 47 appearances in all competitions. Tubbs scored hat-tricks against Altrincham, Wrexham and Rushden & Diamonds, while the longest he went without a league goal was three matches.

····⇥ Striker Matt Tubbs more than repaid his £70,000 transfer fee with a hatful of goals last season to help fire the Red Devils into The Football League.

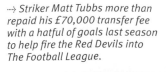

RECORD-BREAKING BRODIE

The Red Devils were labelled the 'Manchester City of non-League' when they splashed the cash in the summer of 2010. Matt Tubbs arrived for £70,000, Sergio Torres cost £100,000, while the deal that took Richard Brodie to the club was reported to be a new Conference record of around £275,000! Brodie managed 11 league goals in 2010/11 but will spend the 2011/12 season on loan at Fleetwood Town, with boss Steve Evans suggesting the striker was homesick.

CONFERENCE RECORDS

Crawley set a new Conference points record as they romped to the title in 2010/11. Steve Evans' side took 105 points from 46 games, winning 31 matches and losing just three times. The Red Devils finished with an amazing goal difference of +63, scoring 93 and conceding just 30. Crawley also set another Conference record for the number of games unbeaten, reaching 30 with a 1–1 draw against York on the last day of the season.

CREWE ALEXANDRA

CREWE'S CONVEYOR BELT

Crewe have earned a reputation for producing top-quality young players through their youth system or signing them from other clubs at a very young age and turning them into stars. David Platt, Robbie Savage and Neil Lennon all made their names with the Alex, while Danny Murphy, Seth Johnson and most recently Dean Ashton all came through the ranks at Gresty Road before moving to top-flight clubs.

← Dario Gradi's eye for talent has unearthed many players who have earned international honours. Wales' Robbie Savage starred at Crewe from 1994–97.

↑ Long-serving boss Dario Gradi is so popular in Crewe that he even has a street in the town named after him!

GRADI'S LONG LEGACY

Long-serving boss Dario Gradi and Crewe have become almost inseparable. Gradi took charge of the club in June 1983 and celebrated his 1,000th game in charge against Norwich in November 2001. He continued as manager until 2000, when he was appointed technical director. Gradi resumed his role as manager for a short spell before the arrival of Gudjon Thordarson and took charge again when the Icelander was sacked. The veteran tactician was still going strong with Alex at the end of the 2010/11 season after almost three decades with the club!

TONY NAILS RECORD

Tony Naylor holds the record for the most goals in a single game for Crewe. Striker Naylor scored five times as Colchester were beaten 7–1 at Gresty Road in April 1993, just a few years after he had joined the professional ranks from non-League Droylsden.

DAGENHAM & REDBRIDGE

A HIGH MARK

Dagenham's record league attendance came on the final day of the 2008/09 League 2 season when they hosted Shrewsbury. A total of 4,791 fans packed in to Victoria Road to watch the Daggers sign off their season with a narrow 2–1 defeat, with Paul Benson scoring the only goal for the hosts.

ROBERTS RE-WRITING HISTORY

Tony Roberts is creating history with every game he plays for Dagenham. Goalkeeper Roberts, who made his debut in August 2000, is already the club's record appearance holder, turning out for the 500th time in a 2–0 defeat at home to Peterborough on April 5 2011. He saved a penalty on his 400th Daggers appearance to earn his side a point against Accrington.

← Goalkeeper Tony Roberts has clocked up almost a quarter of a century in football, having made his debut for QPR in December 1987.

DAGGERS PUT CHESTER TO THE SWORD

Dagenham clearly enjoyed playing Chester City, who went out of business in 2009/2010, with their two biggest Football League victories having come against the Blues. A 6–0 opening-day win on August 9 2008 was secured thanks to goals from Sam Saunders (two), Paul Benson, Dominic Green, Mark Nwokeji and Ben Strevens. Chester were also on the receiving end of the Daggers' second biggest win, 6–2 in February 2008.

GILLINGHAM

STRIKER SUCCESS

Goalscoring duo Robert Taylor and Carl Asaba hold Gillingham's transfer records. Taylor scored 39 goals in 70 matches for the club between August 1998 and November 1999 before Manchester City splashed out £1.5million to sign him – a record transfer fee received by the Gills. The club's biggest outlay was £600,000 to sign Asaba from Reading in August 1998.

···⟩ Gillingham's most expensive signing was Carl Asaba, for £600,000, from Reading. He scored 40 goals for the Gills.

CASCARINO SUITS GILLS

In 1982, Tony Cascarino moved to Gillingham from non-League side Crockenhill in exchange for a set of tracksuits! Republic of Ireland striker Cascarino went on to become a Gills great, scoring 110 times for the club before moving to Millwall for £225,000 in 1987.

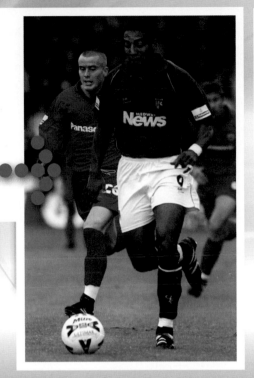

WEMBLEY AGONY TO ECSTASY

Gillingham endured the agony of losing in the play-offs in heartbreaking fashion in 1999 but emerged victorious on their return to Wembley a year later. The Gills were leading 2–0 against Manchester City going into the last minute of normal time in the first final, but amazingly, City scored twice to send the game into extra time and then snatched victory on penalties. However, Gillingham bounced back in 2000 – coming from behind to beat Wigan 3–2.

HEREFORD UNITED

GRAHAM TURNED HIS HAND TO ANYTHING

Graham Turner had spent 47 years with Hereford in June 2010 when he left the club to take charge at Shrewsbury. Turner had held numerous positions at Edgar Street, including chairman and director of football as well as resuming his role as manager following the departure of John Trewick during the 2009/10 campaign. He was first appointed as Hereford boss in 1995 and bought the club in 1998. Arguably his biggest achievement came in 2008 when he was named League 2 Manager of the Year.

⟨··· Graham Turner has spent 46 seasons in football. He made his Wrexham debut in 1964, became Shrewsbury player-manager in 1978 and Hereford boss in 1995.

FAB FOUR FOR STRIKER

Hereford suffered their record defeat in a League Cup clash at Middlesbrough in September 1996. Boro's Italian striker Fabrizio Ravanelli netted four times, while Brazilian duo Emerson and Branco and defender Curtis Fleming were also on the scoresheet in a 7–0 victory. The Teesside club went on to reach the final of the competition that season, losing 1–0 to Leicester in a replay.

CUP MAGIC

Hereford shocked the world of football in 1972 when they belied their non-League status to knock top-flight Newcastle out of the FA Cup. Ronnie Radford's strike from distance is one of the most famous goals in the competition's history, with Ricky George also on the scoresheet for the Bulls in a memorable 2–1 success. Hereford were subsequently drawn against West Ham in the fourth round, where they were beaten in a replay.

MACCLESFIELD TOWN

SILKMEN BOX CLEVER

Macclesfield's record league victory came against Stockport on Boxing Day 2005 when they ran out 6–0 winners at Moss Rose. Strike duo Clyde Wijnhard and Jon Parkin both netted twice, with Martin Bullock and substitute John Miles completing the scoring.

ROOM FOR PARKIN

Jon Parkin has scored the most league goals in a single season for Macclesfield. The big striker netted 22 times in 2004/05. He scored a total of 30 goals in 67 league appearances for the club before joining Hull City in January 2006.

⋯⋗ Jon Parkin's 22 goals for Macclesfield in 2004/05 is the best return by a Town player since they joined The Football League in 1997.

LAMBERT WALKS THE WALK

Rickie Lambert's career has gone from strength to strength since he first made his name at Macclesfield. Lambert was the subject of the biggest transfer fee received by the club when he left for Stockport in a £300,000 deal in April 2002. More recently, he has been banging in the goals for Southampton, and in 2010 he was voted the 30th best player outside of the Premier League.

MORECAMBE

CHAMPIONSHIP DUO STUNNED

Morecambe's maiden Carling Cup campaign made the headlines when they stunned Preston and Wolves. The Shrimps travelled to Deepdale in the first round and claimed a 2–1 victory, with Jim Bentley and David Artell sending North End out of the competition. A trip to Molineux followed, where Morecambe claimed a 3–1 win after extra time. Carl Baker, Jon Newby and Garry Thompson were on the scoresheet. Their run ended in the third round when they were beaten 5–0 by Sheffield United.

⋖⋯ Goalscorers Danny Carlton (left) and Garry Thompson flank manager Sammy McIlroy after Morecambe had beaten Exeter 2–1 in the Conference Play-Off Final in 2007 to win promotion to The Football League.

WEMBLEY GLORY

The biggest day in Morecambe's history came on May 20 2007 when they were promoted to The Football League for the first time. The Shrimps made it to the Conference play-offs, where they beat York over two legs to set up a Wembley date with Exeter. Having fallen behind early on, Morecambe rallied to claim a 2–1 win thanks to goals from Garry Thompson and Danny Carlton. The club played their first Football League match on August 11 2007 – a goalless draw against Barnet.

SHRIMPS CATCH CARL

Carl Baker is the club's record signing, having cost £40,000 from Southport in June 2007. Baker scored 11 goals in his first season with the Shrimps and went on to secure a move to Stockport for an undisclosed fee, which is thought to have matched the club-record £175,000 received when Justin Jackson moved to Rushden & Diamonds in June 2000.

NORTHAMPTON TOWN

GRAYSON IS QUICK OFF THE MARK

Neil Grayson holds the record for the fastest hat-trick in a Northampton shirt. Striker Grayson scored three goals in five minutes against Hartlepool at Sixfields on January 25 1997. The Cobblers went on to secure promotion to the third tier that season, beating Swansea in the fourth-tier Play-Off Final at Wembley with an injury-time goal from John Frain.

← Neil Grayson scored one of the fastest hat-tricks in football history when he netted three times in five minutes for Northampton against Hartlepool in 1997.

COBBLERS KEEP IT TIGHT

Northampton suffered just three away league defeats in their promotion-winning season of 2005/06 – a club record. Town finished runners-up to Carlisle in the fourth tier thanks in no small part to their record on the road.

A LUCKY ESCAPE

The Cobblers finished bottom of The Football League for the only time in their history in season 1993/94, but they still managed to escape relegation. Conference champions Kidderminster were not allowed to take their place as their Aggborough ground did not meet the necessary requirements.

OXFORD UNITED

LEAGUE CUP SUCCESS

Oxford were a top-flight club when they lifted the League Cup in 1986. The Us finished 18th that term, avoiding relegation, and were 3–0 winners against QPR in the Wembley showpiece. It was all too easy for Maurice Evans' side, with goals from Trevor Hebberd, Ray Houghton and Jeremy Charles securing victory. When Oxford dropped into the Conference, it was the first time in the history of English football that a team that had won a major trophy was relegated from The Football League.

OXFORD GRADUATE

The club regained their place in The Football League in May 2010 with a 3–1 victory against York in the Conference Play-Off Final at Wembley. The Us returned to League 2 after a four-year absence courtesy of goals from Matt Green, James Constable and Alfie Potter, who sealed the win in the last minute. They finished 12th in 2010/11.

← Oxford enjoyed their glory years in the 1980s, winning successive promotions between 1983 and 1985 before lifting The League Cup a year later.

DID YOU KNOW?

Match of the Day pundit Mark Lawrenson spent a brief spell in charge of Oxford in the late 1980s. His first attempt at management didn't last long, though, as a dispute with the board over the sale of striker Dean Saunders to Derby saw him leave the Manor Ground three months into the 1988/89 season. Lawrenson spent 14 months in charge of Peterborough between 1989 and 1990, but he is now known for his work on the BBC's popular Saturday evening Barclays Premier League highlights show.

PLYMOUTH ARGYLE

HODGES A HERO

Kevin Hodges earned a place in the Plymouth history books as a player and then went on to manage the club after hanging up his boots. Hodges holds the record for the most league appearances for the Pilgrims – 530 in total. He spent 14 years with Argyle, helping them to reach the semi-finals of the FA Cup in 1984. He took on the manager's role from 1998–2000 and in 2004 was voted part of Argyle's Team of the Century to mark their 100th anniversary as a professional club.

↑ *Kevin Hodges' loyalty to Plymouth was rewarded with two testimonial matches, one in 1988 and another in 1992.*

PILGRIMS' RECORD RUN

Argyle set a club record when they went 19 consecutive league games in one season without losing on their way to winning the fourth-tier title in 2001/02. Their memorable run started with a 3–2 victory at Rushden & Diamonds on August 27 2001, with their 19th game unbeaten coming when they defeated Darlington 1–0 on December 15. The honour of ending their record-breaking sequence went to Scunthorpe, who finally found a way to halt the Pilgrims' progress when they secured a 2–1 victory at Glanford Park a week later courtesy of two goals from midfielder Lee Hodges.

PLYMOUTH'S TEAM OF THE CENTURY

GK	Jim Furnell
DEF	Gordon Nisbet
DEF	Graham Coughlan
DEF	Jack Chisholm
DEF	Colin Sullivan
MID	Kevin Hodges
MID	Ernie Machin
MID	Johnny Williams
MID	Sammy Black/Garry Nelson)*
ATT	Paul Mariner
ATT	Tommy Tynan

* The vote between Black and Nelson was tied

PORT VALE

KEEPING IT IN THE FAMILY

Roy Sproson is Port Vale's record appearance holder with 836 in all competitions. Defender Sproson, who played for the club for 22 years between 1950 and 1972, is joint ninth in the list of all-time Football League appearances with 760 to his name. Roy's nephew, Phil, is Vale's second highest appearance maker with 500.

A SOCA WARRIOR

Chris Birchall earned 22 caps for Trinidad & Tobago during his time at Port Vale, making him the most capped player in the club's history. Midfielder Birchall was the first white player to represent the Soca Warriors for over 60 years, and he lined up against England in the 2006 World Cup finals. He left Vale Park for Coventry in August of that year.

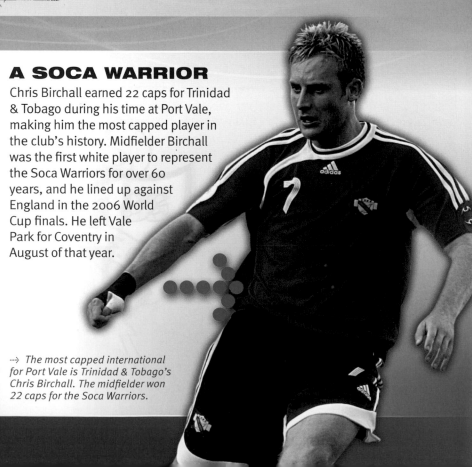

··➔ *The most capped international for Port Vale is Trinidad & Tobago's Chris Birchall. The midfielder won 22 caps for the Soca Warriors.*

BIG FEAT BY LITTLEWOOD

Vale's record win came in September 1932 when they beat Chesterfield 9–1. Another club record was created that day as striker Stewart Littlewood scored six of those goals, the most any Vale player has netted in a single game.

ROTHERHAM UNITED

GOAL FEAST FOR MILLERS

The 2010/11 campaign saw Rotherham score six goals twice in a season for the first time since 2002/03. The Millers were 6–4 winners against Cheltenham in a thrilling clash at the Don Valley Stadium in August, with striker Adam Le Fondre scoring four times. They then destroyed Lincoln 6–0 at Sincil Bank in March 2011. On the opening day of the 2002/03 season, a Darren Byfield-inspired Rotherham side romped to a 6–0 success at Millwall. They also ran out 6–2 winners at Burnley later that term.

CHUCKLES A VISION AT MILLMOOR

The Chuckle Brothers are honorary presidents of Rotherham. The comedy duo are the club's most famous fans and regularly watch their home-town team. An episode of their TV series, *Chucklevision*, entitled 'Football Heroes' was filmed at Millmoor in 1995/96 in which the pair played for the club, with Barry Chuckle crossing for brother Paul to head home what they thought was the winning goal, only to find out that they had scored at the wrong end!

MOORE THE MERRIER

Ronnie Moore led Rotherham to successive promotions in 2000 and 2001. The Millers finished one point behind champions Swansea to move up to the third tier and then secured another second-place finish the following season. The latter promotion was secured with a 2–1 home win against Brentford, with Alan Lee snatching a last-gasp winner.

† *Ronnie Moore is a Rotherham legend, having managed the Millers to successive promotions in 2000 and 2001. He then took the team to Wembley in the 2010 League 2 Play-Off Final.*

SHREWSBURY TOWN

† *Nigel Jemson was Shrewsbury's two-goal hero as Everton were shocked in a 2003 FA Cup third-round tie at Gay Meadow.*

TOFFEES TAMED BY SHREWS

Shrewsbury caused a huge FA Cup upset in 2003 when a double from Nigel Jemson earned them a 2–1 win against Premier League Everton – one of the most memorable results in the Shrews' history. A total of 80 places separated the two teams in the league ladder at kick-off, but the hosts claimed victory when captain Jemson opened the scoring with a superb free-kick and then headed a late winner after Niclas Alexandersson had levelled.

CITY TAKE HART

England's number one Joe Hart started his career at Shrewsbury and the £600,000 Manchester City paid to sign him in 2006 remains a Shrews record. Goalkeeper Hart played 54 games for his home-town club, having made his first-team debut just a day after his 17th birthday in April 2004.

⇢ *Shrewbury's record transfer fee was paid by Manchester City for 19-year-old goalkeeper Joe Hart in 2006.*

ROWLEY RANKS HIGHEST

Arthur Rowley holds the record for the most goals scored in The Football League. The prolific striker netted 152 times for Shrewsbury between 1958 and 1965 to take his career tally to 433 overall. That puts him 54 ahead of the legendary Dixie Dean in the all-time stakes. Rowley managed the Shrews as player-boss for seven years and then stayed on for three seasons after hanging up his boots.

SOUTHEND UNITED

SHRIMPERS MAKE PROGRESS

Steve Tilson led the Shrimpers to back-to-back promotions in 2005 and 2006 as they climbed from the fourth tier to the second tier in impressive fashion. They beat Lincoln 2–0 after extra time in the 2005 Play-Off Final as goals from Freddy Eastwood and Duncan Jupp gave them the edge. The following season they won the League 1 title, pipping rivals Colchester by three points.

⋯⇢ Freddy Eastwood's Football League debut for Southend against Swansea at Roots Hall in October 2004 was spectacular. He scored after seven seconds and finished with a hat-trick.

EASTWOOD GUNS FOR UNITED

Southend stunned holders Manchester United in the fourth round of the Carling Cup in 2006/07 on their way to reaching the quarter-finals – the club's best-ever run in the major cup competitions. A Freddy Eastwood free-kick was enough to see off the Red Devils.

MILLENNIUM MISERY

Southend reached the final of the Football League Trophy two years in a row but lost out on both occasions in 2004 and 2005. They were beaten 2–0 by Blackpool the first time around before their return visit to Cardiff's Millennium Stadium the following season ended with a 2–0 defeat against Wrexham after extra time.

SWINDON TOWN

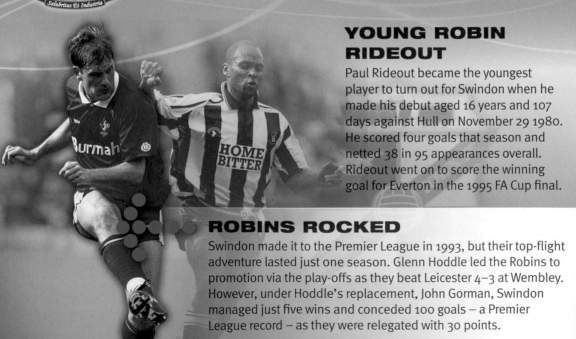

YOUNG ROBIN RIDEOUT

Paul Rideout became the youngest player to turn out for Swindon when he made his debut aged 16 years and 107 days against Hull on November 29 1980. He scored four goals that season and netted 38 in 95 appearances overall. Rideout went on to score the winning goal for Everton in the 1995 FA Cup final.

ROBINS ROCKED

Swindon made it to the Premier League in 1993, but their top-flight adventure lasted just one season. Glenn Hoddle led the Robins to promotion via the play-offs as they beat Leicester 4–3 at Wembley. However, under Hoddle's replacement, John Gorman, Swindon managed just five wins and conceded 100 goals – a Premier League record – as they were relegated with 30 points.

⬅ Glenn Hoddle was player-manager at Swindon when he guided the Robins through the play-offs and into the Premier League in 1993. By the time the following season had kicked off, Hoddle was Chelsea's manager.

CHANGING SEASONS

What a difference a season can make. In 2009/10, Swindon made it to the League 1 Play-Off Final at Wembley, where they were narrowly beaten by Millwall. Then, just 12 months on, the Robins, who had lost star players such as Charlie Austin and Billy Paynter, were coming to terms with relegation to npower League 2. They finished bottom of the table, seven points adrift of safety.

TORQUAY UNITED

TORQUAY'S TOP SCORERS

Sammy Collins	219
Tommy Northcott	150
Robin Stubbs	133
Ron Shaw	106
Ernie Pym	94

IN AT THE SHARPE END

Former Manchester United and England winger Lee Sharpe started his career at Plainmoor. Sharpe was only 16 when he was handed his debut by then Torquay boss Cyril Knowles, but he only played a handful of games before moving to Old Trafford in a £180,000 switch.

⟶ Lee Sharpe's Torquay career comprised only 11 starts, but he did enough as a 16-year-old for Manchester United boss Alex Ferguson to pay £180,000 to sign him.

McNICHOL FEELING RUFF

A dog helped to save Torquay from relegation in 1987! During the last game of the campaign against Crewe – a match Torquay could not afford to lose – Jim McNichol, who had earlier made it 2–1, was bitten by a police dog who thought that the right-back was running towards his handler as he tried to prevent the ball from going out of play. The treatment to McNichol meant a lengthy period of injury time, during which Paul Dobson equalised to keep the Gulls in The Football League!

AFC WIMBLEDON

DANNY THE CHAMPION

Star striker Danny Kedwell scored 23 goals in the Conference in 2010/11 – three more than the previous campaign. The 28-year-old made a blistering start, scoring nine goals in his first 10 matches, while he grabbed a hat-trick in a 4–1 win against Altrincham in February.

⟶ Arguably the most important goal of Danny Kedwell's career was his play-off penalty winner against Luton.

WOMBLING FREE

AFC Wimbledon were formed in 2002 as a result of Wimbledon FC's relocation to Milton Keynes. The club was founded by supporters who were upset that their club had been allowed to leave the area and move 56 miles north to become Milton Keynes Dons. AFC Wimbledon began life in the Premier Division of the Combined Counties League, but an amazing five promotions in just eight seasons saw them start the 2011/12 season in The Football League.

⟶ AFC Wimbledon's players celebrate their promotion to The Football League following their Conference Play-Off Final victory in May 2011.

ARISE AFC

Promotion to The Football League was secured via the Conference play-offs in 2010/11. Having beaten Fleetwood 2–0 away from home in the first leg of the semi-finals, the Dons cruised to a 6–1 victory at Kingsmeadow less than a week later, with Kaid Mohamed scoring a hat-trick. The final against Luton was a much tighter affair, with Danny Kedwell scoring the winning penalty in a shootout after the game had ended 0–0 after 120 minutes.

CUP COMPETITIONS

There is something special about a cup final, whether you are watching two of the Barclays Premier League's big guns going head to head in the FA Cup final or npower League 1 rivals battling it out for the Johnstone's Paint Trophy.

Fans up and down the country dream of a grand day out at a sun-drenched Wembley – the pre-match anticipation, the electric atmosphere inside the stadium and the memories that such occasions inevitably bring.

English football boasts the oldest knockout extravaganza in the world in the shape of the FA Cup, and every year that competition provides some memorable shocks and incredible matches which make it a truly worldwide spectacle.

There are very few other tournaments where a non-league side – with a team possibly made up of tradesmen – can get the chance to pit their wits against an established team from the Barclays Premier League, and every so often pull off a famous victory.

Take Crawley, for example. Not only did Steve Evans' side achieve promotion to the The Football League during the 2010/11 season, but his players also enjoyed a spectacular day out at Old Trafford in front of almost 75,000 spectators, where they gave their all against top-flight champions Manchester United before narrowly losing 1–0 in the fifth round.

The final pitted Stoke – who played the game of their lives to crush Bolton 5–0 in the semis to reach the showpiece – against big-spending Manchester City. It was a tight affair, but Roberto Mancini's side eventually came out on top, with Yaya Toure smashing home the only goal of the game to grab the blue half of Manchester their first trophy in 35 years.

All 92 clubs in the Barclays Premier League and npower Football League are also involved each year in the Carling Cup, and it was another unfamiliar name on the trophy in 2011.

Birmingham snatched a last-gasp win over Arsenal as Obafemi Martins took advantage of a mix-up between Gunners duo Laurent Koscielny and Wojciech Szczesny to tap home and secure a 2–1 victory and Blues' first major silverware since 1963.

But it is often the earlier rounds that can cause the most excitement. Most people would agree that the highlight of the 2010/11 Carling Cup – other than Martins' impressive back-flips – was fourth-tier Northampton's penalty shootout success at Liverpool after a 2–2 draw.

They were given little chance when the draw was made, but the Cobblers put in an impressive display, battling back from a goal down to force extra time and then win on penalties.

Finally, teams from npower League 1 and 2 compete annually for the Johnstone's Paint Trophy.

Carlisle won that particular prize in 2010/11, claiming a 1–0 victory against Brentford to banish the memory of 12 months earlier when they were thumped 4–1 by Southampton.

Cup competitions offer something different from the regular routine of league combat for players and supporters alike – and with plenty of knockout action around, we have never had it so good!

↑ England's main Cup competition trophies, from left to right: FA Cup, Carling Cup, Johnstone's Paint Trophy.

↓ Wembley Stadium hosts all of England's major cup finals, from the FA Vase to the FA Cup and npower Football League Play-Off Finals. In 2011, Arsenal and Birmingham City fans filled it for the Carling Cup Final.

FA CUP

The FA Cup is one of the most famous and oldest competitions in football. Over the years it has seen many great teams, historic moments and memorable upsets. From the first winners, Wanderers, to the current holders, Manchester City, every single season the 'Magic of the Cup' guarantees drama, passion and plenty of excitement.

MOST FA CUP WINS

Team	Wins
Manchester United	11
Arsenal	10
Tottenham Hotspur	8
Aston Villa	7
Liverpool	7
Blackburn Rovers	6
Newcastle United	6
Chelsea	5
Everton	5
Manchester City	5
Wanderers	5
West Bromwich Albion	5

GOLDEN OLDIE

The FA Cup is the oldest domestic cup competition in the world, having been an integral part of English football for more than 100 years. The first competition was played in 1871/72 and had just 15 entrants (compared to more than 700 who took part in the 2009/10 season). Wanderers, a team formed by ex-public school and university pupils, won the first final 1–0 against Royal Engineers at Kennington Oval, although the game was almost unrecognisable from today as back then matches were played without crossbars or nets and the pitch markings did not include a centre circle or a half-way line.

↓ Steve Bruce shows off the FA Cup after Manchester United had beaten Chelsea 4–0 in the 1994 final. Excluding replays, It was the most one-sided final since Bury beat Derby County 6–0 in 1903.

↑ The FA Cup. A popular quiz question asks: 'What is taken to every FA Cup final but is never used?' The answer? The losers' ribbons.

FAMILIAR FOES

The most common FA Cup final pairing has been Arsenal v Liverpool, Arsenal v Newcastle and Aston Villa v West Brom, with each having met three times in the showpiece.

WESTON THE LION CUB

Millwall midfielder Curtis Weston is the youngest player to have appeared in an FA Cup final. The Lions ace, now with Gillingham, broke one of the longest-standing records in football when he appeared as a second-half substitute in the 2004 final against Manchester United. He was 17 years and 119 days old at the time, beating the record of James Prinsep, who was 17 years and 245 days old when he played for Clapham Rovers in the 1879 final against Old Etonians.

QUICK AS A FLASH

Jimmy Kebe scored after just nine seconds in Reading's fifth-round clash with West Brom in February 2010 to make his mark on the competition. Although records are incomplete, the winger's strike is believed to be the fastest-ever goal in the FA Cup proper, although his time has been bettered in the qualifying rounds. Part-time player Gareth Morris, a window fitter by day, scored a goal recorded at just four seconds for Ashton United against Skelmersdale United in the preliminary stages in 2001.

⤍ Jimmy Kebe's goal after nine seconds is believed to be the fastest in the FA Cup proper. Reading drew 2–2 with West Brom, but they won the replay 3–2 after extra time.

⤎ Hereford United players celebrate with a beer after their 2–1 defeat of Newcastle United in 1972. The winner came from Ricky George (middle row, far left).

BEASANT LEADS THE CRAZY GANG

Dave Beasant shot into footballing folklore in 1988 when he became the first goalkeeper to save a penalty in a Wembley final. The shot-stopper dived full length to turn away John Aldridge's spot-kick as 'The Crazy Gang' beat reigning league champions Liverpool in one of the greatest final upsets of all time.

⤍ Dave Beasant shows off the FA Cup after Wimbledon's shock victory over Liverpool in 1988. Behind him is Dennis Wise.

WHAT A SHOCKER

Everybody loves surprises, and the FA Cup is normally full of them as small teams look to get the better of big-name opponents. These shocks, known as 'giantkillings', are what football fans look forward to every year...unless they support the team that has just been knocked out, of course! One of the most famous FA Cup upsets of all time came in January 1992 when Arsenal were beaten 2–1 by Wrexham, who were bottom of the old Fourth Division at the time. Liverpool, Everton and Newcastle are three more teams who have been dumped out by clubs from lower divisions. Manchester United were stunned by then-League 1 side Leeds at Old Trafford in January 2010, with hot-shot striker Jermaine Beckford, now of Everton, scoring the only goal.

A CRICKET SCORE

Preston hold the record for the biggest win in the FA Cup, having scored 26 goals without reply against Hyde in 1887. Striker Jimmy Ross was their hero that day, netting eight times. He scored six more against Bolton in the fourth round and went on to finish the season with 19 in the competition overall – also a record.

THE GIANTKILLERS

Hereford	2–1	Newcastle	(1972)
Stevenage	3–1	Newcastle	(2011)
Wrexham	2–1	Arsenal	(1992)
Yeovil	2–1	Sunderland	(1949)
Sutton	2–1	Coventry	(1989)
Liverpool	1–2	Barnsley	(2008)
Barnsley	1–0	Chelsea	(2008)
Bournemouth	2–0	Manchester United	(1984)
Sunderland	1–0	Leeds	(1973)
Burnley	0–1	Wimbledon	(1975)

DOUBLE DELIGHT

Seven clubs have won the FA Cup as part of a league and cup double: Preston (1889), Aston Villa (1897), Tottenham (1961), Arsenal (1971, 1998, 2002), Liverpool (1986), Manchester United (1994, 1996, 1999) and Chelsea (2010).

THE WORLD'S GAME

The FA Cup final is one of the most watched sporting events in the world with around 484 million people tuning in from all four corners of the globe to watch the 2005 clash at the Millennium Stadium, Cardiff as Arsenal beat Manchester United on penalties.

FA CUP FINAL VENUES

1872	Kennington Oval
1873	Lillie Bridge, London
1874–1892	Kennington Oval
1893	Fallowfield, Manchester
1894	Goodison Park
1895–1914	Crystal Palace
1915	Old Trafford
1920–22	Stamford Bridge
1923–2000	Wembley Stadium
2001–2006	Millennium Stadium, Cardiff
2007–Present	New Wembley Stadium

⟵ The arch over the New Wembley Stadium has rapidly become a famous landmark, even if some traditionalists mourn the passing of the old venue's Twin Towers.

KING LOUIS THE 25TH

Louis Saha scored the fastest goal in FA Cup final history when he put Everton ahead against Chelsea after just 25 seconds in May 2009. The Frenchman got on the end of Marouane Fellaini's headed knockdown and beat Petr Cech with a well-struck shot into the bottom corner. Unfortunately for the Toffees, Chelsea hit back to claim a 2–1 victory. Everton's defeat meant that they finished as FA Cup runners-up for the eighth time, more than any other club.

I CAN'T BELIEVE IT'S NOT BUTTERFIELD

Defender-turned-striker Danny Butterfield scored a hat-trick in seven minutes for Crystal Palace against Wolves in the fourth round of the 2009/10 FA Cup. However, there have been quicker hat-tricks in the competition, with the fastest recorded at two minutes and 20 seconds when Andy Locke scored three times for Nantwich against Droylsden in a qualifier in 1995.

↓ Everton played in five FA Cup finals in 11 years, 1984–1995, winning two. When Louis Saha gave them the lead after 25 seconds of their first final for 14 years in 2009, it led to a record eighth defeat as Chelsea hit back to win.

FIVE-STAR COLE

Ashley Cole became the first player since the 19th Century to win the FA Cup on five separate occasions when he was part of the Chelsea team that beat Everton 2–1 in May 2009. Cole had already lifted the trophy once with the Blues in 2007 when Didier Drogba's extra-time goal secured a 1–0 victory over Manchester United. The England left-back also won the competition three times with Arsenal in 2002, 2003 and 2005. The Gunners were 2–0 winners against Chelsea in Cardiff in 2002, beat Southampton 1–0 a year later and claimed a penalty shootout victory against Manchester United in 2005, with Cole scoring from the spot. He has since won a sixth medal following Chelsea's victory over Portsmouth in 2010.

PLAY IT AGAIN, FULHAM

Fulham hold the record for the most games played in one FA Cup campaign to reach the final. Ties used to be played over and over again until one team won rather than a replay followed by extra time and penalties if the game remained all-square. The Cottagers, playing in the second tier at the time, played 12 games over six rounds of the competition on their way to being losing finalists against West Ham back in 1975.

←⸱⸱ Eric Cantona of Manchester United was the first player to convert two penalties in an FA Cup final, doing so in 1994. In 2010, Portsmouth and Chelsea both failed with a spot-kick – another FA Cup final first.

HAMMERS ARE ALL-ENGLAND CLUB

West Ham's FA Cup-winning side of 1975 was the last all-English line-up to lift the trophy. Alan Taylor scored both goals as the Hammers claimed a 2–0 win against Fulham at Wembley. Their team that day also featured the likes of Billy Bonds, Frank Lampard Snr and Trevor Brooking.

SPOT-ON ERIC AT THE DOUBLE

Eric Cantona made history in 1994 when he became the first player to score two penalties in an FA Cup final. 'King Eric', who was also voted PFA Player of the Year that season, was spot on for Manchester United as they claimed a 4–0 win against Chelsea at Wembley. Cantona's two penalties and a Mark Hughes strike in nine second-half minutes put the Red Devils in control before Brian McClair added a fourth goal late on. Frenchman Cantona also scored the winning goal in the 1996 final as Manchester United beat Liverpool 1–0.

MOST APPEARANCES IN FA CUP FINALS

Manchester United	18
Arsenal	17
Everton	13
Liverpool	13
Newcastle	13
Aston Villa	10
West Brom	10
Chelsea	10
Manchester City	9
Tottenham	9

↑ Alan Taylor of West Ham was the two-goal hero of the 1975 FA Cup final, the last time the FA Cup winners contained only England-eligible players.

A CLASSIC ENCOUNTER

Liverpool's victory over West Ham in 2006 was arguably the most exciting FA Cup final of modern times – with Steven Gerrard proving to be the Reds' hero that day. The Merseysiders were twice forced to come from behind to take the game into extra time, with Gerrard completing the comeback in injury time with a stunning 30-yard volley to haul his side back to 3–3. Both sides went close again in a thrilling extra period before Liverpool goalkeeper Pepe Reina saved from Bobby Zamora, Paul Konchesky and Anton Ferdinand in the penalty shootout.

WELSH WONDERS

The FA Cup has only been won by a non-English team once. Cardiff claimed that honour in 1927 when they beat Arsenal 1–0 at Wembley. They came close to repeating the feat when they made it to the final again in 2008, but they were ultimately beaten by Portsmouth.

←⸱⸱ Steven Gerrard's performance for Liverpool in the 2006 FA Cup final cemented his legendary status at Anfield. The 3–3 draw against West Ham was one of the greatest finals ever.

CARLING CUP

The League Cup holds a special place in the domestic football calendar. Traditionally the first major piece of silverware of the season, the competition is still going strong beyond its 50th year. Current holders Birmingham City claimed the trophy in dramatic fashion in 2011 with a late win over Arsenal.

↑ Keith Cooper has just brandished the first red card in a League Cup final, Andrei Kanchelskis of Manchester United being the unfortunate recipient in the defeat against Aston Villa in 1994.

KAN YOU HANDLE IT?

Andrei Kanchelskis became the first player to be sent off in a League Cup final in March 1994. Manchester United were losing 2–1 to Aston Villa when Russian winger Kanchelskis used his hand to clear the ball off the goalline from Dalian Atkinson's shot. United went on to lose the game 3–1 as Villa's Wales international striker Dean Saunders scored from the resulting penalty.

HARD ACT TO FOLLOW

In 1990 The Football League introduced the Alan Hardaker Trophy, presented to the man of the match in the League Cup final. Hardaker was the former secretary of the League who conceived the idea for the cup competition back in 1960. Nottingham Forest defender Des Walker was the first man to receive the prize, while in 2011, goalkeeper Ben Foster became the first player to scoop the award for a second time. His penalty shootout heroics helped Manchester United to victory against Tottenham in 2009 and two years later another awesome performance allowed Birmingham to stun Arsenal 2–1.

↑ Ben Foster shows off the Alan Hardaker Trophy after helping Birmingham to victory in the 2011 Final – their first trophy in 48 years.

RIISE LEAVES BLUES RED-FACED

Jon Arne Riise holds the record for the quickest goal in the final. It took the Norway international defender just 45 seconds to open the scoring for Liverpool against Chelsea in 2005. It was the Blues who were celebrating at the end of the game, though, as Mateja Kezman's strike in extra time secured a 3–2 victory.

↓ Jon Arne Riise scored for Liverpool in the first minute of the 2005 Carling Cup final at the Millennium Stadium in Cardiff, but Chelsea hit back to win 3–2.

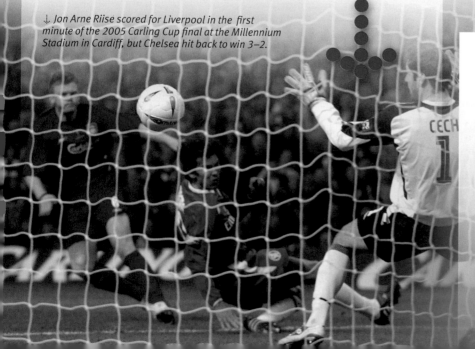

RECENT ALAN HARDAKER TROPHY WINNERS

2011	Ben Foster	(Birmingham)
2010	Antonio Valencia	(Manchester United)
2009	Ben Foster	(Manchester United)
2008	Jonathan Woodgate	(Tottenham)
2007	Didier Drogba	(Chelsea)
2006	Wayne Rooney	(Manchester United)
2005	John Terry	(Chelsea)
2004	Boudewijn Zenden	(Middlesbrough)
2003	Jerzy Dudek	(Liverpool)
2002	Brad Friedel	(Blackburn)
2001	Robbie Fowler	(Liverpool)

CLIVE IS GOAL MACHINE

Tottenham legend Clive Allen has scored the most goals in one League Cup campaign. He netted 12 in the 1986/87 season as Spurs reached the semi-finals. They were eventually beaten by arch-rivals Arsenal over three games – two legs and a replay – with Allen scoring three times in the process. The prolific striker scored 49 goals in total that season, with 33 coming in the league, as he was named the PFA Player of the Year.

⇢ *Clive Allen (arm raised) celebrates scoring the first goal of the 1987 League Cup semi-final second leg against Arsenal with Spurs team-mates Gary Mabbutt (left) and Paul Allen.*

MINNOWS UPSET THE BIG BOYS

The League Cup has thrown up its fair share of shocks over the years but perhaps the most memorable came in 1995 when York City, playing in the third tier at the time, claimed a sensational 3–0 win against Premier League giants Manchester United at Old Trafford. David Beckham and Ryan Giggs were playing for the home side, but that didn't faze the Minstermen, who secured a remarkable upset. In 2010, League 2 Northampton pulled off a stunning penalty shootout success against Liverpool at Anfield after holding the Reds to a 2–2 draw.

↑ *Northampton Town added their name to the list of League Cup giantkillers with a famous shootout victory over Liverpool at Anfield in 2010/11.*

⇢ *Frankie Bunn was fantastic on plastic and his six goals for Oldham in the 7–0 rout of Scarborough on the artificial turf at Boundary Park in 1989 remains the competition's individual scoring record.*

MOST LEAGUE CUP FINAL APPEARANCES

Liverpool	10
Aston Villa	8
Manchester United	8
Arsenal	7
Tottenham	7
Nottingham Forest	6
Chelsea	6

HURST HOLDS GOAL RECORD

England's 1966 World Cup hero Geoff Hurst shares the landmark for scoring the most League Cup goals in a career. Hurst, who famously netted a hat-trick for England against West Germany, scored 49 goals overall in the competition playing for West Ham and Stoke. He holds the record jointly with Ian Rush, who managed the same feat with Chester, Liverpool and Newcastle.

⇠ *Geoff Hurst was a real cup star. His 49 goals is a League Cup record, but he also won the FA Cup and European Cup Winners' Cup with West Ham, to say nothing of his 1966 World Cup final hat-trick for England.*

BUNN HITS BORO FOR SIX

Frankie Bunn holds the record for the most goals in a single League Cup tie. Striker Bunn scored six goals for Oldham in a 7–0 win against Scarborough in the third round in October 1989. The Latics went on to reach the final, where they were beaten 1–0 by Nottingham Forest. Bunn was forced to retire in 1990 through injury.

JOHNSTONE'S PAINT TROPHY

For those clubs further down the league pyramid, the Football League Trophy, currently the Johnstone's Paint Trophy, offers the chance of silverware, and a memorable day out at Wembley. The competition, which began in 1983, is popular with both players and supporters in the lower reaches of the English game.

SIXTH TIME LUCKY FOR CUMBRIANS

Carlisle appeared in a record sixth Football League Trophy final in 2011, with a 1–0 victory over Brentford allowing them to join the list of clubs who have won the competition twice. The Cumbrians reached the Wembley showpiece for the second year running – they lost 4–1 to Southampton in 2010 – with Peter Murphy's early goal enough to secure a narrow win against the Bees. Carlisle's first Trophy success came in 1997 when they beat Colchester on penalties following a goalless draw.

SAINTS DRAW A CROWD

The highest attendance for a Trophy game other than the final came in the 2009/10 competition when Southampton hosted MK Dons at St Mary's Stadium in front of 29,901 spectators. The previous best was 24,002 at Birmingham City's St Andrew's in 1994/95.

LAST FIVE JOHNSTONE'S PAINT TROPHY FINALS

2010/11	Carlisle	1–0	Brentford
2009/10	Southampton	4–1	Carlisle
2008/09	Luton	3–2	Scunthorpe (extra-time)
2007/08	MK Dons	2–0	Grimsby
2006/07	Doncaster	3–2	Bristol Rovers

⬇ Carlisle secured their place in the record books with victory over Brentford in the 2011 Johnstone's Paint Trophy final.

MOST FOOTBALL LEAGUE TROPHY WINS

Bristol City	2
Port Vale	2
Birmingham	2
Blackpool	2
Stoke	2
Swansea	2
Wigan	2
Carlisle	2

TO HULL AND BACK

The Football League Trophy was introduced in 1983/84. The first final was scheduled to be played at Wembley but damage to the pitch caused by the Horse of the Year show saw the game switched to Hull. Hull actually made it to the final that year, but they were beaten 2–1 by Bournemouth.

⬆ The Football League trophy in its current guise, the Johnstone's Paint Trophy. It was won in 2011 by Carlisle, 1–0 against Brentford at Wembley.

PENALTY HEROES

Three finals have been settled by penalty shootouts. Mansfield beat Bristol City 4–3 after the game had finished 1–1 in 1987, while Swansea were 3–1 winners following a 1–1 draw with Huddersfield in 1994, with goalkeeper Roger Freestone the Welsh club's hero that day as he saved the decisive spot-kick. Carlisle won the trophy via a penalty shootout in 1997. They beat Colchester 4–3 after a goalless draw in normal time, with Peter Cawley and Karl Duguid missing from 12 yards for the losing side.

THREE-SY DOES IT

No team has won the Trophy by more than three clear goals. Bristol City beat Bolton 3–0 in the 1986 final, while Bolton claimed the title with a 4–1 victory against Torquay three years later and Blackpool inflicted the same scoreline on Cambridge in 2002. The 2009/10 competition also ended 4–1, with Southampton claiming their first silverware since 1976 with victory against Carlisle.

↑ *Swansea goalkeeper Roger Freestone helped his club win the trophy in 1994 with a crucial save in the penalty shootout.*

TROPHY MADNESS FOR HATTERS

Luton won the 2009 competition but were unable to defend their title after they were relegated from The Football League in the same season. The Hatters finished bottom of League 2 that year but at least had something to celebrate when they beat Scunthorpe 3–2 at Wembley. Claude Gnakpa was the Hatters' hero, scoring the winner in extra time.

FAMOUS NAMES

Some famous names have won the Trophy over the years, making it a prestigious piece of silverware for those in the lower reaches of English football. No fewer than six sides who competed in the Barclays Premier League in 2010/11 have lifted the prize, with Birmingham, Blackpool, Bolton, Wigan, Wolves and Stoke among the former winners.

INCE IS THE DON

MK Dons' success in 2008 was a landmark moment in the history of the club. Their 2–0 victory over Grimsby in the final secured the Dons their first piece of silverware. Paul Ince, in his first season as manager, saw his side cap a superb season by going on to win the League 2 title. However, the Dons could not repeat their heroics the following year and defend the Trophy. After receiving a bye into the second round, they were knocked out of the competition by Bournemouth.

⋯⋙ *One of the highlights of Paul Ince's first spell in charge of MK Dons was victory in the 2008 Johnstone's Paint Trophy final, the first silverware collected by the club in its current guise.*

THE BOY DUNN GOOD

Iain Dunn was the first player in British football to score a golden goal in the Trophy of 1994. The golden goal method, which failed to catch on, meant that the game ended immediately after a goal was scored by either side in extra time. Striker Dunn earned Huddersfield a 3–2 victory against Lincoln, although the Terriers went on to lose to Swansea on penalties in the final.

←⋯ *Golden goals (and silver ones, too) were a short-lived football innovation. Introduced in England for the 1994/95 Football League Trophy, Iain Dunn of Huddersfield was the first man to end extra time early when he scored against Lincoln.*

INDEX

ACKNOWLEDGEMENTS

This book would not have been possible without the help and co-operation of Football DataCo Limited, the Premier League, The Football League and the clubs themselves, as well as the talented and dedicated team of journalists and researchers at Press Association Sport.
On behalf of Press Association Sport:
Author: Andrew Carless
Head of Content: Peter Marshall
Copy Editor: Andrew McDermott
Research: Patrick Harness, Neil Morgan, Simon Plunkett
Contributors: Alaric Beaumont-Baker, Duncan Bech, Roddy Brooks, James Cann, John Curtis, Dominic Farrell, Andy Hampson, Ross Heppenstall, Carl Markham, Tom Rostance, Matthew Sherry, Andrew Sims, Damian Spellman, Simon Stone, Sean Taylor, Jim van Wijk, Jonathan Veal, Mark Walker, Stuart Walker, Drew Williams

PICTURE CREDITS